GLOBALIZATION AND CULTURE AT WORK

Globalization and Culture at Work

Exploring Their Combined Glocality

by

Stuart C. Carr
*Te Kura Hinengaro Tangata, School of Psychology,
Massey University, New Zealand-Aotearoa*

KLUWER ACADEMIC PUBLISHERS
BOSTON / DORDRECHT / LONDON

A C.I.P. Catalogue record for this book is available from the Library of Congress.

ISBN 1-4020-7845-5 (HB)
ISBN 1-4020-7943-5 (e-book)

Published by Kluwer Academic Publishers,
P.O. Box 17, 3300 AA Dordrecht, The Netherlands.

Sold and distributed in North, Central and South America
by Kluwer Academic Publishers,
101 Philip Drive, Norwell, MA 02061, U.S.A.

In all other countries, sold and distributed
by Kluwer Academic Publishers,
P.O. Box 322, 3300 AH Dordrecht, The Netherlands.

Printed on acid-free paper

All Rights Reserved
© 2004 Kluwer Academic Publishers, Boston
No part of this work may be reproduced, stored in a retrieval system, or transmitted
in any form or by any means, electronic, mechanical, photocopying, microfilming,
recording or otherwise, without written permission from the Publisher, with the exception
of any material supplied specifically for the purpose of being entered
and executed on a computer system, for exclusive use by the purchaser of the work.

Printed in the Netherlands.

Acknowledgements

This manuscript is dedicated to Tony Marsella, for believing in it, and in me, throughout. Grateful credit is due to Steve Atkins, for coining the term *glocality* during one of our many carpool discussions on "pro-social I/O." Thank you to all the research collaborators whose studies, case studies, and creative sparks, are the lifeblood in this work. This includes a special vote of appreciation to the many academic readers of this book whilst it was still in draft embryonic form: Steve Atkins; Richard Fletcher; Kerr Inkson; Peter Johnston; Leo Marai; Mac MacLachlan; Karin Menon; Don Munro; Bridie O'Reilly; Madalyn Parlet; Tod Sloan; and Jennifer Stillman.

This project was generously supported by a grant from the School of Psychology at Massey University in New Zealand/Aotearoa. Professional copyediting assistance for this project was provided by Jude Fredricsen. Thanks to all the publishing staff at Kluwer-Plenum in Dordrecht – and especially Cathelijne van Herwaarden, Marie Sheldon and Herma Drees – for your support and understanding along the way (extra appreciation to Herma for helping the book across the finishing line).

Most importantly of all, a huge Thank you extends to my Family, in New Zealand, Aotearoa, and in Jersey, Channel Islands, for tolerating the absences of mind, body, and spirit.

Contents

Preface   xi-xii

1 Globalization   1-20

    1. What is Globalization?   1-3
    2. Localization   3-4
    3. Glocalization   4-5
    4. Some Foundational Theory   7-10
    5. Glocality at Work   10-15
    6. A Case in Point   15-20
    7. Conclusion   20

2 Culture   21-47

    1. Introduction   21-22
    2. Country-level Studies   22-27
    3. Individual Values   27-32
    4. Organizational Culture   32-36
    5. Occupational Culture   36-38
    6. Glocal Positioning   38
    7. Cultural Positioning   38-40
    8. Link to Glocality   40
    9. The Generality of Escalation   40-42
    10. Theories of Positioning   42-45
    11. Cultural Re-positioning   45-46
    12. Interpretation   46
    13. Summary   47

3 Achievement   49-75

    1. A Brief History of Achievement at Work   49-53
    2. *n* Ach in Social Context   53-54
    3. *n* Ach in Work Context   54-59
    4. Research on Motivational Gravity   59
    5. A Primary Strand: Measures of Motivational Gravity   59-61
    6. A Secondary Strand: Influences of Gravity on Work Behavior   61-70
    7. Systems Approach   70-73

8. Managing Motivational Gravity	73-74
9. Conclusion	75

4 Pay   77-103

1. A Theoretical Foundation	77
2. Behavioral Theories of Work Motivation	78
3. Task-focused Theories of Motivation	78-80
4. Relationship-focused Theories of Motivation	80-87
5. Research on Double De-motivation	87-91
6. The Case	95-97
7. Managing Pay Justice	97-103
8. Conclusion	103

5 Power   105-131

1. The Concept of Empowerment	105-106
2. Defining Teamwork	106-107
3. The Mantra of Diversity	107-108
4. Contingency Approaches	108-110
5. A Glocal Analysis	110-111
6. An Acid Test	111-112
7. Teams through Development	112-114
8. Mental Models	114-116
9. An Approach to the Fundamental Question	116-120
10. A Glocality?	120-121
11. The Broken Promise	121-123
12. Case Analysis	123-127
13. Managing the Broken Promise	127-130
14. Conclusion	130-131

6 Learning   133-157

    1. Boundary-less Careers   133-134
    2. Boundary Conditions   134-137
    3. Utilising the Immigrants We   137-144
        Already Have
    4. An Empirical Test of SIT, SAT,   144-147
        & SDT
    5. Implications for Policy and   147-153
        Practice
    6. Beyond Migration   153-154
    7. A Synthesis   154-156
    8. Conclusion   156-157

References   159-186
Index   187-194

Preface

All books are written from a point of view, and in that sense are implicitly biased. Prefaces are logical places to try and externalize some of those implicit biases, and to that extent partly reduce them for reader and author alike. This book, and the research reported within it, contains a number of such prejudices.

First and foremost, the book is relatively micro in its level of analysis. This is a focus only. The analysis and research presented in the volume fully recognize that a variety of elements, both micro and macro, constitute the systems that most of us call 'work." Work behaviors are linked, for example, to structural issues, like mergers, and to economic issues, like share crises. One of the conduits making these linkages happen is human perception. Mergers and crises are represented in perception, and perceptions, as Kurt Lewin reminds us, continually influence work decisions and actions. Today's leading examples of such influences at work, and on work behavior, are the perceived effects of globalization and localization. Because those perceptions are so central to work behavior, their influences are central, also, in this book.

As well as being behavioral issues, globalization and localization are issues of power and politics. So what are the politics, and political assumptions, in this book? Resisted, for example, is any assumption, often implicit in work behaviour studies, that people are intangible human "resources." Instead, people in this book are viewed as tangible agencies in work life. Within the more economically "developed" world for example, competition for jobs is now increasingly waged not between employees, but between employ*ers*. It is *they* who often must "compete," in order to become "employers of [*employee*] choice." Taking that zeitgeist to its logical conclusion, there is no reason in fact why employees should not "select" organizations, rather than the other way about (K. Inkson, personal correspondence, March 18, 2003). As the balance of power continues to shift in this way, the study of work behavior will need to shift with it. It will need to serve less the interests of organizations and more the interests and aspirations of people, both as individuals and as groups.

This last point implies that the study of work behavior, when narrowly conceived as "organizational" behavior, is adrift from, and out of touch with, a developing global consciousness. This book argues that the predominant models of individual and group behavior, at work, need re-animation. "Individual differences,' for example, are not as 'dyed-in-the-wool" or as omnipresent as the traditional and neo-traditional literature implies. Much of this literature, for instance, is heavily individualistic, even though individuals can sometimes transform themselves from loosely coupled aggregates into socially dynamic teams. As this example (and many others in the book) suggest, there is today more than ever an inherent flexibility in work psychology. To begin respecting that enhanced fluidity and dynamism, we need fluid and dynamic concepts.

The expectations for such concepts are high. They are expected, for example, to cover a range of different types of work-related repertoires, without ever over-positioning their subject matter into crass or offensive stereotypes. At the same time, these new concepts are expected not to lose sight of what it means to have a sense of "self," "us," 'other,' and "others." Balancing legitimate concerns like this, between perpetual movement and, at the same time, a sense of continuity in personhood, is a tall order. Yet it is not an unrealistic one. A first step in the right direction, for instance, is to engage in good faith with critical perspectives on work behavior.

Critical approaches to work behavior scrutinize not only work behavior itself, but also our own discursive practices, as "scholars," about it. Accordingly, this book both begins and ends with a critical analysis of the key competing discourses found in the research literature around work behavior. Those discourses, like any other, function as conceptual lenses. They allow us to appreciate work behavior from a diversity of perspectives. Perhaps then, they offer the best hope for capturing the diversity of our subject matter.

This diversity assumes many forms. Many workers today for instance are bicultural or even tri-cultural. They are intrinsically capable of reflecting cultural diversity in their own work behavior. To fully appreciate that frequently found capacity for variation, and for multiple forms of identity, we need to focus not just on work behavior per se, but also, on its various meanings. Meaning itself is often best communicated through the lens of qualitative theory and methods. This book dons that lens. In the spirit of pluralism outlined above, it strives to include a balance of both qualitative and quantitative research. Thus, this book contains, for example, just as many research case studies as research sample surveys.

In addition to being pluralistic in methodology, a focus on meaning has other key implications. First of all, it leads us to consider affect (or emotions) as central to understanding work behavior. The book discusses, for instance, a wide range of emotions, from envy and jealousy through to pride and prejudice. Secondly, a focus on meaning leads us to consider the meaning of work in wider, i.e., community context. Work behavior is neither structurally separated from, nor does it function independently of, its societal roots. As an example of this, the concept of "job satisfaction" is ceding ground, today, to the wider-ranging concept of "work-life balance." Related to this broader ambit for studying work behavior, people are also increasingly working away from a single physical location called "the workplace." Against shifting backdrops like these, it makes sense to say that the study of work behavior is becoming more socially responsive and more socially responsible. Many organizations in fact are involved directly in working for the community. Their reasons for being are not for profit, but pro social, ranging from enhancing public safety to assisting with international peacekeeping and famine relief. Reflecting those enhanced scopes of practice, "pro-social" organizations, and especially the employees and clients for whom they work, have a strong voice in this book. Listening to such voices, I believe, is one of the great plus-ups in globalization, not to mention a wonderful opportunity to develop the study of work itself.

Stuart Carr
Auckland, 2004

Chapter 1

Globalization

The initial stimulus for writing this book is the experience of travel. Not just travel in the literal sense of the term, i.e., physically moving from one country or place of work to another (Clifford, 1997). Travel also brings people@work toward us, rendering work life into travel-without-moving. Travel might thus be a useful metaphor for re-appreciating the way that work behavior continues to evolve (Hermans & Kempen, 1998).

Metaphors become useful by eventually extending our understanding of work behavior (Inkson, Arthur, Pringle & Barry, 1997). To achieve that extension of understanding, however, a metaphor has to first resonate with people's existing experiences (Ottati, Rhoads & Graesser, 1999). So, how well does the concept "travel" resonate with "work" as we know it in its present form? Most of us will recognize diversity in our work – whether in the people we meet, the technology we use, or the processes and practices that we encounter and enact every day of working life: Our local workplace is increasingly international. As one commentator pithily observes, "the differences between cross-national and intra-national diversity have become increasingly blurred" (Schneider, 2001: 342). Travel, therefore, is a promising and timely metaphor for work, because it reflects the everyday familiarity of diversity heading toward us.

Contained within this familiar experience of diversity is one particularly salient – some might even say overriding – example of travel-without-moving. This is commonly referred to – in everyday work life and beyond – as our encounters with globalization.

1. What is Globalization?

To many, if not most of us, globalization means influence by stealth, and from a particular direction. True, once in a while, some idea or practice perceptibly emanates from outside of the Western hemisphere, either penetrating "the West" or, more likely perhaps, migrating to other "non-Western" settings (e.g., Posthuma, 1995). But, by and large, most of the influence in globalization appears to emanate and diffuse outwards from *within* "the West." "The West" is, in turn, often just a euphemism for the United States of America (USA). In the study of work behavior, for example, few scholars would deny that research and theory from the USA has for some time been represented disproportionately in the behavioral literature. This book is a response to that imbalance. It speaks directly to a sense of disquiet that many of us feel: That there is actually far, far more to work behavior than "the literature" – from its home base in the USA – would have us believe.

Using our travel metaphor, a logical way of beginning to articulate this disquiet is to take a closer look at what it is, precisely, that is perceptibly traveling toward us. Take, for example, a paper published by Lawler and Finegold (2001), entitled, "Individualizing the organization: Past, present, and future." As the title amply suggests, the paper sees as a "core issue" in organizational dynamics "how to design organizations and jobs that meet individuals' needs" (2000: 1). These needs purportedly span, for instance, personalized employment contracts, pay and benefits packages, and personalized leadership styles. Lawler and Finegold consider the satisfaction of individual needs such as these to be vital to attracting and retaining the best employees; to improving customer satisfaction with service; and to stimulating profitability. In fact, Lawler and Finegold conclude that, "variety within species is critical to their survival. To the degree that this is true of organizations, it suggests that organizations that are individualized are more likely to outlive those that aren't" (2000: 14).

Neo-Darwinist conclusions such as these make excellent mantras for the globalization of individualism. Their take-home message is that radical individualism has already arrived, at least for the most perceptive among us. By championing that call, esteemed writers such as Lawler and Finegold position themselves in the vanguard of a globalization of individualism at work. At the same time, they also attempt to position the rest of us as camp followers, in a "libertarian" train of change and innovation.

This insinuation may be partly correct, insofar as individualistic thinking and assumptions, overt and implicit, already pervade much research and writing on work behavior. But despite that somewhat depressing possibility, there are also significant contradictions within the libertarian thesis, and the broader zeitgeist whose bidding it performs.

The most obvious of these contradictions is that the thesis undercuts its own arguments against standardization. It is arguing for individualism *itself* to become a standard, and in that sense for it to become just another manifestation of "one size fits all." This standardization of individualism does not respect, for instance, all those millions of employees and managers alike, who often prefer – for reasons either personal or cultural – to give more emphasis to the group, and to social, rather than personal, achievement. Even to the more individualistically minded among us, making prized possessions out of a minority of high-flying "core resources" (2000: 12) positions the majority as commodities of a lower sort, whose lot in work life is to be the base of a demeaning "performance pyramid." This is socially divisive, offensive, and oppressive. Thus, the radical individualization that Lawler et al. proclaim is actually, in point of fact, anathema to the mutually respectful workplace that they claim to envision.

A second contradiction in the message of the paper is that many of its supposedly individual differences are actually group similarities. Prime illustrations of this are "cultural" and "gender" differences. In many work situations (e.g., in bicultural workplaces), and during gender discrimination cases, groups like this, and their supporters, readily identify with each other. They find more to unite them into groups than to divide them up as individuals. Variance between groups temporarily exceeds the variance within. In Lawler et al.'s field of vision, bonds like that are overlooked. This short-sightedness is all the more obvious because it ignores a vast but predictably "non-American" (predominantly European and Australasian) literature (for an overview, Hogg & Terry, 2000). That literature tells us that, in many settings, the work behavior of individuals is governed not so much by their individual identities, as by a shared, social identity. Thus, it begins to look as if

Lawler and Finegold's analysis, far from being objective and detached, is actually deeply imbedded in its own individualism.

The sharpest indicator of this imbeddedness – this social identity with individualism – is that the paper fails to see, or to understand, the backlash that individualism creates. In many work, management, education, and research-oriented settings, outside of the USA at least, there are strong sentiments that American managerialism, and especially its inherent individualism, has gone beyond the pale. Just as one size does not fit all *within* America, neither does one size fit all *outside* the USA. Hence we continue to hear calls, albeit less frequently published than their global "mainstream" counterparts, for more culturally respectful, and in that sense, localized, theories of work.

2. Localization

The essence of all localized perspectives on work behavior, in theory, is that they remain anchored in a local cultural perspective on work behavior, with which people "on the ground," in that particular locality, socially identify. From this inherently social identification, the lion's share of variance in work behavior is attributed to, and explained in terms of, influence by local norms. Thus, relatively localized writers on work behavior often group themselves, and their study of work behavior itself, under the descriptive term "Indigenous."

By definition, these Indigenous approaches to work behavior are not easily encapsulated in one article or chapter. Neither are they easily articulated into a single authored book. Instead, the closest we can often get to an encapsulated statement about localized perspectives on work behavior is an edited collection of readings. To maximize those readings' cohesion, these edited volumes generally focus on a particular sector or region of the world, the inhabitants of which share socio-economic or socio-cultural similarities despite their differences. Thus, we find edited books on, for example work motivation in "developing" economies (Kanungo & Mendonca, 1994), or work cultural values in countries across Asia (Kao, Sinha & Wilpert, 1999).

The latter collection of readings is a good example of the Indigenous approach to work-related behavior. The book focuses on Indigenous cultural values and their primary role in work settings. It contains engaging chapters on, for instance traditional Japanese models of leadership and their capacity to lift Japan out of economic recession (Fukuda, 1999); the importance of social achievement and family dynamics in organizations in India (Gupta, 1999); the benefits of balancing workplace relations with social equity and reciprocity in Chinese Confucianism (Liu, 1999); traditional views about leadership in Thailand (Komin, 1999); and the nature and complexion of management according to Islamic values (Ali, 1999). It is an undeniably fascinating read, and provides many points of stimulation for contemporary and future research (Carr, 1999).

At the same time though, while the authors advocate diversity, the book simultaneously advocates a kind of uniformity. As one Indigenous reviewer of the book succinctly concludes, "The book sticks more or less to one theme: It is not one world, it is many worlds" (Xin, 2001: 571). In that way, this and other Indigenized perspectives on work behavior do not restrict themselves to baulking at globalization. They also seek to repel it completely, by, for example, implying that the values of individualism cannot exist alongside their more traditional, collectivistic counterparts. Thus, and as Xin's critical review cogently points out, we run up against another fundamental inconsistency – another implicit position that "one size fits all."

To sum up, contemporary students and scholars of work behavior, more than ever before, face an apparent paradox. On the one hand, there are supposedly overriding global – or at least globalizing – principles in the way that people behave at work. This is the mantra of globalization. On the other hand, there are also – supposedly – enduring local realities that make each context in which work takes place largely unique. This is the mantra of localization. Which of these positions is "correct," is the question implicitly posed by the wider literature. Surely, however, that is the wrong question to ask. This book, for instance, grew from a feeling that the study of work behavior can move beyond these zero-sum games. People at work are just as often engaged with the latest global trends, as they are with their local traditions, even when these two appear to contradict each other (Hermans & Kempen, 1998).

3. Glocalization

The essence of a "glocal" perspective is that work behavior is increasingly the product of two interacting, and often competing, cultural influences – globalization and localization (Robertson, 1995). Glocalization has already established itself as a concept in tourism and marketing, where operating glocally has become translated into the now familiar and arguably hackneyed phrase, "think global, act local" (Tai & Wong, 1998). In tourism and marketing, this often means strategic planning in which the local uniqueness of a product or locality is regarded as globally attractive, and in that sense, a source of competitive advantage. In the marketing of health services too, there have been calls to pluralize health systems, in order to match the local-cum-global beliefs about health held by many health service clients (Carr, Mc Auliffe, & MacLachlan, 1998). In these ways, the normal usage of the term "glocal," in the business and human services literatures, has to date focused on glocalizing the systems in which people work.

But what about the people who work in those systems themselves? When we move to a more micro level of work behavior, i.e., of the kind adopted in this book, it is clear that glocality, as a concept and a mentality, has made fewer inroads. This lack of engagement with glocality and glocal consciousness, in the study of work behavior, is ironic. Glocality is integral to, and infused throughout, much of today's work behavior. To give one example, and as Lawler and Finegold cogently remind us, contemporary work systems tend to encourage individualistic self-promotion. Such systems, a sense of glocality warns us, may underestimate the possibility of localized backlashes at the behavioral level, by the collectivity. In other words, global cultural norms (favoring self-promotion) will sometimes conflict with traditional local norms (favoring achievement by the group).

Further examples of global–local interactivity would include global reforms such as (a) pay diversity, (b) project teams, and (c) boundary-less careers. Again, each of these ideas in principle interacts with local traditions, for instance traditions that stress (a) pay equality, (b) not "relying" on others, or (c) selecting "local" over "foreign" workers. How do people at work handle such tensions if and when they arise? Of course, we should remember too that global and local interactions do not *always* resonate together in a negative way: Even the existence of tensions, as we shall see, highlights new opportunities – for individual and group alike – to choose to work both enjoyably and creatively. First of all, however, we need to see those opportunities in the first place. And a key concept for enabling us to do that, the book will argue, is glocality.

3.1. What glocality is *not*

There are at least two forms of cross-cultural management that might claim, at this point, to already *be* glocal. Each of these however is demonstrably not reflective of glocality as conceptualized in this book.

Firstly, there is a cross-cultural approach which inherently claims that the "dimensions" of culture, for example from individualism to collectivism, are universal (globality), whilst at the same time specific positions adopted within them, by specific cultural groups, are not (locality). According to this view, certain management principles – the ones that are consistent with the positions – will generally work, whilst others – the ones that are not consistent with the positions – will likely not. A prototypical example of this kind of approach to cross-cultural management can be found in the following observation, made by Javidan and House:

> The U.S. is among the high performance-oriented countries. To a typical American manager, effective communication means direct and explicit language. Facts and figures and rational thinking are important pillars of communication…. But people from other cultures do not necessarily share these attributes. People from lower performance-oriented cultures like Russia or Greece tend to prefer indirect and vague language. They are not too comfortable with strong results-driven and explicit communication. Hard facts and figures are hard to come by, and not taken as seriously, even when they are available. To a typical Greek manager … (2001: 302).

Quotations like that above are not hard to find in the cross-cultural management literature (for another prominent example, try for instance Lewis, 1999). Despite these and other authors offering sincere caveats against stereotyping cultural groups, those same cautions seem to end up being overridden by a more utilitarian notion. The notion, usually implicit, is that the gain to be had from stereotyping, in terms of economic purchase on work group behavior, is somehow worth the loss in social capital (Hickson & Pugh, 2001). On this basis, whole groups are subsequently positioned in an essentially immutable manner within a single identity. As Javidan and House's conclusion illustrates, these forms of positioning invite us to exclude definitively whole groups – often the "non-Western" ones – from "global best practice." Ironically, therefore, these cross-cultural forms of positioning can end up being over-generalized, ethnocentric and, often, just plain inaccurate.

A second type of remonstration with our approach comes from a more subtle form of positioning. In this vein of cross-cultural management – more difficult to find in the literature than the first – a distinction is drawn between constructs that are "etic" (or global) and work behaviors that are "emic" (localized). *Etic* constructs are found universally; *emic* behaviors are surface reflections of those constructs, or sometimes principles, in local context (Triandis, 1995). A prime example of this etic–emic distinction is found in the literature on leadership. Leadership styles are globally described as being either task- or relations-focused (from, for example Lewin, Lippitt & White, 1939; Misumi & Peterson, 1985; Sinha, 1990; Dunphy & Stace, 1993; Aycan, Kanungo & Mendonca, 2000; Eagly, 2003). According to the cross-cultural etic–emic literature, how each of the two basic styles of leadership are best expressed is defined culturally. Thus, task and relationship foci can be expressed with more or less formality (e.g., according to cultural beliefs in hierarchy), and with more or less attention to group, as distinct from individual, needs (e.g., according to degree of collectivism versus individualism).

Despite this nod to social context and cultural contingency, the etic–emic approach, in cross-cultural management, still positions one cultural group (and its leaders) into fixed modes of expression (Ratner & Hui, 2003). In leadership, for example, it is not conceivable in the model that a leader can *vary* the way his or her leadership styles are expressed, either within a single – but multicultural – group of workers, or when moving from one cultural context to another. Successful leadership in multicultural settings, and across changing contexts generally, becomes a logical impossibility. So, too, does the theoretical optimum leadership strategy, namely *combining* both task and relations styles in a way that is appropriate contextually. Compounding this difficulty, the etic–emic approach also makes no real allowance for flexibility on the part of "followers," whose own preferences may also of course shift according to circumstance. In the final analysis therefore, the etic–emic approach becomes hoisted on its own pétard.

3.2. What glocality *is* and *can* be

In direct contrast to the approaches above, a glocal lens assumes that leadership and other work behaviors are more inherently fluid, interactive, and changeable (Earley, 2002).

Firstly, for instance, people at work are not only surrounded by diversity; they also reflect and encapsulate it. This is a travel metaphor writ large, with individuals themselves incorporating internally diverse cultural repertoires. Those people may, for instance, be migrants, or the first or second generation of migrant families and settlers. Whoever they are and wherever they come from, their experiences render significant numbers (not all) of them equally at home with elements of global work culture, like those outlined by Lawler and Finegold (2000), and with their own traditional cultures of work, as outlined for us in Kao et al. (1999). This plurality renders them capable in principle of identifying with multiple positions and points of view. In a word, global and local identities are often "integrated" (Berry, 1997).

Secondly, and related to the first point, the work behavior of glocal selves and groups is inherently socially interactive. Different identities, from global to local, can be invoked by social factors that become important at any particular time. These social factors include, for instance, group composition, or inter-group competition (Hogg, 2001). Glocalized workers thereby adjust their leadership style, and follower-ship style, to "fit" the cultural context at the time, whether it happens to be global or local. For example, the same group may behave relatively informally while global, relatively "egalitarian" work norms are primed; but the same group can also behave more formally, for example if relatively "hierarchical" traditions are brought to mind.

The latter contingency can happen if, for instance, the latest imported fad at work antagonizes core traditions. These traditions might stress, for instance, (a) respect for elders and leaders and/or (b) resistance to perceived imperialism and hegemony.

Such shifts in forms of cultural identity have implications for how we study work behavior. Ipso facto, if work behavior itself is inherently fluid – if behavior at work has become more pluralistic – then our study of it needs to be pluralistic, too. As we have seen, however, leading thinkers and writers in the field are still regarding work behavior through a largely global lens, whilst others in the wider literature are adopting an inherently more localized perspective. Each of these forms of discourse is, of course, appropriate when the work behavior *itself* is enacted predominantly in one mode or the other (as indeed it often is, and will continue to be). But to the extent that work behavior often transcends these positions, the discourse itself must transcend them, too. Otherwise, the literature will remain detached from the totality, and the fluidity, of its subject matter.

4. Some Foundational Theory

Dislocated discourse like the above would also be turning its back on the available theory of work behavior. For example, Social Identity Theory (or SIT) is a social psychological model of change, anchored in societal groups, that was first proposed in the latter part of the twentieth century (Tajfel, 1978). Since its inception, SIT has been progressively, and lately, extensively, applied to work groups and work behavior (e.g., Hogg & Terry, 2000). SIT argues that, as well as growing individually, people at work also need to affiliate socially. In particular, SIT proposes, people at work need to identify with, and feel proud of belonging to, diverse kinds of group (e.g., Haslam, 2001). Pride of this kind is often derived through social and inter-group comparison, namely by achieving collective differentiation from other groups (out-groups). According to SIT, such differentiation helps to maintain the integrity of the in-group's *culture*. According to Tajfel, this twin requirement, for both cultural differentiation and cultural integrity, applies equally well to minority and majority groups. Thus, much of SIT explicitly focuses on the dynamic interaction between these groups – minority and majority – as each of them strives to preserve and develop its own sense of identity in an ever-changing, and interconnecting social world.

Of course, preserving cultural integrity is also a central challenge in the face of globalization. SIT implies, for instance, that work practices need to reflect a balance of (a) individualistic *and* (b) group, i.e., social, concerns (Carr, 1996). Too much individualism by implication will threaten group identities, while too much collectivism will stifle individual concerns. Hence, SIT can be said to focus on the dynamic interaction between different forms of identity – one more global, the other more local. For example, to the extent that workers are at the time concerned with social identity, "individualization" is likely to fan a collective backlash. However, if the organizational climate at the time is instead preoccupied with internal competition and strife, then individualized programs may resonate not negatively but, perhaps, positively with workers' expectations. Thus, one of the key ways in which SIT respects the flexibility of work behavior is through its engagement with the idea of thresholds for change, between for instance individual and social identity, and global to local forms of action.

4.1. A mirror to ourselves
As well as respecting the diversity of its subjects, SIT also respects the diversity of its subject matter. It can be applied, reflexively, to the kinds of discourse found in the literature on work behavior itself. As we have already seen, the groups in this (literary) arena include at least two main protagonists. On the one hand, we can identify with the scholars who are researching and publishing from within a US "mainstream" schema for work behavior. On the other hand, we can identify with those scholars, fewer in number (as we have seen), who live outside of the "mainstream" but are also researching and publishing in mainstream publications (e.g., that are domiciled in the USA). SIT suggests that if these two largely opposed groups are to begin communicating with each other, thereby illuminating complementary aspects of work behavior, the more "dominant" group must recognize its own implicit biases, while the less powerful group must overcome its fears of domination (Empson, 2001). Only then – according to the theory – will the two groups reach a more peaceful and productive coexistence.

In SIT, the three processes just proposed are termed *assimilation, anti-conformity,* and *integration*.

4.1.1 *Assimilation*
According to SIT, during assimilation, a less privileged group experiences pressure from a more privileged group to blend itself into a socially dominant mainstream. Such processes are often found, for instance, in organizational takeovers and mergers (McEntire & Bentley, 1996). Assimilation may be achieved initially by some individuals, who manage to "cross over" and adapt themselves to the dominant group's ways of thinking, feeling, and acting (Terry & O'Brien, 2001). This change can, in principle, become a model for others to follow, except when the new converts continue to be treated by the majority group as second-class citizens (Terry, Carey & Callan, 2001; see also, Ashkanasy & Holmes, 1995). Processes like this, i.e., being positioned into second-class citizenry, would include the study of work behavior itself. In that domain, for instance, we have seen how Indigenous perspectives are often positioned – in the eyes of the mainstream at least – at the margins of the publishing enterprise.

4.1.2 *Anti-conformity*
If the dominance and implicit arrogance of a mainstream continues, with no real attempts by the majority to fully integrate and respect the views and experiences of a minority, that minority will eventually, and according to Tajfel, inevitably, reactivate its latent need for positive distinctiveness. For instance, during this process – according to SIT – cultural cringe becomes local pride. In organizational mergers as an example, lower-status groups turn their previously "weak" points into strengths. They take pride in their distinguishing features as a minority group (van Knippenberg, van Knippenberg, Monden & de Lima, 2002). There is a risk with such localized tactics however: Because the agenda for development continues to be set by the majority group, the minority group defines itself by what it is not rather than by what it is, and to that extent falls into bad faith with itself. To the degree that this lack of awareness persists, genuine localization and Indigenization at work is compromised (Sinha, 1989). Instead, in its place, there is a continuing stand-off – and thus stalemate – between a mainstream who keep thinking, acting and

unconsciously emanating assimilation, and their more localized counterparts who continually seek to revive tradition in an implicitly romanticized form.

As an alternative to stand-offs like the above, SIT suggests that global and local outlooks, e.g., on work behavior, can be integrated in at least two mutually inclusive and complementary ways.

4.1.3. *Integration*

One way for minority groups to find their own voice, without isolating themselves from the global mainstream, is for them to independently identify domains in which they genuinely excel. A good example of this can be found in the literature on entrepreneurial behavior within Indigenous communities (Ivory, 2003). In many of these local settings, competitive edges in the global market can be developed through drawing on pre-contact (and, by definition, independent) traditional local values (Rugimbana, 1996). Such processes are inherently less viable, however, in the study of work behavior itself. After all, the goal for scholars of work behavior is the exact opposite of gaining competitive advantage over each other. Instead, and rather like in an organizational merger perhaps, the goal is more likely to involve developing a sense of common purpose (Gaertner, Dovidio, & Bachman, 1996). Thus, a glocal goal, in studying work behavior, is to find a way for the different perspectives, both global and local, to communicate with each other.

Helping to address that kind of goal, SIT suggests a second path to glocality. This path entails the minority finding a way to do its own thing alongside, but not completely "apart" from, the majority. In mergers, for instance, each party to the merger, regardless of 'status,' might rediscover respect for its own cultural strengths and the unique contributions they make towards the new workplace as a whole (Terry & Callan, 1998). As an example of a not dissimilar process outside of mergers, in New Zealand/Aotearoa there is a bicultural work practice called *whānau interviewing*. In Māori world views, the *whānau* includes the extended family, and in whānau interviewing, a conventional employment selection interview is biculturated: In addition to traditional panel-to-candidate interviews, Indigenous Māori candidates are interviewed in the presence of members of their extended families and in accordance with Māori protocol. Such culturally familiar practices can give candidates and selection panel alike a fairer tilt at managing the job selection process. Beyond these justice concerns however, whānau interviewing is also a legitimate alternate form for conducting job selection, one that respects cultural tradition without simply being a reaction against more wider, global practices: In whānau interviewing, there is no turning of backs on wider, relatively global practices at work. Instead, in this approach to job selection, both local and global systems are balanced and integrated, practically and ethically, into one glocality.

What the example of whānau interviewing also tells us is that glocality is a mentality. Studying and practising work behavior glocally is all about pluralism. The glocal (selection) scholar, and the glocal (selection) practitioner work in both modalities – global and local – in parallel. She cultivates a relatively detached consideration of what is likely to work, and be fair, from a bicultural point of view. Whether in daily practice or when conducting work behavior research, "going glocal" means making balanced considerations of both (a) the latest global concerns, like interviewing individually, as well as (b) enduring local traditions, such as respecting family traditions and collectivistic definitions of "self" and selfhood.

Glocal melds like these are best introduced more fully by a brief preview of the contents of the book.

5. Glocality At Work

5.1. Culture (Chapter 2)

In the wider debate on globalization, it is often implied that globalization equals the attempted eradication of local culture. Such all-or-nothing dichotomies overlook the possibility that globality has a culture too. As many of us would probably accept, global culture is heavily imbued for instance with "individualism." Elements of culture like this will interact with local cultures – the latter often stress, for example, the group, and the collective. Given such interactivity, and the shifting "culture-scapes" it inevitably creates, we need to achieve two goals before the book gets fully underway. Firstly, it is argued, we need to construct some reasonably reliable "compass points," that will enable us to navigate the cultural landscape at work using relatively parsimonious points of reference. Secondly, it is argued, we need to explain *how* global–local interactions take place at work, by tracing any regularities in the pathways that individuals and groups often take, as they pass through the cultural landscape earlier described.

At first sight, the complexity of cultural systems is daunting. This is partly because they criss-cross a range of levels. The lattice includes, for example, societal cultures, organizational cultures, professional sub-cultures within organizations, departmental cultures, and cultures within workplace teams. Even within those various "layers," which we might conveniently picture as shrinking concentric "rings" of culture surrounding work behavior, there are conflicting views, in the literature, about the dimensionality of cultural space and its chief landmarks. As well, cultural behavior is often hard to *see*, thereby making it hard to *measure*. Culture is less and less visible, for instance, as we pass from comparatively visible artifacts, like office layouts and dress codes, to explicit values verbalized on questionnaires, through to cultural assumptions that are implicit in everyday discourse (Schein, 1990, 1996). Yet the latter may exert the more profound influences on actual work behavior (Schein, 1996). Adding further complexity to this picture, people at work are often contradictory – for example their rituals and implicit assumptions may be at odds with the work values that they overtly, and often sincerely, espouse.

There is a way out of this complexity however.

Firstly, and foremost, the overall picture of culture becomes much less daunting once we realize that the dimensionality of culture space is more a question of focus than of "fact." Compass points are not "real," they are social constructions designed to navigate and "make sense of" a landscape in two basic dimensions. Two particular compass points are in fact readily available to us. These are individualism–collectivism and belief in hierarchy–egality (Probst, Carnevale & Triandis, 1999). Thus, behavior at work often reflects, for example, an interaction between (a) global norms, that stress either individuality or egality, and (b) local norms, that stress either collectivity or hierarchy.

Secondly, people at work regularly position each other into global and local cultural *stereotypes* (Giacalone & Beard, 1994). At least two theories, SIT and

Social Facilitation Theory (or SFT) (Thompson, Nadler & Kim, 1999), suggest a mechanism for these forms of "cultural positioning," i.e., mutual stereotyping, to happen (Tan & Moghaddam, 1996). In brief, the presence of others (SFT), and especially diverse others (SIT), socially facilitates (enhances) well-learned (cultural) repertoires (Glynn & Carr, 1999). Forms of mutual positioning like these render work behavior painfully predictable, even in a work environment that is potentially very flux-like and fluid. But the same mechanisms also suggest *new* forms of glocality. If cultural positioning is possible, so too must be *re*positioning, and the breaking *out* of, rather than merely *into*, mutually divisive stereotypes. "Waking up" to this kind of capacity for change (MacLachlan, 2003), by "trying on" different perspectives both local and global, is termed *glocal repositioning*.

5.2. Achievement (Chapter 3)

A fine example of glocal repositioning can be found in how the literature on work behavior conceptualizes "achievement." This in fact has tended to be conceptualized similarly to "leadership" (House & Aditya, 1997). Achievement has been heavily individualized and "psychologized" into a trait-like commodity. However, if we adopt a more localized instead of globalized perspective, we see that the individualization of achievement is actually inconsistent with many prominent and enduring socio-cultural systems. Even at the level of small groups, work teams may be part of globalization but their inherently localized ethos is liable, too, to create expectations that achievement will be social not just individual. From a glocal perspective therefore, performance management systems that emphasize achievement "by and for the individual" may end up incurring as many as 360 degrees of social restraint, i.e., from peers, supervisees, and supervisors.

Our chapter explores this range of possible social influences, using a metaphor of *motivational gravity*. Motivational gravity often arises from the dynamic interplay between two key forces. These comprise (a) global norms that favor individual over social (or group) achievement, and (b) local group, organizational and societal norms that favor social achievement on behalf of the collective (Carr & MacLachlan, 1997). Social tensions from these forces create strains and ambivalences for individuals, groups and organizations alike. Yet they also create opportunities as well. Motivational gravity can, for instance, act as a civilizing agency on the "up-or-out," "dog-eat-dog" mores that radical individualism sometimes engenders. Motivational gravity, too, can encourage teamwork, and, in general, leadership "from the middle." Thus, gravity can be managed for the good of both individual and group alike, once we become aware of its inherent and dynamic glocality.

5.3. Incentives (Chapter 4)

One possible way of unintentionally fostering negative gravity at work is by designing systems of remuneration that appear unjust. Chief among the various forms of remuneration is pay, which brings us to the concept of pay diversity. Pay diversity is widely reflected, for example, in pay-for-performance, individual contracts, enterprise bargains, and international assignments for commercial and humanitarian organizations. Our chapter on remuneration adopts a contrarian attitude toward pay diversity in each of these situations. The chapter questions the received wisdom of pay diversity and all that it represents. A starting point for this devil's advocacy is the fact that pay diversity always takes place in a social context. In this peopled landscape for remuneration, diversity in pay (a global norm) becomes pay relative to others (a local reality). Relative pay like this, it is argued, is a question of work (in)justice (Colquitt, Conlon & Wesson, 2001).

According to theories of work justice, pay diversity always involves at least two major parties. On the one hand, there will be a higher paid individual or group. On the other hand, there will be a lesser paid individual or group. What does this basic fact enable us to predict about work behavior in each of the two relative pay groups? Imagine, for example, that we take the domain of *distributive justice*. This term refers to a perception that finite resources have been shared in a just and fair manner between key work group stakeholders. According to Distributive Justice Theory, there are three major principles in terms of which available resources may be justly (and unjustly) distributed. These principles are (a) need, (b) egality, and (c) equity. The common principle in (a) to (c) however is that people will react to perceived injustice by restoring a sense of balance.

If workers become focused on (a) need as a basis for reward, the *less* well paid, whether as individuals or as a group, will feel angry, gravitational, and generally disaffected. The same applies if (b) egality is salient at the time. Whenever (c) equity is salient, too, the underpaid will react by withdrawal and other counter-productive work behaviors, thereby restoring the sense that outcomes are proportionate to inputs (Adams, 1965). In the situation of a *higher* paid individual or group, the same three principles (a) to (c) predict an alternative form of de-motivation. A combination of Equity Theory and SIT, for instance, suggests that the worker or group will either increase their inputs (effort) to try and match their raised outcomes, thereby ultimately becoming stressed, or – more likely perhaps – in the course of time they will inflate their inputs psychologically, in order to match their inflated outcomes in a material (i.e., pay) sense. Since neither of these outcomes is optimal for work performance ("If I am better than you, I do not need to work as hard to do my job"), we would expect a drop in work motivation compared to if pay had been *less* diverse.

Overall therefore, whatever basis our individuals and groups use to judge the justice in their pay, both less well paid and better paid individuals and groups will start to become de-motivated. There will be a *double de-motivation* (Carr & MacLachlan, 1992/3; MacLachlan & Carr, 1992). In case this prediction sounds too contrarian and counter-intuitive, a range of field and laboratory research, within inter-individual and inter-group situations, across a wide range of organizational contexts and settings, now supports the double de-motivation hypothesis. This emerging literature is reviewed in the chapter. The core point in the review, however, is that viewing global pay reform in local context enables us to spot an otherwise overlooked, not-talked-about issue (of social justice) with pay diversity itself. Problem recognition like this, of course, is a first and necessary step to problem resolution.

The same glocal lens that allows us to critically "see" the possibility of double de-motivation also suggests a range of options for managing it once it has already occurred, and – better still – for preventing it from happening in the first place. Options on the prevention side range, for instance, from improving selection decisions (made by potential employers and potential employees alike), to designing more glocally appropriate incentive systems. Essentially, these systems each incorporate both locally and globally valued forms of remuneration, that are in accordance with the level of plurality of beliefs about work pay justice held amongst the working stakeholders themselves. An elementary example of that plurality is the so-called "Pay-[for]-Performance Matrix. This type of pay-and-remuneration system rewards work performance through a combination of group and individual rewards, thus respecting the mix of both individualist and collectivist aspirations that teamwork often engenders.

5.4. Empowerment (Chapter 5)

As the above example indicates, pay diversity both contributes toward double de-motivation and suggests some solutions, and even advantages, to it. A further key to the managing double demotivation is empowering a group to have culturally appropriate levels of "voice" in the process of designing, implementing and delivering pay systems (Van den Bos, Vermunt & Wilke, 1996). Such initiatives toward encouraging more voice from employees, reflect a wider, global zeitgeist toward empowerment in organizations (Spreitzer, 1995). Empowerment is epitomized most clearly of all in the concept of teamwork, which has become part of the global lexicon at work today. Teams, for example, are widely seen as vehicles to "surf the knowledge wave" ("two heads are better than one;" "nobody is smarter than everybody"). Teams are also seen to provide a way of capitalizing on processes like social support and social facilitation (above). By fusing together both global (productivity, creativity) and local concerns (social needs), the entities that we call workplace teams are inherently glocal.

Despite that inherent glocality, teams and teamwork are still being promulgated as "one size fits all." It is superbly ironic that theories of teamwork remain essentially individualistic. They tend to stress, for example, diversity in "personality," and choosing "individual" differences that complement rather than antagonize each other (e.g., Belbin, 1997). A detailed review of the literature on teams reveals, however, that successfully implementing teams is a question of both global *and* local considerations. To revisit an idea on which this book is based, a more glocal perspective holds that it is important to find locally relevant metaphors that resonate positively with the potential team members' own implicit, and largely local, models for working together (Gibson & Zellmer-Bruhn, 2001). Thus, teamwork, at the ground level, is intrinsically glocal.

Perhaps the most outlandish and faddish aspect of this unmistakably global push for teams is that no one, as yet, has demonstrated that work "teams" are any different, in work behavior terms, from work "groups." A promising theoretical base for launching research on this question, and some preliminary research using it, is described in the chapter. Prototype Theory is an inherently glocal way of listening to how "teams," and "teamwork," are actually constructed socially, in local settings. A prototypes approach to team design, for instance, empowers the team itself to describe the associations that it already has in mind, with respect to what teamwork means. In that way, by "tuning into" pre-existing, local metaphors for team design, prototypes research is a process-based approach that endeavors to respect both global and local norms, and which actively resists the notion that one size fits all.

Introducing teams into a work setting can require a lot of emotional labor. It can, for instance, from the outset, emotionally threaten the power base and invested commitment of supervisors already "in" the previous, more traditional system.

Supervisors who are asked to empower others can reasonably be anticipated to resist any *dis*empowerment for themselves! According to some observers, one common way of dealing with this dissonance is for supervisors to assimilate the rhetoric of empowerment, whilst at the same time retaining their (relatively hierarchical) routines for managing people that they used, successfully, in the past. This is a glocal process, partly implicit perhaps, par excellence: Not only does glocality function at the individual level, through the supervisors' own ambivalence toward teams, but it also creates pressures socially, within the work group itself. To be specific, by coupling the globalised rhetoric of empowerment with the local practice of traditional supervision, the situation is created of an over-promise (of empowerment) and an under-delivery on that promise (actual continuing delivery of hierarchy). This discrepancy, between what writers like Argyris (1998) have termed *espoused theory* and *theory-in-use,* is a potentially damaging and demoralizing form of broken promise.

5.5. Learning (Chapter 6)

Perhaps the most destructive and divisive form of broken promise of all is found, today, in the global jobs market. A key way of empowering the self, in the world of global migration and travel, is to move from one work setting to the next. Much of this global mobility, nowadays, is metaphorical. It takes place, for instance, through highly powered e-teams, whose physical location, as individual members, can be extremely widespread. A second form of mobility, more literal but still vital for international cooperation, is the expatriate assignment (or EA). This has been researched widely (Inkson, Arthur, Pringle, & Barry, 1997). But a third, and so far clearly under-researched form of mobility, of greater significance perhaps than the others, is global migration. This form of mobility is often work-related, and realized by unskilled and skilled workers alike. The common motivation is often to leave a country-of-origin to build a safer and more prosperous life in the country-of-destination. To that end, skilled migrants are often encouraged to enter the country-of-destination by immigration systems that award "points" for qualifications and experience, and implicitly promise "a good life" in the new country.

The poignant irony in these boundary-less careers, however, is that they are often impeded by human factors relating to job selection in the country-of-destination. Travel may broaden the mind of the traveler, but not necessarily the mind of the host. Despite the immigration systems that encourage skilled migrants to enter the country-of-destination, the skilled immigrant often experiences an intolerable range of barriers to finding full employment. These can include, for instance, selection biases operating against job candidates from one country-of-origin over another, which may even prevent them from securing any kind of skilled job whatsoever. This is a massive broken promise for those people. A review of the research reveals that "brain waste" of shameful proportions, via local biases of various kinds, is found globally. Thus, in major cities around the world, it is not unusual to find highly skilled individuals either unemployed or grossly underemployed if one considers the skills they have to offer (Atkins & Fletcher, 2003).

For any country or society, this is a tragic waste of talent, and a massive drain on social capital. In order to begin removing those barriers to personal, organizational and national development, emerging research has utilized theories such as SIT. SIT makes some rather counter-intuitive predictions pinpointing which countries-of-origin will be least preferred. For example, candidates originating from countries that are perceived to be more similar to the country-of-destination may actually, all else being equal, be *less* preferred compared to candidates whose country-of-origin is comparatively "different." Counter-intuitive predictions like these signal potential management issues, for instance, with regional trade blocs. Those blocs are often based, in part, on an implicit assumption that similarity is relatively attractive to employers, and that skilled labor pools will consequently be correspondingly free to move unimpeded from country to country within the bloc itself (Dore, 1994). Contradicting these notions, the lens of glocality suggests a different picture. Amongst employers in the country-of-destination, we predict, and test, an inverse (negative) resonance with candidates whose country-of-origin is overly *similar*.

The emerging evidence on this question is consistent with the prediction of an inverse resonance effect. However, the same research also reveals the importance of other factors. These factors include, for instance, the implicitly perceived socio-economic dominance of the country-of-origin, compared to the country-of-destination. Candidates from countries-of-origin that are lower in the global hierarchy, at a schematic level, will generally have less of a fair chance of being selected for the job, even though their skills may be just as high. Findings like this illustrate again that global and local interests interact in work settings, at the perceptual level. In that sense, and to return to a point made in the Preface to this volume, perceptions at work are inherently glocal in character.

In order to draw these and other glocal processes into one integrated model, the book will conclude with a summary of the range and depth of glocal processes in work behavior. In order not to steal that thunder, but at the same time perform a similar, summarizing function, we can end this chapter with a sample of glocal research. The following case study encapsulates a range of glocal processes, all of which interact with each other to form one coherent, behavioral system. That capacity, for coherent and graspable interactions, is in turn a key strength of case study research (Bachiochi & Weiner, 2002).

6. A Case in Point

6.1. The Buick Bar & Grill

After 18 months of market research, a consortium of North American investors selected an Australian coastal city, in which they planned to develop the prototype for a chain of entertainment centers throughout the country. The Buick Bar & Grill concept was to be a multi-purpose complex consisting of a 200-seat capacity restaurant, nightclub, cocktail bar and a theme bar emphasizing Australian sporting icons. Facilities were top of the range. No expense was spared on the fitting out of the venue in order to obtain a uniquely North American atmosphere, and to ensure that the staff would have the most modern equipment and comfortable working environment.

The manager of the complex, and part-owner, was a North American, Kirk Reed. Reed was still in his early thirties but had already acquired much experience in the North American hospitality industry. After leaving school at age 16, Reed got his first job as a kitchen hand in a local restaurant. Four years later he owned it. By the time he was 25, he was also part-owner of two American bars. Reed was a self-made man who had worked his way to his current position, and who believed that any individual with motivation and energy was capable of doing the same.

In November 2001, advertisements were run in the newspaper calling for applications to positions as bartender, cocktail waitperson, bar/food runner, cook and kitchen-hand. The ads were visually exciting and emphasized the fact that the Buick Bar & Grill was to be an exciting workplace, "rapidly expanding ... highly motivating" and full of opportunities. In excess of 1800 people applied for the 77 vacancies.

Selection interviews were two-tiered. Company trainers, personally recruited by Reed in North America, carried out a first interview. As well as conducting future training, they would also later act as temporary managers of specific sections – kitchen, restaurant, and bar. Reed himself carried out a second interview. The interviews were fast-paced, informal, had no standard structure, and varied in duration from candidate to candidate. Previous qualifications were not an issue. The criterion for job selection was to impress Reed with one's own enthusiasm, motivation, and desire to succeed. The 77 successful candidates were not informed of the positions they had won. Instead, they were congratulated and invited to attend a two-week training program.

At the outset of the training program, all new staff members received detailed employment manuals and job descriptions. Many staff members were quite surprised that they had been placed in jobs for which they had no prior experience. Reed then explained the concept of the Buick Bar & Grill in detail. He was an extremely fluent and interesting speaker who held the audience's attention very well. His energetic nature and his desire for success were obvious, and he continually referred to the management and staff of Buick's as a "family". Reed placed much emphasis on teamwork and communication, and he pointed out that the franchising of Buick's would commence within six months. As such he was looking for "peak performers ... staff with the little bit more that separated them from the crowd;" who would be promoted to trainee managers, with the long-term goal of managing Buick's clubs in various locations around the country.

Reed also explained the pay system at Buick's. Regardless of job description, age, experience or qualifications every staff member (excluding management who were on a salary) was to receive a flat rate of $10 per hour. Penalty rates and overtime rates did not apply. It was stressed that all 77 staff members were to start off as "equals in the family". Those who "soared above the already high standards set at the Buick Bar & Grill" were to be rewarded with pay rises, promotions above the other staff, and a variety of other benefits (e.g., free drinks and meals).

Training was intense and combined direct hands-on work, role-plays and observational learning (modeling). The kitchen staff, the restaurant staff, and the bar staff were trained as separate teams by their own particular trainer. During the training process, Reed spent equal amounts of time with each of the three groups. During this time he offered words of encouragement, gave pep talks and repeatedly remarked that he was looking for outstanding individuals for promotion.

During training, three of the 20 kitchen staff unexpectedly resigned. All three were qualified chefs and claimed that it was unfair and demeaning to them that they were to do the same tasks as "unqualified" individuals who had no previous cooking experience. Furthermore, they claimed that the dishwasher was not equal in pay and status with the chefs. These resignations did not seem to worry Reed, who stated that they simply made the task of identifying peak performers in the kitchen team easier – only 17 staff members now needed to be monitored for progress.

Despite these resignations, each of the teams now developed into highly cohesive groups. This cohesion was encouraged formally through team-building exercises, games, and various initiatives developed by Reed. The groups also became more cohesive outside of work. After the day's training, which finished around 10 PM, each of the team leaders would take their respective group out for a "few quiet drinks". Friendships were quick to build, and considering the relatively small amount of time the members of the group had known each other, the group cohesion was surprisingly strong.

Opening night was a resounding success. All staff members were rostered on, and except for first-night jitters, everything went smoothly and professionally. At a staff party afterwards, Reed congratulated the group and reminded everybody that he was looking for individuals who excelled, in order to promote them.

With the initial orientation, training and opening night out of the way, work began in earnest. Each of the three teams handled their tasks well, and everyone worked competently. Each of the separate teams made decisions on a group basis. In the kitchen, for instance, decisions were not ratified unless every member of the group agreed with them. This enhanced group cohesion even more, to the point where individuals felt uncomfortable receiving any praise from Reed in front of their colleagues. Those who received praise in front of the group would often refuse to accept the compliment, insisting that it be given to the group as a whole.

Within a month of opening, Reed was placing pressure on the team trainers to identify the individual peak performers for the possibility of promotion. The trainers replied that all of the team members were working well, but none seemed to be making any effort to stand out from the group. This, however, was not producing any negative effects on the operations. The team members were close-knit and working well together.

A week later, after much deliberation, Reed called a staff meeting to announce to all, that promotions had been given to three staff members. Nicholas, a recent university graduate had received the largest promotion, rose from waiter to trainee manager. Jason, a recent Higher School Certificate graduate was promoted from food runner to floor supervisor, and Karen, who had worked in the hospitality industry for a number of years, was promoted from card girl to nightclub supervisor. Nicholas, Jason, and Karen, now had greater responsibilities and the power to delegate tasks to the rest of the staff members.

Four other promotions had been offered to various individuals, but none had accepted the offer. Reasons given for this included: not wanting to rock the boat; feeling uncomfortable about being in charge of friends; and the prospect of no longer being a member of the group. Reed explained that they would still be team players, and put their fears down to lack of responsibility.

Tension now began to rise between Nicholas, Jason, and Karen on the one hand, and the ordinary staff members on the other. Staff felt that they should not have to answer to any of these three, and many heated arguments ensued. Staff members often ignored Nicholas and Jason's requests, and those that were heeded were done so under protest. During breaks, Nicholas, Jason, and Karen were ignored by the rest of the staff, and much of the informal conversation amongst staff members consisted of complaints, and negative remarks concerning the three new managers.

It soon came to Reed's attention that the separate teams were operating ineffectively under the charge of the new managers compared to the trainers. Customer orders were often wrong, productivity had dropped, arguments frequently broke out, and the teams generally seemed apathetic. Reed had also received numerous anonymous complaints from staff members regarding the three new managers. He subsequently began to think that the new managers were ineffective. Upon close investigation however, Reed found that Nicholas, Jason, and Karen were working extremely hard, and within the operational guidelines which he had set for them.

Reed now deduced that the problems being experienced were due to "troublemakers," and sacked ten staff members. At a staff meeting he described this sacking as "cutting out an insidious cancer from within the organization". Staff members were now instructed in clear tones that the slightest form of resistance against any requests made by Nicholas, Jason, or Karen, would be met by instant dismissal.

Within two weeks morale had plummeted amongst staff at the Buick Bar & Grill. Five staff members had been sacked or resigned, Reed was distrusted and resented by the ordinary staff members, and Jason and Karen had both resigned. Their explanation was that they felt ostracized by the majority of the staff members. The low morale, and the increasing rate of staff turnover, led to a drop in the quality of work being carried out by remaining staff members. This often led to customer complaints and dissatisfaction.

In March 2002, poor sales at the Buick Bar & Grill forced the company into the hands of receivers. Reed wanted to try and trade Buick's out of debt, but he no longer had either the staff or the finances to do this. It had taken four months for the Buick Bar & Grill to close down all operations until a new buyer could be found.

Source: Extracted and adapted from McLoughlin & Carr (1994).

6.2. What went wrong at the Buick Bar & Grill: A glocal analysis
6.2.1. *Glocal repositioning.*

First of all, the management of Buick's failed to appreciate the local as much as the global. Initially, there may have been a serendipitous positive resonance between the US consortium and with the sporting traditions that are often venerated and valued in Australian society. These resonances arguably produced an initial glocal positioning into a team ethos. Not long afterwards, however, there was a sharp change of tack, back toward a stereotypically US-style individualism, and individualistic systems of promotion. This was accompanied, too, by an individualistic preference to look for blame in individuals instead of inside the systems of working and leadership themselves. Such changes of tack went completely against the grain of mateship that, up till then, Reed had inadvertently so successfully encouraged. Now, an evident lack of respect for local cultural realities began to reposition each party – "leaders" and "led" alike – back into essentially divisive, mutual stereotypes of each other.

6.2.2. Motivational gravity.

Continuing with the theme of cultural sensitivity, Reed ultimately managed to remain insensitive to stereotypically "Australian" traditions of mateship. These tend to emphasize, for instance, radical egalitarianism and collectivism. In particular, the management of the Buick Bar & Grill failed to notice or appreciate the danger of what these Australian workers termed the "Tall Poppy Syndrome" (Chapter 3). Briefly, Tall Poppy Syndrome, as it is known across Australasia (Australia and New Zealand), entails cutting "tall poppies" (or high individual achievers) down to size, a type of scything action that, according to research presented later in the book, is frequently precipitated in workplaces elsewhere. Through a glocal lens, a tall poppy syndrome might have been preventable at the Buick Bar & Grill, for example by using stock-in-trade techniques like clearly structured job evaluations, realistic job previews, and well-defined performance and promotion goals (Chapter 3, this volume).

6.2.3. Double De-motivation.

Pay, or rather relative pay, was a major de-motivating factor at the Buick Bar & Grill. For the comparatively underpaid group, it clearly left a sour taste in the mouths of those employees who were left behind during the promotion rounds. This aftertaste in turn contributed toward a great deal of rancor in the majority's work behavior. For the promoted individuals, too, their pay "superiority," over their former co-workers and mates, was anything but a social blessing. For example, there were four individuals who declined the promotion offer (and the pay rise that went along with it). Even amongst the three who did accept the rise, two of them soon resigned. To those extents, there are clear indications, in the Buick Bar & Grill, of double de-motivation.

6.2.4. A broken promise.

The initial successes at Buick's were largely due to the team spirit that Reed and his colleagues managed to unleash. Ultimately, however, there was no genuine respect given to the locally important values that underpinned this initial success, namely for example that performance and promotions should be managed on a collective, rather than on a purely individual basis. Similarly perhaps, there was no real recognition of the notion that achievement there is often stereotyped as underdogs managing to 'scrape' a living, rather than high-flyers managing to 'soar above the rest'. At the core of the fiasco however was an over-promise of empowerment and an under-delivery of radical individualism – a broken promise. Instead of raising expectations about empowerment and then backflipping into promoting individuals once collective momentum was underway, the Buick's management may have been better off, in the long run, not promising empowerment at all. At the least, the limits to empowerment ought to have been spelled out in advance, through clear job descriptions, promotion rules, and realistic job previews. In this way, potential employees might have chosen their employer more wisely, or at least lowered their expectations to meet the realities of the job more squarely.

6.2.5 Inverse resonance.

Last, but not least, mobility, and our original travel metaphor, is at the heart of the case study. Reed comes to Australia from America. America comes to

Australia with Reed. So, for the Australians working at Buick's, travel comes to them. With that mobility, there soon come clear inverse resonances between the two belief systems, i.e., frictions that are partly attributable to similarities between the two cultures. Those similarities arguably entail for example reasonably comparable sporting values, work ethics, and a form of cultural individualism, in which every worker is as good as their master. In the final analysis therefore, even Reed did not have a totally boundary-less career. Quite the contrary – his first major career failure was due to a human factor, an inverse resonance.

7. Conclusion

The overall suggestion from this brief analysis of the "rise and fall" of the Buick Bar & Grill is that a glocal lens helps us probe into – and realize more clearly perhaps – other vital nooks and crannies in work behavior systems. Personally, I do not believe that the dynamics of this particular workplace – some of which many of us will recognize – would have been quite so visible without the kind of lens that glocality provides. Delivering on that promised sense of acuity is a yardstick against which the rest of the book can now be judged.

Chapter 2

Culture

> Culture consists of patterned ways of thinking, feeling and reacting, acquired and transmitted mainly by symbols, constituting the distinctive achievements of human groups, including their embodiments in artifacts; the essential core of culture consists of traditional (i.e., historically derived and selected) ideas and especially their attached values.
>
> *Source*: C. Kluckhohn (1951: 86).

> ... the effort for these years to live in the dress of Arabs, and to imitate their mental foundation, quitted me of my English self, and let me look at the West and its conventions with new eyes: they destroyed it all for me.
>
> *Source*: T. E. Lawrence (1926/7, 1997: 14)

1. Introduction

An interesting feature of Kluckhohn's definition of culture above is that it was originally written to define "culture" broadly, i.e., beyond work itself. Despite that wider, societal ambit however, the definition is often cited in narrower, occupational circles (e.g., Aycan & Kanungo, 2001: 390). Evidently, Kluckhohn's definition of culture captures what for many scholars is an essence of culture, whenever it is found and wherever its influences manage to extend. In that sense, it provides us with a working definition of culture with which to begin this chapter.

A further interesting feature of Kluckhohn's definition is that it excludes organizational climate. In this chapter too, culture is differentiated from climate, which consists more of atmospheric factors such as aggression, motivation, or trust (Moran & Volkwein, 1992). Climate factors such as these are discussed in detail later in the book, firstly under motivational gravity (Chapter 3), then as double de-motivation (Chapter 4) and broken promises (Chapter 5), and, finally, as inverse resonance (Chapter 6). Underlying each of these climate-related processes, however, is the presence and influence of culture. Culture, therefore, comprises the underlying values and assumptions held, made, and above all lived on a daily basis within any work group (Ashkanasy, Wilderom & Peterson, 2000).

Our definition of culture, as Kluckhohn's definition implies it should, also spans multiple levels. Those levels range from country-level analyses of societal cultures; within-country individual differences in those values (usually in fact either within a single country or across a pair of countries); to organizational cultures. Organizational cultures include various sub-cultures, from departments within the organization to the micro-cultures of workplace teams. Organizational cultures also embody and intersect with cultures of occupations, for example amongst a company's in-house or out-sourced engineers and accountants. Many of us will recognize these various levels of identification. We regularly don them, and inhabit them, each in turn, over the course of a working day. Logically therefore, and as the quotation from Lawrence above presages, a key challenge in studying culture at work is to develop theories about how different forms of cultural identity transit from one kind of identification to the next.

One of the key lenses for understanding cultural transitions like the above is glocalization. For example, *occupational values* (and norms that are relatively global) may take precedence during disputes about industrial safety; whereas *societal identity* (a more localized form of positioning) will come to the fore when a group of foreign expatriates arrive, "overpaid and over here," to work on our employer's latest international project. It is therefore disappointing that much of the literature on culture at work has ignored this kind of fluidity and plurality. Instead, the study of culture at work has been largely a-theoretical (Aycan & Kanungo, 2001). Specifically, the literature has concentrated on building models of measurement only. These models have focused on describing in detail the n-dimensionality of cultural space at one kind of level; and on the content of those (proposed) dimensions, principally in terms of espoused values. It is fitting, therefore, that we begin our journey through work and culture with an overview of the foremost models for measuring cultural values at work.

2. Country-level Studies

The glue that both binds country-level studies together, and, in addition, helps to set them apart, is that they each treat one country (and sometimes region) as one research "participant." Scores for questionnaire items, normally focused on work-relevant values, are averaged for each country (or region) participating in the survey. In most studies, each country's participants then effectively become one line of data in an exploratory factor analysis, of the country-level responses on a questionnaire. Although a reasonable descriptive term for this kind of approach generally would be *inter-national*, the approach has actually become known, in the literature, as *ecological*. The context for coining this term *ecological* was the influential study of work culture at IBM worldwide (Hofstede, 1980; for a recent restatement and overview, Hofstede, Triandis, Smith, Bond, Fu & Pasa, 2001; for a more critical point of view, again focused largely on measurement, Spector & Cooper, 2002).

2.1. Hofstede's IBM study

The original 1980 publication of this study has recently been revised (in Hofstede, 2001) and thereby gone on, reportedly, to become a most cited work in the social sciences (Yoo & Donthu, 2002). Many readers will know the details of Hofstede's work itself, which was an organizational survey of 40 (and later 50) countries, represented by over 100,000 employees of a single multinational company, IBM. The core result to emerge from this survey was a four-dimensional mapping of ecological culture space, into individualism–collectivism; power distance (belief in hierarchy and keeping social distance between strata); uncertainty–avoidance (desire for the security and certainty of rules); and – most contentiously – "masculinity–femininity." The latter, according to Hofstede, reflects the degree to which "male" values (supposedly emphasizing "assertiveness" and "acquisitiveness') tend to prevail in a society over their "softer" and supposedly, also, more "feminine" counterparts (e.g. the stressing of "interpersonal relations", and "companionship").

2.2. The Chinese Culture Connection

Between Hofstede's first and second editions (1980a, 2001), a fifth value dimension has been added to the work-related culture-scape. In the latter half of the 1980s, a group calling itself "The Chinese Culture Connection" conducted an ecological study of its own (1987). The questionnaire used in this ecological survey was reportedly anchored in a Chinese Confucian, i.e., relatively localized, regional perspective, instead of the perspective of a relatively "Westernized" global corporation. Participating in the study were 22 countries (i.e., $N = 22$). Based on exploratory factor analysis, the ecological data from these 22 countries suggested that, in addition to the factor vectors reported by Hofstede (1980), a fifth dimension in work-related cultural values should be considered. This dimension is termed *Confucian work dynamism* (The Chinese Culture Connection, 1987). The dynamic component in Confucian work dynamism stems from a relative emphasis on a subset of traditional Confucian values that advocate looking *forward* in time, as compared to other traditional Confucian values, that advocate looking for guidance *backwards* in time, i.e., to the wisdom of the past. With these broad distinctions in mind, Confucian work dynamism is nowadays often described, in more general terms, as short- (relatively tradition-oriented) versus long-term (future-looking) orientation (e.g., Smith, Peterson & Schwartz, 2002).

2.3 Are the ecological categories linked to work behavior?

In the latest edition of his (1980a) work, *Culture's Consequences*, Hofstede (2001) suggests that a combination of individualism—collectivism, power distance, uncertainty—avoidance, masculinity—femininity, and short/long-term orientation, constitute, in the values domain, a new "Big Five" not unlike the Big Five in personality (McCrae & Allik, 2002). Three of the values-related Big Five — individualism—collectivism, power distance, and temporal orientation — have demonstrated their potential to predict behaviour statistically. In one study for instance, Hofstede's country-level indices of individualism—collectivism and power distance outstripped a range of conventional demographic markers to statistically predict compliance with group norms (Bond & Smith, 1996). In another study, The Chinese Culture Connection's ecological index of Confucian work dynamism (temporal orientation) was linked statistically, at an ecological level, with economic growth (gross national growth) from 1965 to 1984 (Hofstede & Bond, 1988). More recently, research has begun to examine ways in which ecological work values translate to work behavior, again at the ecological level, in the form of managing work "events" (Smith et al., 1994 to Smith et al., 2002). These events include, for example, correcting poor worker performance, or dealing with faulty workplace equipment. Evidently therefore, ecological indices of work behavior have predictive potential, and scholars of them are now moving closer to using them to help predict, in an ecological sense, actual work behavior.

2.4. Trompenaar's waves of culture

Adding to the ecological databank, and its taxonomies of work-values dimensions, is a well-known study reported in Trompenaars and Hampden-Turner (1998). In this study, conducted originally by Trompenaars (1994), there were 55 countries represented by 30,000 managers from 30 multinational corporations. In comparison to the values Big Five system recently proposed by Hofstede (2001), the taxonomy that has emerged from Trompenaars' work is not fundamentally different from its predecessors. Instead, it offers a relatively differentiated view of some of the Big Five. With respect to power distance for instance, the Trompenaars' schema distinguishes between (a), status that is earned by *achievement*, versus (b), status that is earned by conferral (or birthright), which Trompenaars terms *ascription*. Thus it may be possible, in a conceptual sense, to integrate some of Trompenaars' differentiations with the values Big Five.

Such integration is however seldom undertaken in the literature itself. Even now, the literature is only just beginning to integrate the different versions of ecological dimensions empirically (Smith et al., 2002; for an early rare exception, Smith & Bond, 1993). Thus, a researcher, or manager, or consultant, who reads the ecological literature hoping to find a sense of unity, is likely to be disappointed. With avoiding that shortfall in mind, Table 2.1 synthesizes some major n-dimensions of culture, proposed to date in the ecological literature, into a conceptual map.

Table 2.1 Mapping work behavior in ecological culture space

Hofstede (2001)	Trompenaars	Schwartz	GLOBE
Individualism-Collectivism	Individualist-Communitarian	Self-direction Benevolence Stimulation Hedonism	Individualism Group pride
	Neutral-Affective Universalist-Particularist	Universalism Conformity	Humaneness
Power distance	Achievement-Ascription	Achievement	Power distance
	Specific-Diffuse Internal-External	Power	Performance orientation
Uncertainty Avoidance		Security	Uncertainty-Avoidance Assertiveness
Masculinity-Femininity			Gender-differentiation
Work Dynamism	Time	Tradition	Future orientation

From Table 2.1, some of Trompenaars' constructs, such as individualism and planning, overlap squarely with the Big Five. Other concepts from the Trompenaars schema, as depicted in Table 2.1, occupy more of a penumbral zone between two categories of the Big Five. In that sense, they redraw some of the boundary stones. For example, in Table 2.1 the concept of internal–external (locus of control for work behavior) borders both power distance and uncertainty–avoidance. Table 2.1 also indicates that still other concepts in the Trompenaars schema, like being *neutral* (rational) versus *affective* (emotional), and the bipolar dimension that ranges from *specificity* (being direct) to *diffuseness* (being indirect, subtle), add gradations to the earlier concepts (for a nice example of these, Albert, 1996, on emotional expressiveness versus stoicism in controlling desires).

2.5. Schwartz's Value Survey

The Schwartz Value Survey involved some 44,000 people, representing 47 nations (Schwartz, 1997). Schwartz chose to focus not on managers or other business personnel, as his predecessors had done. Instead, he focused on teachers and school students. The rationale for this choice of participating occupations was that schools, and the classrooms within them, are vital conduits for the transmission of cultural values. The interesting possibility that this extant rationale creates for us, however, is that it compares cultural dimensions across different contexts – business and educational services. To the extent that this comparison reveals any consistent constructs and themes, those dimensions can be considered to be cross-contextually robust (Strohschneider, 1999).

From Table 2.1, signs of robustness are clearly evident. Just as we experienced with the schema proposed by Trompenaars (1994), we are able to conceptually identify points of congruence and convergence with the earlier dimensions. For example, some of the overlapping constructs include individualism with self-direction, and work dynamism/planning with tradition orientation. As well, we also see in Table 2.1 additional refinements to the basic constructs suggested in earlier studies. The additions include, for instance, *stimulation* (liking excitement) and *hedonism* (living for pleasure). Each of the latter is clearly relevant to work behavior and work motivation, and is probably linked more closely with individualistic than collectivistic forms of action. To that extent therefore, they map to the individualistic "pole" of the individualist–collectivist dimension.

2.6. The GLOBE project

The country sample in the GLOBE project, introduced in Chapter 1 (this volume) is $N = 62$. These 62 nations are represented by a total of approximately 18,000 managers, working across a range of industries from food to telecommunications (Javidan & House, 2001). From Table 2.1, the GLOBE project claims to have identified nine ecological factors relevant to leadership behavior. This focus on leadership (rather than work behavior generally) means that we should be careful about making direct comparisons with the other studies represented in Table 2.1 (which have had a broader focus on work groups as an ensemble). Nonetheless, leadership is central and pivotal within work behavior generally, since much of what goes on at work invariably reflects leadership and follower-ship, or the lack of these, in some way. To that extent therefore, the GLOBE taxonomy warrants being featured in our comparison of general ecological models summarized in Table 2.1.

From Table 2.1, the factors emerging from the GLOBE project map, to varying degrees, onto the core constructs classified in earlier studies of work behavior at the ecological level. The cross-model linkages range from the isomorphism of individualism and of power distance, through to adding components such as *humaneness* (which is defined as "belief in social support and harmony," 2001: 301) and *performance orientation* (which is defined as "seizing the initiative", either individually or collectively, p. 300). Thus, once again, with a little conceptual mapping like that in Table 2.1, it is possible to appreciate more clearly how the various models of work culture, proposed in the ecological literature, are not necessarily – as the literature might imply – contradictory.

2.7. A critique of ecological approaches

Even without any manifest contradictions, the ecological literature still raises for us the question of *which* measurement model is the more appropriate, overall, to choose, i.e., the most valid, useful, etc. To answer that question, we can turn for help to the literature on individual differences in personality. This literature on personality suggests in fact that the question "Which model?" is actually something of a straw man. In the literature on dimensionality in personality, there has arguably been a maturing of outlook. Instead of asking 'which' model, and associated number of dimensions, should prevail, the number of traits to be measured is seen to be context-dependent. That is, the number of traits to be measured depends on the degree of differentiation and focus required, by the task at hand (Fisher & Boyle, 1997).

To illustrate what this means and how it works in practice, we can imagine that a practitioner is questioning the likely culture-fit, ecologically, of a possible nationwide training course in "assertiveness," or, alternatively, being "direct" in workplace negotiations and discussions. Here, as in many other types of question, the task at hand indicates which measurement constructs are most appropriate. From Table 2.1, some measurement models have relevant constructs; others do not. Taking baseline (and later, evaluation) measures from respectively the GLOBE, or the Trompenaars schema, may be more fitting than using, say, either Schwartz's or Hofstede's measures. Likewise, if a consultant or work group is considering whether to implement selection by past record (as in past behavior interviewing) or selection based on prospects (as in situational interviewing), the dimension of time orientation, and any instrument-set within the "work dynamism" row of Table 2.1, would be ecologically germane. Thus, once we adopt a relatively pluralistic attitude toward the models themselves, and recognize their essentially social constructivist (sense-making) functions, the overall terrain in the ecological literature becomes less disorienting.

A second, and perhaps more weighty criticism of the ecological approach stems from its aggregation of scores across whole national populations. A precondition for aggregating into groups is to first demonstrate that there is more variance between groups than there is within. Yet many nation states today are actually extremely diverse both ethnically and culturally – raising doubts about the validity of casting people into "nation states" in the first place (Schneider, 2001). Attribution Theory, for instance, cautions extensively about over-homogenizing groups outside our own (Carr, 2003b). Ipso facto therefore, a danger in ecological approaches – more than ever in this age of global travel – is that they help to perpetuate stereotypes that simply have no foundation.

Even when a national consciousness is salient, ecological approaches may be over-positioning the people they seek to describe. In countries like Sweden and Australia, for example, workers often describe themselves as paradoxical hybrids of both individualism *and* collectivism (respectively, for instance, Daun, 1991; and, more recently, Ashkanasy & Falkus, 2003). Clearly, the kind of (ecological) schema portrayed in Table 2.1 does not readily allow for this level of complexity, subtlety, and change. Instead, the schema in Table 2.1 stubbornly implies that societies, and the workers within them, *cannot* be individualist *and* collectivist, or humble *and* assertive, at different points during the same working day.

Projects like GLOBE have gone some way toward addressing this issue. They have, for example, recorded both actual and ideal ecological behavior (e.g., Ashkanasy, Trevor-Roberts & Earnshaw, 2002). Analyzing these gaps may help reveal where people at work hanker for what they are not, or do not have, and can thereby start to engage with motivational pluralism. Yet gap analysis like this still does not compensate for the inability of ecological indexes to capture actual changes of identity, from one context to the next (Ashkanasy & Falkus, 2003). In the Buick Bar & Grill case for instance (Chapter 1, this volume), individualism gave way to group pride once work became sport-like and team-driven. Moreover, the same collectivism later created a climate of gravity when individuals were singled out for promotion. Transformations of identity like these, we have seen, are the very stuff of glocalization (Chapter 1, this volume). Ultimately therefore, perhaps the most serious criticism that can be made of the ecological approach is that it cannot, by definition, capture cultural transitions.

3. Individual-level Values

In drawing this last observation, we have ourselves switched foci. We have surreptitiously moved from taking ecological snapshots, to tracing small work group dynamics within a single, small-group setting. The measurement of culture at this kind of level, i.e., at the level of individuals and individual differences, has been extensive. Such models have to be segregated, at least for the moment, from their ecological cousins. An elementary reason for this segregation, conceptually and in measurement terms, is that measuring devices developed at the ecological level are not necessarily appropriate to use at the individual level. As Schwartz has pointed out for instance, at the ecological level power-distant societies tend to value, simultaneously, both the shunning and seeking of power: Societies that value humility also tend to value dominance (1994). At the level of individual differences however, belief in humility and belief in dominance rarely appear together. They are too far apart, logically and psychologically, for most people to handle. Thus, what constitutes work "culture" at level of measurement (a) does not necessarily constitute it at level (b).

Disjunctions like this do not, however, prevent the broad constructs in Table 2.1 from translating well across different levels of measurement. Most of us, for instance, will recognize the general constructs in Table 2.1 within our workplace; in our work experience; and within ourselves as individuals. Schwartz is one investigator who has broached this issue of crossover, empirically (1997). Specifically, he has replicated the broad factor pattern of his values taxonomy in Table 2.1, *within* societal groups (as well as between them). In a similar fashion, the concept of uncertainty–avoidance, in Table 2.1, emerges also in the factor-analytic research focusing on individual differences – where it is termed *looseness–tightness* (Triandis, 2002).

Most of the research in the individual differences domain, however, has focused on one particular pair of value constructs – individualism and collectivism.

3.1. Individualism–Collectivism

Much of the early conceptual work on individualism and collectivism can be found in various collaborations between Triandis and Hui (e.g., Hui & Triandis, 1986). In this study, social scientists around the world were polled about the core elements of individualism and collectivism. The resulting poll produced convergences in seven key domains. These were: considering the costs and benefits of decisions; sharing material resources; sharing of non-material resources such as time and effort; susceptibility to social influence; self-presentation and face-work; sharing of outcomes; and feeling involved in others' lives (Hui, 1988). Thus, although the concepts of individualism and collectivism were originally envisaged to have a community-wide remit, the dimensions that actually emerged are each clearly relevant to the world of work.

From this early conceptual analysis, Hui went on to develop specific items for a scale called INDCOL (for Individualism–Collectivism). The INDCOL instrument has since spawned a range of instruments built around the same or similar core themes. One of the most interesting features of the original INDCOL scale was its explicit acknowledgement that the same individual or group manifests differing degrees of individualism and collectivism in differing social contexts. Amongst these contexts were included the home; the community; and work. For instance, the INDOL sub-scale for a work context contains items about helping colleagues who need advice and guidance; and about asking for personal advice from superiors (1988: 35). Items like these, through the distinctive context-focused sub-scales they constitute, imply that the same group will behave individualistically in one context, but in a relatively more collectivistic manner in the next. To an extent, therefore, INDCOL scales have, from their beginnings, implied the presence of glocality in work behavior.

Despite that implication, INDOL scales have not often been used to indicate any extent to which people can change their orientation within the same – for example work – context. Instead, much of the research endeavor around the original instrument and its derivatives has consisted of examining cultural groups, or pairs of groups, as if they were somehow each of them fixed entities (Oyserman, Coon, & Kemmelmeier, 2002). In an early illustrative and influential example of this genre of study, Hui obtained responses on the INDCOL from known individualist and collectivist groups. These two groups were then compared on the INDCOL, to see how often, and by how much, their responses differed. In that cross-cultural comparison, the greatest score difference between the two groups was found on the sub-scale measuring collectivism at work (Hui, 1988: 24, Validation Study 1). Such early analyses, whilst partially validating the scale, also imply to a reader that the differences between the cultural groups are relatively fixed rather than fluid, and especially so at work.

Much of the research on individualism and collectivism by Triandis and colleagues has focused on the etic–emic distinction drawn in the previous chapter (e.g., Triandis, Bontempo, Villareal, Asai & Lucca, 1988). In the latter study, Triandis et al. first of all focused on refining the measure of individualism within one national setting, the USA (1988: 330, Study 1). Other studies in the paper compared samples from two national settings, using exploratory factor analysis. These factor-analytic studies have explored both factor overlap and, as well, constitutive elements in those factors that are culture-specific. Collectivism, for example, incorporates different specific beliefs depending on the precise nature of the group's salient out-groups and their histories of interaction together (1988: 336). Taking this idea of social context further, in more recent research Triandis has argued that individualism and collectivism are moderated by the degree of egality versus belief in hierarchy in which they are also imbedded (Triandis & Gelfand, 1998). Thus, according to Triandis et al., work behavior reflects a combination, or rather intersection, of both INDCOL *and* belief in egality–hierarchy.

3.2. Belief in Egality–Hierarchy

According to this revised and expanded model of work values, there are at least four basic factors, or referent points, in personal culture space: (1) In *horizontal collectivism* people see themselves as equal, and as not submitting to authority; (2) in *vertical collectivism* the individual defers to an in-group; (3) in *horizontal individualism,* people, as individuals, seek to "do their own [individual] thing," without in theory infringing on the rights of others to "do theirs;" (4) and in *vertical individualism,* the individual engages in a rat race. This is the classic "up-or-out" philosophy that arguably characterizes much of the cultural ethos in contemporary globalization (Chapter 1, this volume).

Triandis and Gelfand (1998) have claimed validity for this four-factor model on the basis of convergence with a range of predecessors. One of these predecessors, for example, is a values taxonomy proposed by the social psychologist Rokeach (1973). Rokeach's schema included political values, which in turn can be categorized not just in terms of individualism versus collectivism, but also the degree to which they endorse the concept of freedom (an essentially vertical dimension). Convergence is also claimed, by Triandis and Gelfand, with respect to a social anthropological model proposed in Fiske (1991). Like Triandis and Gelfand's model, Fiske's model structures social systems into four basic dimensions: (1) *communal sharing* (in which resources are pooled and distributed on the basis of need); (2) *authority ranking* (in which resources are pooled and distributed according to rank); (3) *equality matching* (where resources are distributed on the basis of equality between individuals); and (4) *market pricing* (in which individuals receive outcomes for individual input). These categories overlap well with (1) horizontal collectivism, (2) vertical collectivism, (3) horizontal individualism, and (4) vertical individualism (also, Singelis, Triandis, Bhawuk & Gelfand, 1995).

In addition to linking their model to pre-existing theory, Triandis and Gelfand's fourfold classificatory system has been probed empirically. Again, this has been done using exploratory factor analysis, with individual-level samples spanning a range of different ethnic backgrounds (see for example, from Singelis et al., 1995, to Probst, Carnevale, & Triandis, 1999). The factor structure and item content of the instrument developed and tested by Triandis and Gelfand appears to be relatively robust. As well, some items in the model are explicitly work focused (e.g., "It is important that I do my job better than others"). Thus, the fourfold classification system advanced by Triandis and colleagues seems especially relevant, in principle, for studying behavior at work.

3.3 Are the categories linked to work behavior?

The four categories being proposed by Triandis and colleagues have the potential to become a new 'big four' in culture-related values at the individual level. Exploring that potential, the research literature has studied linkages between (1) to (4) and work-related behavior. In one study for example, participants scoring relatively high (versus low) on vertical individualism were comparatively uncooperative in a zero sum (prisoner's dilemma) game between individuals; and they became relatively cooperative (in order to keep own profits maximized) only when the competition involved their own group versus an out-group (Probst et al., 1999). Thus, in this and other examples within the study, the data comport with Triandis' observation that measuring horizontal and vertical components of collectivism and individualism is more informative than measuring individualism and collectivism per se (1991: 187).

3.4. Critique of the four-factor model

What exactly does 'four factors' mean in this context? Clearly it is convenient, and useful, for researchers to have each differentiation of individualism-collectivism represented on a single numerical index. But should we reify these indices into a four-dimensional culture space? Perhaps instead we can conceptualize the dimensions more parsimoniously. On a priori grounds for instance, the four factors might be under-girded by just two, more basic dimensions: (1) individualism-collectivism; and (2) belief in hierarchy. Indicating (1), at least one classic publication on culture and the self suggests that individualism and collectivism can be expressed independently of the power structures that surround them (Markus & Kitayana, 1991; see also, Bhawuk, 2001). Indicating (2), degree of belief in egality-hierarchy, Triandis et al. themselves have observed that, "Social distance is ... a concept that is understood in all cultures in which the question has been asked" (Triandis, McCusker & Hui, 1990: 1018; see also, Sidanius & Pratto, 1999). Thus, we can envisage the four indices that Triandis and colleagues have usefully described as reflecting different and distinctive positions on a values grid (Carr, 2003b).

```
                        Vertical
                           |
                           |
VERTICAL INDIVIDUALISM     |     VERTICAL COLLECTIVISM
                           |
                           |
Individualist ─────────────┼───────────── Collectivist
                           |
                           |
HORIZONTAL INDIVIDUALISM   |    HORIZONTAL COLLECTIVISM
                           |
                           |
                       Horizontal
```

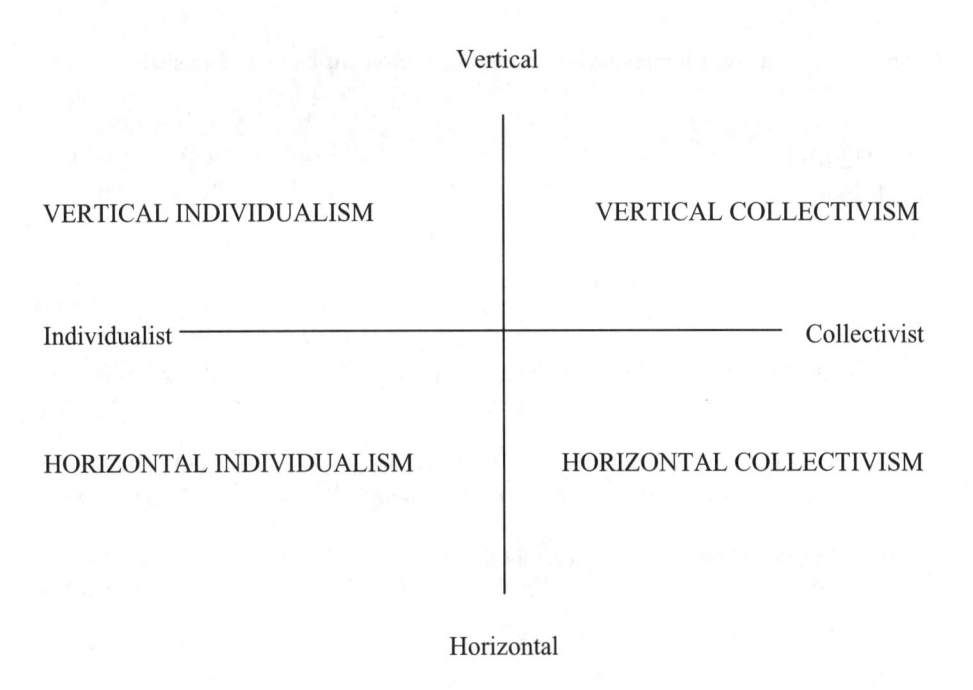

Figure 2.1 A values grid

Source: Adapted from Carr, Bolitho, & Purcell (1999)

The essence of the parsimonious model presented in Figure 2.1 is that individuals' descriptions of their values, about relations between themselves and others, tend to combine together to form distinctive "cultural patterns" (Probst et al, 1999, p. 175). Those patterns in fact are even embedded in some of the items in the Triandis et al instrument itself. Examples of these items are provided in Table 2.2. From Table 2.2, we can see that the items are in fact inherently double-barreled. They refer simultaneously to specific combinations of verticality and collectivism, horizontality and collectivism, horizontality and individualism, and verticality and individualism. Such double barreling would help participants' numerical responses, on the items themselves, to cluster into four factors, rather than the two more fundamental, and conceptually distinguishable, dimensions presented in Figure 2.1. Thus, there are several grounds, both theoretical and methodological, for adhering to the conceptualization offered in the values grid – without dispensing with the essential fourfold classification of cultural patterns proposed by Triandis and his colleagues.

Table 2.2 **Items from horizontal–vertical/individualism-collectivism scale**

VALUE RESPONSE DIMENSIONS	EXEMPLAR ITEM (Bi-clausal)	EMBEDDED/ PROPOSITIONS
Vertical Collectivism	It is important to me that I *respect*/ /the decisions made by my *groups*	Verticalism + Collectivism
Horizontal Collectivism	I feel good when I *cooperate*/ /with *others*	Horizontalism + Collectivism
Horizontal Individualism	I rely on *myself* most of the time/ /I rarely *rely* on others	Individualism + Horizontalism
Vertical Individualism	It is important that I do *my* job/ /*better* than others	Individualism + Verticalism

Source: Triandis and Gelfand (1998, Table 2, emphases and clause separators ['/'] have been added)

Beyond the concepts of individualism-collectivism and horizontality-verticality, the literature on individual values has perhaps not explored the culture-scape as widely as its ecological counterpart. For example, despite a possibility that many of the relatively differentiated ecological concepts in Table 2.1 could, in principle, be useful at an individual level of analysis, most of the research, to date, has focused on the individual equivalent of individualism-collectivism and power distance. Nonetheless, those facets are each undoubtedly central to behavior at work. Given that centrality, plus the fact that this book is pitched at a more micro level than the ecological, much of the rest of our discussion uses the four metaphorical poles in Figure 2.1. More accurately in fact, our discussion will focus on how behavior at work moves *between* the four points of reference.

4. Organizational Culture

In the 'ecological' and 'individual differences' literatures briefly described above, the value dimensions, and the forms of identity that they support, have been conceptualized by the researchers quite broadly, often being only indirectly related to work, rather than being directly or exclusively 'organizational' in focus. Yet cultures of work itself exist 'at' work, as well as in and around it. After all, just as societies are groups, so too are organizations. Admittedly, cultures of work, at work, may be less central in the lives of people. Yet they are also, by definition, more easily primed and proximal with regard to work behavior itself. And, just as societies and communities contain sub-groupings, so, likewise, do organizations. Some of these groups are formal and others are more informal. Whatever their level of formality however, many work-related groups are often forms of cultural community (Burroughs & Eby, 1998). Outside of formal organizational boundaries also – for example in freelance work, independent consulting, and temping – people still work and behave in meaningful work groups (Alach & Inkson, 2003). Thus, wherever we turn in work life, the culture of the work group, and in particular its cultural values, are crucial for understanding work behaviour.

4.1. 'Work group culture:' What precisely is it?

Like its ecological counterpart, the study of culture at work only really took off during the 1980s (Schein, 1990). At that time, Schein argues, there was a realization that "one needs concepts that permit one to differentiate between organizations within a society" (1990: 100). Today, with organizational de-layering and the greater emphasis on teamwork, it is being claimed in some quarters that work group cultures have taken over from the more "structural" components of organizations as a key influence on work behavior (Ferris, Perrewe, Anthony, & Gilmore, 2000: 26). Despite this growth of interest in organizational culture however, Schein's (1990) 'older' model continues to hold considerable sway. Part of the reason for that enduring prominence is the conceptual clarity with which Schein's model announces itself.

Firstly, and consistent with Kluckhohn's definition of culture at the opening of this chapter, work group culture can be observed, according to Schein, through a work group's symbols and artifacts. These include, for example, company logos, written or unwritten dress codes, symbols, and rituals. Not surprisingly perhaps, these artifacts and rituals have tended to be studied, in the literature on work behavior, by organizational anthropologists (Davidson, Manning, Timo & Ryder, 2001).

Secondly, and again consistent with Kluckhohn's classic definition of culture, work group cultures can be observed through espoused work group values. As we have seen, this has been the medium of measurement preferred by both ecological and national studies of culture (above). Jointly, ecological and national studies of culture tend to have been carried out by scholars in two major discipline areas: cross-cultural management studies; and cross-cultural "social" psychology. Ironically however, these same two discipline areas have not ventured squarely into organizational culture per se. Instead, a largely separate literature on organizational culture values, has developed within management studies and, to a lesser extent perhaps, industrial/organizational (I/O) psychology.

Thirdly, and most importantly perhaps, Schein adds value to Kluckhohn's opening definition of culture generally, by himself articulating a need to tease out the implicit assumptions latent in work groups. These assumptions, which have been far less studied than their consciously available cousins, need not be consistent with each other, and may even contradict explicitly articulated values (Argyris, 1998). A little ironically perhaps, implicit cultural assumptions have been discussed in the literature on international human resource management, in particular under the expatriate assignment (or EA) (Dowling, Schuler & Welch, 1994). To the extent that the EA is often about – in the published literature – "global" emissaries interacting with "local" hosts, such discussions can be said to be glocal.

How can these implicit assumptions, whether among expatriates and their hosts, or among workers in multicultural settings generally, including multi-organizational settings, be gauged and measured? According to Schein, interviews and questionnaires can be used to articulate the espoused values. These in turn can then be compared and contrasted to the subtexts contained in the symbols and rituals - the latter, Schein implies, may reveal some of the influence of hidden, i.e., implicit, assumptions. Any inconsistencies between espoused values and the implicit assumptions can then more easily be corrected, if so desired and appropriate by employees themselves. Schein is suggesting here that ethnography, and other forms of case methodology, might be used to explore intra-cultural inconsistencies. That kind of pluralism would also include perhaps critical discursive approaches, since these often focus on externalizing contradictions and raising awareness generally about the implicit assumptions that guide much of everyday work behavior. Yet as well, Schein's message is also consistent with a central thesis in this book – that work behaviors are often inherently pluralistic and dynamic.

4.2. Dimensions of work group culture

The field of organizational culture is currently less developed than its ecological and individual differences counterparts (Ogbonna, 1996). This is partly because of (a) commercial sensitivities and also (b) division over the issue of culture versus climate; but also, perhaps, because (c) the literature has not drawn too much from literature *outside* of the specifically "work" domain. The literature we have already reviewed, for instance, suggests that much of what goes on *inside* of work is influenced by cultural values in wider society, *outside* of work itself (see also, Templer, Beaty & Hofmeyr, 1992). Thus, the field of organizational culture has arguably experienced a hiatus in understanding, or indeed not even seen at all, the nexus between cultures *of* work and cultures *at* work.

This idea of a nexus between organizational and societal groups, through their respective cultures, becomes more insistent still, once we consider Schein's own (leading) taxonomy of organizational cultural values (1990: 114). Although not all of the dimensions of organizational culture are identical to the dimensions found at the ecological and individual levels (organizational environments are not identical to their ecological, i.e., national cousins), many of the elements in Schein's taxonomy do nonetheless resemble the same broad themes already depicted in Table 2.1. For example, Schein's "the nature of human relations" includes the issue of whether relations are structured inter-individually or on the basis of "groupism" (1990: 114). This concept sounds very much like individualism and collectivism. The same point – parallel concepts – applies as well to "the organization's relationship to its environment," i.e., the question, "Does the organization perceive itself to be dominant, submissive, harmonizing, searching out a niche?" (1990: 114). The underlying concept here, in turn, sounds like power distance (at the ecological level) and believing in horizontality–verticality (at the individual level).

Another concept in Schein's taxonomy is the question of "need for rules." This clearly reflects uncertainty avoidance at the ecological level and looseness–tightness within countries. A further issue proposed as core by Schein – that of "defining truth" – resembles Trompenaar's concept of emphasizing being "neutral" (i.e., emphasizing being rational). An issue that Schein terms *homogeneity versus diversity* reflects what Schwartz terms *conformity* and *self-direction* (at both ecological and individual levels). Finally, Schein proposes a conceptual dimension about the perceived nature of time, which includes "orientation toward the past versus the future," and the way that time is managed (linear versus parallel tasking). Once again, from Table 2.1 we can link this concept about organizational culture to orientation toward time.

Overall therefore, there is a significant degree of overlap, at the conceptual level, between the constructs and dimensions of organizational culture and the constructs and dimensions of societal/community-related culture.

These theoretical linkages, across organizational and societal/community domains, are backed by relevant measurement data. There is empirical research, for instance, measuring both sense of collectivism at work (Burroughs & Eby, 1998) and also the ways in which time is managed (Munro, Carr, MacLachlan, Kwang, & Bishop, 1997; see also, Bluedorn, Kalliath, Strube & Martin, 1998). As well, and as we have implied already, there is a plethora of instruments, both published and unpublished (commercially sensitive), that claim to measure work group culture. Despite the apparent weightiness of detail across these measures – even those that are freely available – a closer inspection reveals, again, a degree of overlap with measurement models at other levels. To take one example, the Organizational Culture Profile (or OCP), measures factors that include *structure,* the *development of the individual,* and *planning* (Ashkanasy, Broadfoot & Falkus, 2000). These factors relate respectively to power distance, degree of individualism, and orientation to time. Clearly therefore, these (and other) dimensions of culture space, at work, are not overly dissimilar to the dimensions of culture space in wider society.

Parallels like the above are fascinating, because they imply that transitions between frames of reference can be relatively smooth and seamless. Indeed, if the models contained in their respective literatures on culture each have any validity, then transitions between different scopes of identification must be the norm not the exception. Such transitions would be particularly interesting if we could show that social identification with organizational values significantly influences work behavior. This possibility is inherently intriguing because, if such identification processes influence work behavior, then *changing* the sphere – transiting from one form of identification to another – will influence it, too.

4.3. Is work group culture linked to work behavior?

There is now a growing empirical literature on the capacity for work group cultures to link to work group behavior (for a critical overview, Ogbonna & Harris, 2002). A classic example of this linkage can be found in Sheridan (1992). In Sheridan's study of work behavior in accounting firms, employees were less likely to leave a group whose culture of work stressed interpersonal relationships than they were a group with a strong focus on individual performance. This group of accountants needed social networks, and providing them made the workplace a better "fit" for them. Similarly, and in an example of more recent research, managers whose socio-cultural traditions (about belief in hierarchy) were reflected in their group culture at work were less work stressed than their poorer aligned counterparts (Joiner, 2001). Thus, the research on organizational culture begins to invite us to consider a new possibility: that culture links to work behavior through an *interface* between one type of value system and the next (Hermans & Kempen, 1998).

This idea of cultural interfaces is best illustrated through the literature on organizational mergers and takeovers. A common technique for determining the degree of "fit" between merger partners, and thereby for preparing workers for handling the change before it happens, is a "culture fit" analysis (Weber, 2000). One such technique for example is called the *Merger Potential Analysis* (Schlaeger, 2002). In Merger Potential Analysis, Schein's values and artifacts are assessed in both groups, and the widest points of difference (the "gaps") are identified. Merger potential is then operationally defined as the magnitude and frequency of the gaps. As we saw in the opening chapter, few mergers are perfectly balanced in terms of the power, prestige, and status of the two "partners." This means that the term *merger* is often partly a misnomer, and that the term *takeover* would actually be closer in some senses to the way that mergers are actually experienced: Perceptually, "merger" often means a more globally positioned entity taking over our more locally positioned enterprise. To that extent, gap analysis, as it searches for points of agreement and potential discord between the key stakeholder groups, one more powerful and the other less, is an exploration in glocality.

4.4. Critique of organizational culture models

As with studying culture ecologically and individually, the study of work group cultures has progressed to the point where measures of it are being used to predict outcomes like staff retention and quality of work life (e.g., stress and strain). Like its counterparts at those other levels, work group culture space can also be navigated with some crude but nonetheless robust compass points. These include the relative emphasis put on individual versus collective good; and the endorsement of hierarchy versus egality. Finally, and again like its outside cousins, work group behavior can be navigated using more finely differentiated features of the culture space, such as the value placed on rationality versus emotionality in problem solving; and through homogeneity (and conformity) versus self-direction.

Ironically, however, commonalities such as these, between the various levels of culture, have not been widely recognized in the literature on work group culture itself. This means, unfortunately, that the potential for transitivity, between differing forms of cultural identity, has not been recognized either. Transitivity in general could be critical in helping to negotiate cultural difference with others at work. That possibility is highlighted nicely for us in the literature on yet another form of culture at and of work - occupational culture.

5. Occupational Cultures

According to Schein, "occupational communities have at least three identifiable cultures of their own, which continually interact with each other in organizational and work settings" (1996: 236). These core elements are "operators" (or workers in "the line" as distinct from the more general category, "staff"); "engineers" (or technology specialists); and "executives" (a community of Chief Executive Officers, or CEOs).

5.1. Operator cultures

This is the most general and diffuse category of the three. It includes both "line managers and workers who make and deliver the products and services that fulfill the organization's basic mission" (1999: 236). Because this group is most frequently the target of change interventions, it is also, according to Schein, the most researched and measured.

By implication, therefore, there are at least two relatively under-researched groups who sit outside of this corpus, who often have their own, relatively neglected view on work.

5.2. Engineering cultures

Under the label *engineer,* Schein includes all technologists and purveyors of technology in work settings. These include, for example, technocrats, information technologists working in IT, and employees working in IT support (Kunda, 1992). According to Schein, the "common occupational culture" of engineers is imbued, for example, with "performance orientation" (Table 2.1). A potential problem with this type of culture, according to Schein, is that it sometimes clashes with a more industrial relations-oriented position adopted by operators (see also, Workman, 1993). In Triandis' terms, therefore, engineering cultures, in their dealings with operators, are often relatively individualistic (versus collectivistic) and vertical (versus horizontal), compared to their operator counterparts.

5.3. Executive cultures

According to Schein (1996), executives are often torn between loyalty to their shareholders and the profit motive, versus respect for the people who work to earn that profit and their issues, e.g., workplace empowerment. The result of these inner tussles, between loyalty to a group and loyalty to profit, according to Schein, is that the profit motive – and responsibility to the shareholders – usually wins out. Most executives, according to Schein, will eventually "unconsciously collude with the engineers in wanting to minimize human factors" (1996: 238). Thus, according to Schein, the scene becomes set for an inter-group conflict, between, on the one hand operators, and on the other hand, both engineers and (senior) management.

5.4. Interactive schemata

According to Schein, two out of these three groups, i.e., engineers and executives, "have their roots in larger worldwide occupational communities" (1996: 238). This suggests that they (professional engineers; CEOs and their shareholders) function partly like a diaspore; and that their identity is comparatively globalized. By implication, the third group (operators), which does *not* have the same wide parentage according to Schein, often adopts a form of identity that is relatively more localized (1996, pp. 236–237). Despite the fact that we are oversimplifying here for the moment (e.g., empowerment and teamwork are part of globalization, too), the theoretical possibility that Schein's argument is raising is that interactions between occupational cultures take place in a work glocality.

5.5. Critique

How, precisely, do different cultural positions, like those above, interact? According to Schein, we do not yet really know. But there are at least two fundamental questions with which any new analysis of such a challenging issue must immediately and unhesitatingly engage. Firstly, how is it, given all the multiplicity of identifications that our review has discussed, that people at work do still position themselves relatively stably? After all, much behavior at work, including cultural positioning and counter-positioning, is often crashingly predictable. Secondly, if we can explain some of the processes underlying cultural positioning, can we also apply the same principles to understanding and promoting cultural *re*positioning? The rationale here is that if people at work are capable of stepping into cultural roles, and then inhabiting them a little too rigidly, they are nonetheless equally capable of stepping out of them when a change of behavior is desired, either by others or, more importantly, by themselves.

6. Glocal Positioning

A good entrée to glocal work dynamics, and a response to our first question in the paragraph above, can be found in Giacalone and Beard. These writers describe an interaction pattern that is sometimes observed between Western managers who have been expatriated into host societies where daily positions inside the glocality of work are stereotypically less individualistic, and more power distant:

> Communication style can be classified as being either direct or indirect…personal [self focused] or contextual [role focused] … [and] instrumental or affective ... When attitudinal differences between speakers exist, for example, it results in the instrumental speaker attempting attitude change in his or her receiver, whereas the affective speaker will simply change subjects … as a consequence, the … tactics employed are reinforced and the probability of their use in the future increases … For example, if the American expatriate uses a direct communication style and seeks to 'clarify' his intentions regarding a matter, he may inadvertently give the impression to [a host counterpart] (whose culture exhibits an indirect style) that he is impudent. Similarly, the [expatriate] may misinterpret the communication of a [host counterpart] using an indirect style as being sneaky, concealing, or disinterested. (1994: 623–624, 628, parentheses added)

7. Cultural Positioning

Translating the above into the language of this chapter, and concepts in Table 2.1, our prototypical expatriate begins from a position of relative individualism and egality, including a belief in one-to-one directness (specificity). By contrast, the host worker begins the same interaction from a different position, by being positioned toward collectivism and belief in hierarchy (including diffuseness). This configuration of initial positions, however tentative they may be at "Time 1" (or "T") enables us to superimpose Giacalone and Beard's scenario onto an organizational equivalent of the values grid. This is laid out for us in Figure 2.2. Admittedly, this schema focuses on just two dimensions of culture at work, and is to that extent impoverished. But it nonetheless provides some handy metaphorical compass points for starting to understand what can happen in the glocality at "T + 1".

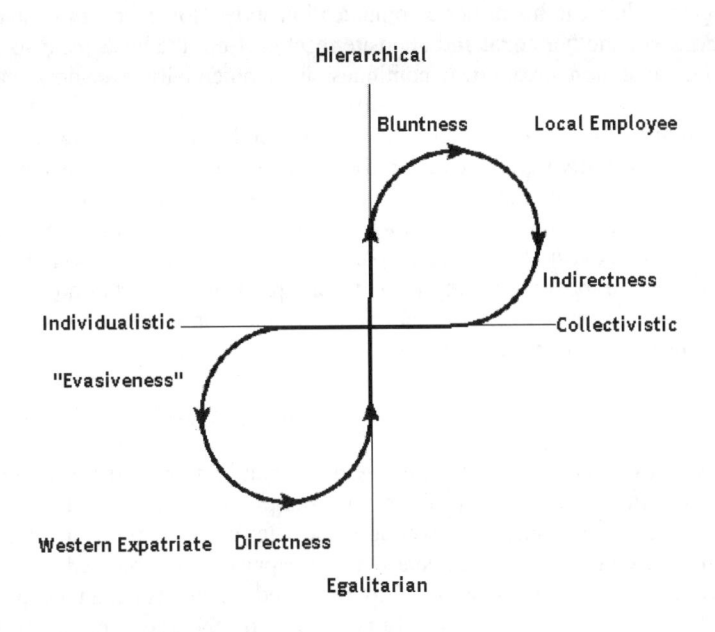

Figure 2.2 **Escalating glocal work dynamics**

Source: Carr (2003b: 16)

7.1. Systems theory

From Figure 2.2, the manager has started from a position of tending to believe in one-to-one directives at work. From that position the manager speaks comparatively bluntly to the individual employee, whose performance is perceived by the manager to be falling short of a required 'performance' orientation. From Table 2.1, being 'specific' and 'neutral' (matter-of-fact, coldly rational) can be linked with positions that are relatively egalitarian and individualistic (Table 2.1). At the same time, however, the operator employee whose position is relatively collectivistic and hierarchical, is tending toward social harmony and indirectness, *not* individual bluntness. As well, the operator employee also feels relatively uncomfortable with a one-to-one communication pattern, at least with overseas supervisors, whose position of power requires them to respectfully keep a little more (power) distance.

Unaware of this essentially different perspective on the same interaction, the expatriate manager, from the outset, speaks a little too directly to the host employee. This employee's first reaction, to the over-bluntness, is to keep the conversation as indirect and as harmonious as possible. To the manager however, such forms of positioning look and feel like evasiveness; and even perhaps like a smoke screen for incompetence (which sometimes it can be, but not on many occasions like the present work event). Now, more than ever, the expatriate feels that the host worker needs "straightening out," and some straight *talk*. The expatriate manager therefore becomes even more direct in his or her communication style. However – of course – that in turn elicits yet another equal and opposite reaction from the host. And so the process of communication breakdown continues, in a potentially ever-downward spiral.

In systems theory terms, such downward spirals are termed *escalation* (Senge, 1992). The prototype for escalation dynamics generally is arms racing. In any arms race, and as is essentially depicted in Figure 2.2, each party's actions, and reactions, steadily and cumulatively reinforce the differences, rather than the potential similarities, between the concerned parties. The end result of this continual and reciprocal form of positioning, systems theory predicts, is a reinforced and consolidated intransigence. In short, each party to the communication steadily reinforces the other's stereotypes of itself.

8. Link to Glocality

The systems dynamic portrayed in Figure 2.2 can be interpreted as a living example of a recurring glocality. It features, for example, a global emissary in the form of the relatively individualistic traveling expatriate; and it features a form of backlash against the culture of management that the expatriate is perceived to bring with him. As Schein and others have forcefully reminded us, surveys cannot capture such dynamics. At best, they "freeze frame" some of the more obvious and articulable stages and states in (for example) our escalation process. Through the lens of systems theory however, and with the aid of the diagram in Figure 2.2, we can see something else. We capture in motion how a relatively global and pro assimilation attitude, which is what the expatriate implicitly holds, rather easily becomes a self-fulfilling prophecy. At the same time too, a not dissimilar self-fulfilling prophecy occurs for the "local employee." This process is partly attributable to the local person's anti-conformity, against relatively global norms – in short, to backlash. In addition, neither of the parties is either willing or able to take the perspective of the other – neither is ready to appreciate the situation's inherent glocality. As a result of this twin shortfall, any potential to break the cycle is never fully realized. We end up with a glocal standoff.

9. The Generality of Escalation

Although the scenario depicted in Figure 2.2 is couched inside a common work scenario overseas – in the EA – our travel metaphor (Chapter 1) suggests that this kind of encounter, and the dynamic it produces, is found in more everyday work settings. Those everyday settings range for example from in-country intercultural work assignments; to work e-teams that are geographically widely dispersed; to workplace encounters that take place in a context of international tourism; or indeed a customer service exchange of any kind (in the event that the customer positions himself or herself toward collectivism and hierarchy, the dynamic would still work, because they would again feel uncomfortable being spoken to in a relatively direct manner by a customer service agent). Thus, the forms of positioning, and stereotype reinforcement depicted in Figure 2.2, may be more common than they first appear.

9.1. To the shop floor

A good example of how the escalation dynamic permeates everyday work behavior can be found amongst the occupational work cultures identified by Schein. In particular, we can predict the dynamics among interacting occupational work cultures of technicians (or engineers) and shop floor (or operators). As we have seen, these positions, like those adopted by our expatriate and host in Figure 2.2, are relatively glocal. In Figure 2.3, we have envisaged how these interactions might escalate into mutually stereotypical forms of cultural positioning and associated work behaviors. From Figure 2.3, the relative focus of each group, on task versus (industrial) relations, steadily reinforces and delineates the other. In this system, any initial tendency on the part of engineers toward a "performance" orientation, and away from human relations, is steadily reinforced by the operators' comparative focus on (industrial)-relations factors. Thus, the more the operators react against the task focus of the engineers ("Performance" orientation, extrinsic rewards), the more the engineers are positioned, and position themselves, into a stereotype of their own occupational culture. The net result, in systems theory terms, is an escalation of mutual stereotyping.

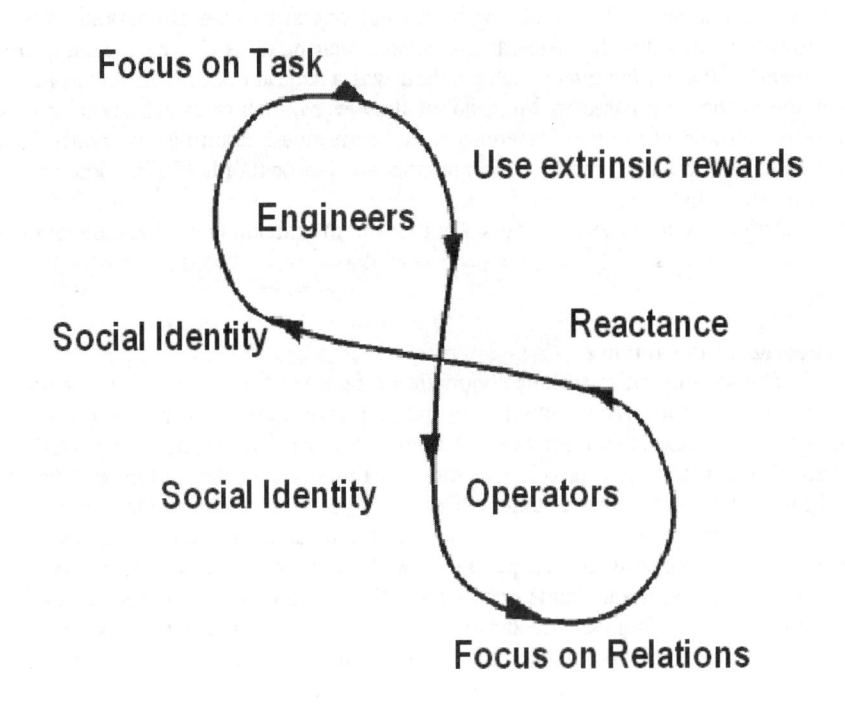

Figure 2.3 Differing occupational identities interact to produce positioning effects in the workplace

9.2 Some qualifications

An important caveat to Figure 2.3 is that these systems dynamics are inter-group and longitudinal. They depict what can sometimes happen, in the longer term, when each form of social-occupational identity, engineers and operators, are left to their own devices without other factors intervening to trip the circuitry of vicious circles. In addition, the concept of social identity means, by definition, that these groups will not necessarily interact with their own members, i.e., in-group, as they do with out-groups (like, for engineers, the operators). Quite the contrary in fact, as is suggested in Sheridan (1992, above), engineers may well interact with each other more as individuals, and in that sense with more of a relationship focus (Howard, 2003; see also, Ingram & Parker, 2002, below). A possible example of such interpersonal interactivity, within groups rather than between them, is software engineering teams (Chapter 5, this volume).

9.3. Conclusion

The key point of Figures 2.2 and 2.3 is that people sometimes slip unawares into overly rigid work behavior patterns. These mutually reinforcing processes of escalation are not confined to intercultural exchanges in the relatively "exotic" sense of culture, i.e., during international assignments. They apply, also, to exchanges between occupational cultures of engineers and operators, and shop floor versus management (Carr, 2003b). As Carr suggests, such patterns can be meaningfully termed *double Pygmalion effects*. Pygmalion was a sculptor who believed so much in his statue that she came to life, and in double Pygmalion effects, two groups mutually reinforce each other's stereotype of themselves, resulting eventually in a loss of social capital (mutually antagonistic stereotypes); plus a breakdown of communication that disrupts production.

The irony in all this of course, is that the interaction could have developed otherwise.

10. Theories of Positioning

The starting point for any Pygmalion effect, by definition, is some kind of predisposing tendency. The sculpting metaphor thereby signals to us a limit to the system dynamic's explanatory power. Neither of the two figures above offers us any insights about why people position themselves initially into the particular form of social identity, at any one time, that they do; nor indeed why they might choose one particular identity, at any one time, at the expense of another (Tan & Moghaddam, 1996). As I have now suggested, people at work regularly position and re-position themselves in different quadrants across the values grid (Figure 2.1). For example, they may become individualistic during competitions *within* departments, and yet collectivistic during competitions *between* them. In that sense, Figures 2.2 and 2.3 are simply reminders that work behavior is not indelibly fixed in one or other of the quadrants of the culture-scape. The influences of culture, in any glocality, are more fluid than that. To discover how positions change however, we need to look in more detail at where we position in the first place, at the outset of the interaction. And to achieve that step, we need, firstly, to briefly review three major theories relevant to work behavior. These theories are: SIT (Chapter 1); SFT (or Social Facilitation Theory); and Realistic Conflict Theory, or RCT (Taylor & Moghaddam, 1994).

10.1. SIT and cultural positioning

In an early exposition of SIT, Tajfel (1978) argued that people inhabit both social (or group) and personal identities. Crowds can coalesce for a one-off event like a sporting contest, and so, too, can people at work behave as individuals in one setting but as team players in the next. The question arises therefore, what is a sufficient condition for a social (versus individual) identity to become activated in the first place?

According to Tajfel, it actually takes very little to either temporarily replace an individual identity with a social one, or, indeed, one social identity with another. In a range of national settings, and population groups, Tajfel and colleagues have repeatedly demonstrated what they term a *minimal group effect*. Whether in experimental or field settings, the mere fact of naming a social cluster, even when that cluster has very little in common with each other, has apparently been sufficient to produce discriminatory judgments against an equally nominal out-group. Nominal groups, i.e., groups in name only, react to each other in prejudiced ways, for example they will distribute resources in an inequitable manner, and even take pay cuts to maintain a pay advantage over the perceived out-group rival (Carr, 2003b). The key point according to Tajfel, however, is that simply priming people with a reason to identify with each other, no matter how nominal, is often sufficient to invoke instead a social identity – and by implication, too, perhaps, replace one social identity with another. Thus, from job selection to performance appraisal, different social identities continually influence work behavior (Fadil & Moss, 1998).

10.2. SFT and cultural positioning

The central proposition in SFT is that the presence of others creates arousal, which makes more likely, or "socially facilitates," an enactment of responses that are already well known, or "socially dominant" (Aiello & Douthitt, 2001). Anyone who has ever felt their well-rehearsed, over-familiar business presentation "go into automatic pilot," achieving a state of 'flow' in front of the audience, has experienced a social facilitation effect. A key feature of the social facilitation process, however, is that the dominant response is not invariably a 'correct' one. In the same way that a poorly rehearsed business presentation can be facilitated into a shambles (by amplifying responses and repetitions that are incompetent), so, too, can any kind of pre-existing repertoire be socially facilitated by the presence of others. Thus, in theory, our over-familiar and self-stereotypical repertoires as operators, or as engineers, or as CEOs, can also be socially facilitated by the mere presence of others, via the arousal this produces.

Some of the best examples of SFT processes can be found in the early literature on cross-cultural communication (Bochner & Perks, 1971). In Bochner and Perk's study, Australian and Asian participants interacted cross-nationally or intra-nationally. When they interacted cross-nationally, they gave more "ethnic" responses than when they interacted intra-nationally. It was as if the presence of a different nationality was sufficient to prime a keener sense of socio-cultural identity. Likewise perhaps, cross-cultural contact sometimes produces what has been termed a *reaffirmation* of pre-existing cultural beliefs and prejudices, i.e., local backlash (Kosmitzki, 1996). In each case however, the presence of others, from another cultural background or group, is sufficient to position the people coming into contact with each other into their most familiar routines and implicit assumptions.

The developmental aspects of such social facilitations have been demonstrated in outdoor training for cultural integration (Ying-yi Hong, Wong, Chan, Chi-yue Chiu, Ip, Ho-ying Fu & Hansen, 200. In Ying-yi Hong et al.'s study, summer camp exposure between Hong Kong-born participants and Chinese immigrants to Hong Kong produced different changes depending on the participants' pre-contact, initial attitudes toward immigration. Amongst the Hong Kong-born participants with *pro*-immigration attitudes beforehand, the contact experience promoted greater acceptance of the immigration issue. There was a positive resonance. Amongst the participants with pre-contact *negative* attitudes toward immigration however, attitudes toward immigration became more negative. The resonance in this group was an *inverse* one (Chapter 5). In both cases however, there was a process consistent with the kinds of systems dynamic depicted in Figures 2.2 and 2.3. There was a social facilitation of pre-existing preferences, including a social facilitation of cultural identity.

Interestingly, this cultural positioning effect does not require the people to be physically present during the contact. A recent study of the social facilitation process examined social loafing, or free-riding, in culturally different work groups (Earley, 1993). Using in-tray exercises as the measure of performance, Earley found that relatively individualistic managers, both within the USA and within, on average, more collectivistic settings in China (relatively vertical collectivist) and Israel (relatively horizontal collectivist), socially loafed in simulated group as compared to individual work settings. In SFT parlance, the implied presence of others ("You are participating with other managers from …") enhanced a dominant response of individualism. By contrast, within a relatively collectivistic work setting in China or in Israel, and among the relative collectivists within the US-based sample, an implied presence of others *enhanced* performance compared to working alone. Again, therefore, the presence of others socially facilitated a dominant social response – in this case culturally positioning the workers into relatively traditional, "collectivistic" repertoires.

What these examples all reveal is that social facilitation is compatible with social identification. In a nutshell, socio-cultural identification *itself* is often socially facilitated. A pithy and poignant example of this form of positioning, at another level, is found in the literature on the influence of gender composition in workplace teams (Ingram & Parker, above). Ingram and Parker's (qualitative) study, which took place within engineering classrooms, found that gender-stereotypical behaviors were more commonly reported in mixed gender teams than in teams composed all of one gender. Specifically, all-female teams, unlike their mixed-gender counterparts, did not conform to stereotypical patterns for women at work. Since the key difference between the teams was social context (presence of males versus not) these data suggest that males and females (in part) mutually positioned themselves into their respective stereotypes through the social facilitation of gendered social identities. Through this mutual process, as well, the kind of "engineering culture" envisaged in Schein (above) is itself subject to sub-typing, for example on the basis of gender (for a different example, Bloor & Dawson, 1994).

10.3 RCT and cultural positioning

Realistic Conflict Theory posits that whenever resources are scarce, it is realistic (and rational) to expect individuals to band together to compete for them

(Taylor & Moghaddam, 1994). For example, in a recent study conducted in the Netherlands, Dutch workers who positioned and aligned themselves organizationally, pre-threat, within a work ethos of individualism were more likely, post-threat, to exaggerate that individuality (Jetten, Postmes & Mc Auliffe, 2002). According to Jetten et al., this was partly their way of showing solidarity to salient group norms (of individualism). Such interpretations imply roles for both SIT and SFT. The central point of the study, however, is that external adversity helps galvanize even the most individualistic among us into a sense of group. Such adversity-affiliation is also a psychological basis for example of Outward Bound courses (Carr, 2003b). In disaster management, too, circumstances of adversity often bond victims and helpers alike into a common, social identification (Paton & Stephens, 1996).

The mechanism of adversity-affiliation is, again, complementary to both social facilitation and social identity. Firstly, arousal is central in the examples above, from the arousal of an interdepartmental competition to the arousal of an instinct to survive, during an emergency. Secondly, in Tajfel's minimal group studies, and arguably for social identification to work, there is often an implied threat of some kind, through limited resources or threat to group pride (Turner, 1975; and, more latterly, Haslam, 2001). The more general, third point however, is that all three processes – social identification, social facilitation, and realistic conflict – often take place conjointly.

If we now revisit the glocality portrayed in Figures 2.2 and 2.3, we can more fully appreciate *why* people at work begin to position themselves into mutually antagonistic stereotypes of each other. In the first place, global travel – both literal and metaphorical – makes local and global identities salient. In the second place, the presence of other cultural identities, whether they be relatively globalized or relatively localized, arouses and enhances already internalized, and possibly implicit, local and global stereotypes. In the third place, the presence of diversity, insofar as it is perceived as threatening access to finite resources like jobs and privileges, or group pride, will foster affiliation with pre-existing groups, and to that extent, also, a degree of realistic conflict.

The *good* news in all this is that the same three processes create the potential for all the parties to reposition, and, by implication, realign with each other (Pun, 1990). Given our argument that SIT, SFT and RCT are often integrated into an overall process of cultural positioning, we should be able to find at least one example of cultural *re*positioning, that encapsulates, and demonstrably depends on, all three types of process happening together. Such an example can be found in a study of work performance in team settings (Glynn & Carr, 1999).

11. Cultural Repositioning

The participants in Glynn and Carr's study were business students and future managers. Their task was an in-tray exercise, which was completed in one of four behavioral conditions. In the first of these conditions, the participants believed that they were working alone. In a second condition, they believed that they were working on the same task with others, whose identity was left relatively diffuse. This "aggregate" condition, being relatively low on social/group cohesion, replicates the kind of condition that is classically used to investigate social loafing, i.e., free-riding. In a third condition, the participants were informed that they were representing, along with others working on the same task, their own faculty (partly analogous perhaps to an organizational or professional sub-culture). Finally, in a fourth condition, the participants were led to believe that they had been inadvertently placed in the "wrong" faculty team (i.e., they found themselves representing a faculty that was not their own). As our measures of work behavior, we took three principal measures of task performance. These were: ability to organize the in-tray; level of accountability demonstrated; and demonstration of appropriate analytical skills (see key below).

The key results of this study are presented in Figure 2.4. Compared to working alone in the first condition, participants in the second, aggregation condition, as predicted, displayed social loafing. Performance dropped when individuals believed that they were part of a relatively non-cohesive aggregate. From Figure 2.4, performance was also relatively low, and to that extent, de-motivated, in a fourth, out-group condition, where participants had earlier been informed that they were representing a rival faculty. In condition three however, where the participants had been minimally primed that they were part of a faculty inter-group effort, performance and motivation were highest across all performance domains.

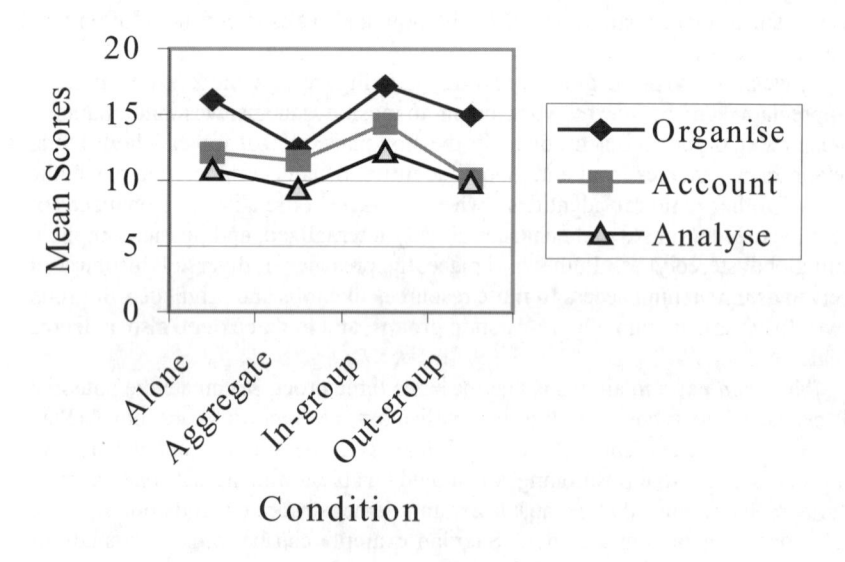

Figure 2.4 Mean performance scores under varying social contexts

Source: Glynn and Carr (1999)

12.1. Interpretation

In terms of theoretical processes, the performance in the in-group condition in Figure 2.4 can be attributed to at least three factors, or group processes. In the first place, a particular social identity was primed by the experimental instructions. In the second place, that social identity was socially facilitated by the perception that others were working on the same task. In the third place, this social facilitation took off when it was perceived that there was a rival team working on the same task – i.e., when there was realistic conflict (for the pride of winning). In the aggregate condition by contrast, the presence of others facilitated a different, and ultimately less efficacious response – individuality and self-concern – and thus a minimum level of working to get through the task. This study therefore implies cultural – and glocal – repositioning, through the transit from cultures of individualism (alone and aggregate conditions) to cultures of collectivism (in- and out-group conditions).

13. Summary

Returning to our travel metaphor introduced at the beginning of the book, we can now say that in the face of cultural and other forms of diversity, it is by no means inevitable that people at work will position themselves at loggerheads. Changing and variable work contexts are capable of priming, arousing and reinforcing a wealth of different social identities. These identities can be positioned and re-positioned, however, within a finite number of socially constructed compass points. Those metaphorical points of reference range for example from individualistic to collectivistic, power distant to egalitarian, and global to local (also, Taylor & Yavalanavanua, 1997). To the extent that points of reference are socially shared, people at work and scholars of work can, in principle, navigate each other's cultural landscape, and could do so, in practice, in a way that is far more generative than the existing literature on culture, at work, implies. Thus, a core mistake arguably made by cross-cultural management has been to take cultural positioning at face value, and even to feed into that process in a self-fulfilling way.

In the chapters that follow, our journey will be somewhat different. Through a vehicle of emerging research, we will explore the dynamics of cultural positioning and repositioning in some detail. In the interim, however, the key point to this chapter, and our best preparation for the journey to come, is to remember the following: Although cultural diversity and identity are complex, they are not completely unpredictable, nor are they unmanageable. On the contrary, one of the keys to managing them, both for our selves, and alongside others, is to respect their inherent glocality, and the debt this fluidity owes to culture.

Chapter 3

Achievement

> An important issue in social regulation in almost every society is the conflict between encouraging individual initiatives and promoting pro-social behavior ... how to maintain a balance between encouraging personal striving and constraining the manner through which personal striving is expressed has been a long-standing problem in almost every social philosophical system.

Source: Chi-yue Chiu & Yong-Hi Hong (1997: 172)

Me, We.

Source: Mohammed Ali

In the preceding chapter, it was argued that cultural identities regularly interact with each other, creating work behavior that is potentially either rigid or fluid, depending on the degree to which it is mutually stereotyped. A prime example of these intercultural dynamics, according to Chapters 1 and 2, is glocalization. Bringing that process to life, this chapter examines how stereotypically global cultures of achievement that are predominantly individualistic, interact with more localized cultures of achievement that are more collectivistic – through their socio-cultural values, workplace traditions, and micro-cultures of mateship in self-managed teams. As a result of donning this glocal lens on achievement-in-context, we identify new "climates for achievement." These can be negative (discouraging) or positive (encouraging, motivating). Accentuating the latter, the chapter ends with an opening out onto new vistas for managing achievement, which is then explored in the rest of the book.

1. A Brief History of the Study of Achievement at Work

The study of achievement as some of us know it began with the taxonomic efforts, by Henry A. Murray in the USA, to classify a "core" set of human needs based. These were extracted from his predecessors' writings on individual differences in personality, and tested in a series of group assessments (Murray, 1938). One of the products of this project was the Thematic Apperception Test (or TAT) (Murray, 1943). The basic rationale behind the TAT was to provide test-takers with ambiguous pictures – such as a schoolboy wistfully, or perhaps ambitiously, daydreaming – and to give the test-taker license to "project" their inner motives into the picture via their own creative narratives about it. According to Murray, the more a particular need was alluded to in the resulting storytellers' texts, the more salient that need must be to the storytellers themselves. Amongst 28 such needs identified by Murray and his team, was a *need for Achievement*, abbreviated to *n* Ach. This particular need subsequently became the most researched of all Murray's core needs. (Peck, 1975).

1.1. Phase 1: A concept defined

Chief among the researchers making *n* Ach so prominent was D. C. McClelland (1987b). In multiple publications, McClelland and colleagues provided the work research literature with its best-known and most enduring definition of *n* Ach. According to this definition, people high in *n* Ach are focused on "seeking success in competition with a standard of excellence." This oft-repeated definition captures succinctly at least three core features of achievement motivation: competing to win; striving to continually improve performance; and motivating the self toward those continual improvements (Franken & Brown, 1995). Features like these, of course, render *n* Ach directly relevant to the world of work. This is especially so in a global culture that stresses personal achievement as one of its core tenets.

1.2. Phase II: Ecological research

In the initial research on *n* Ach at work, McClelland adopted an approach that was ecological (Chapter 2, this volume). Achievement levels for societies past and present (at the time) were gauged through various adaptations of Murray's tests of projection, including, for example, cultural myths and stories. These indices were then for example correlated with measures of economic development several decades later (McClelland, 1961). The resultant correlation coefficients were often positive and statistically significant, thereby supporting a linkage between (a) levels of *n* Ach in a particular cultural group, and (b) that cultural group's prospects for future economic development.

1.3. Phase III: In-country research

1.3.1. *Small-to-Medium Enterprises (SMEs)*.

One of the proxies for economic development, used by McClelland, was ecological level of entrepreneurial behavior (1961). Buoyed by findings that this, too, was linked to *n* Ach, McClelland and his colleagues undertook an ambitious program of behavioral and economic engineering. They designed programs in *n* Ach and entrepreneurial skills for potential business people in "developing" countries (McClelland & Winter, 1969). In an evaluation of one of these interventions in India, conducted two years after the initial training in *n* Ach, found that its trainees had made more profit, employed more people, and invested more money, than an equivalent group of controls. Other interventions, in different "developing" areas, were reportedly also successful in SME development (see for example, McClelland, 1987a). Thus, *n* Ach has been linked to economically successful work behavior both *between* countries (at the ecological level, above) and *within* them (at the level of individual differences) (Chapter 2, this volume).

1.3.2. *Middle management*.

The role of individual differences in *n* Ach has also been explored, extensively, in a less interventionist manner. In one discernible wave of these studies, individuals high in *n* Ach were found to prefer moderate (i.e., attainable) goals over goals that were both more easy and more difficult – and thus less attainable (Littig, 1963; McClelland, 1965; Atkinson & Rayner, 1974). According to the classic definition of *n* Ach above, this preference is partly attributable to individuals high in *n* Ach being more highly motivated to win, and to continually seek to better themselves. Logically, each of these drives is more likely to be realized by adopting challenging *and* attainable goals, rather than challenging but *un*attainable ones. In addition, and again consistent with the classic definition, people high in *n* Ach tend to want to closely control their own destiny. This means that they like to receive prompt feedback from their work environment. Each of these propensities helps to make them not only entrepreneurial, but also relatively effective as middle managers. (McClelland & Boyatzis, 1982; Stahl, 1983).

1.4. Phase IV: Questionnaire research

Being entrepreneurial and managerial are not the sole work behaviors to be linked to *n* Ach. During the 1970s, *n* Ach was linked to a number of other behaviors that are directly relevant to globalization (Chapters 1 & 2, this volume). A principal investigator of *n* Ach during this era was Hines. Hines used structured questionnaires, rather than projective measures such as the TAT, to measure *n* Ach. He managed to replicate the earlier research, with projective tests, by establishing a link between *n* Ach and entrepreneurial behavior (Hines, 1976). In addition, Hines also linked *n* Ach to assimilation into mainstream culture (1973b), persistence of *n* Ach during migration and resettlement (1973c), and labor mobility (1973a, 1976). Thus, n Ach became linked, amongst other things, with the motivation and the courage to travel (Chapter 1, this volume). This link between *n* Ach and travel makes it relevant to a number of themes in this book, from embracing opportunities for international work (Chapter 4, this volume) to undertaking migration to build boundary-less careers (Chapter 6, this volume).

By the 1980s and 1990s, questionnaire measures of *n* Ach had multiplied (Reeve, 1992: 290). Integrating many of these measures together is an instrument developed by Cassidy and Lynn (1989). Specifically, Cassidy and Lynn's questionnaire contains sub-scales for measuring (a) excellence, (b) competitiveness, (c) mastery, (d) work ethic, (e) dominance (over others), (f) status aspiration, and (g) acquisitiveness (focus on money). Arguably therefore, the modern conception of *n* Ach, in a global economy, has two major facets – one more "intrinsic," which is related to McClelland's original definition and (a)–(d) above, and the other more "extrinsic," which is related more to impression management and (e)–(g).

1.5. Phase V: Rejuvenation

Today, *n* Ach remains an influential concept in the study of work behavior. For example, it is still used to select mid-level leaders (Stricker & Rock, 1998; Winter, 2002) and entrepreneurs (Cromie, 2000; Friese, 2003). Recently, the concept of *n* Ach has also been merged with goal setting and discrepancy theories (Chapter 4, this volume). Briefly, the idea here is that what motivates achievement behavior at work is not simply *n* Ach itself, but more the gap between *actual* and *ideal* levels of achievement (Langens, 2001). Langens has used an index of gap like this, for example, to re-analyze McClelland and Winter's original (1969) intervention, in India, on training entrepreneurs for small business development (above). According to Langens' recent re-analysis, trainees who were high in both *n* Ach *and* work-related self-discrepancy immediately after the training also had the highest probability of becoming SME-active two years later. Thus, "continuous improvement" in entrepreneurial work behavior may depend on a certain amount of *tension* between personal and social systems, for example if workers are seeking their personal success and excellence against a backdrop of prevailing – and horizontally or vertically collectivistic – mateship.

1.6. An assessment

There can be no doubt that *n* Ach has proved itself a robust explanatory concept for describing and part-explaining leadership behavior at middle-management level; and also entrepreneurial behavior in small business development settings. Those rejuvenations of *n* Ach notwithstanding however, and whether we adopt its earlier (psychodynamic, implicit) or later (impression management, conscious) definitions, the construct of *n* Ach and the study of it has remained heavily individualistic (see also, Hofstede, 1980b). Our analyses in Chapter 2 (this volume) suggest that this conceptualization is not the only form of achievement motivation – and so not the only pathway to economic progress. Conceptually, there is absolutely no reason why "achievement" should be construed exclusively as *personal* achievement (Diaz-Guerrero, 1977). Measures of *n* Ach from the twentieth century, for example, failed to predict economic growth for the years 1950–1977 (Lewis, 1991). In *n* Ach's stead, one could argue, economic growth overlapping with this period was partly predicted, statistically, by indexes like Confucian work dynamism (Chapter 2, this volume; Hofstede & Bond, 1988). For an example at a more micro level, today's workplace teams are overtly expected to achieve – partially at least – on a collective rather than an individual basis (Chapter 5, this volume).

1.7. Social achievement

Despite the evident potential for multiple definitions of achievement motivation, when we examine the literature on achievement motivation at work, there is very little research on achieving "socially," i.e., on behalf of, in conjunction with, and through the work group. Some literature does remind us about the existence of social achievement, for example in relatively impoverished and collectivistic settings (Lawuyi, 1992; Oshodi, 1999). These kinds of study are by no means dismissive of personalized forms of achievement motivations (see also, for example, Mehta, 1977; and Munro, 1983). Yet, by comparison with the literature on *n* Ach, and especially in today's organizations, where social networking and "working through others" is at a premium (Ferris et al. 2001), the literature on social achievement in the workplace is inadequate (The Afro-centric Alliance, 2001).

To sum up then, there is evidently an imbalance, in the literature on work behavior, toward individualistic rather than collectivistic forms of achievement motivation. To some extent, the inattention to social achievement simply reflects the relatively individualistic discourse on work behavior, which currently prevails in the global publishing media themselves (Chapter 1, this volume). However, the lack of respect for social achievement, in this same literature, also belies an overemphasis on personal achievement in the rhetoric of "performance" at work itself. According to our opening quotes, and the title of this book, these views of achievement are incomplete (Adkins & Naumann, 2001). Specifically, they leave us doubly bereft: First of theories and research about social achievement; and second, on how to balance the individual with the social. Thus, what an over-individualistic, and more recently over-globalized, view of achievement is missing, is an understanding of how groups "*constrain* the manner through which personal striving is expressed" (above, emphases added).

2. *n* Ach in Social Context

A first clue about the consequences of ignoring this issue - fundamentally a question of balance - is contained in the original evaluation of *n* Ach training in India, by McClelland and Winter (1969). According to McClelland (1987b), the tendency to adhere to traditional customs was higher amongst the program's "successes" than amongst its "failures." This pattern is described in McClelland as "the opposite of what might be expected" (1987b: 563). That surprise, however, arguably stems from an implicitly individualistic and globalistic view of achievement itself. From a more collectivistic and glocalistic counter-perspective, the findings make reasonable sense: Any individualistic achievement-striving among McClelland's new trainees was more acceptable to the community, and so ultimately more workable and sustainable, when it was balanced by a degree of respect for tradition.

Of course, this interpretation is retrospective and, to that extent, inherently speculative. For example, the custom in question (observing Rahukal, a period of siesta during the business day) was not overtly "collectivistic." Evidently therefore, we require more direct evidence that collectives will indeed act to "constrain the manner through which personal striving is expressed," and that they will demonstrably do so as a way of reasserting a value of achieving on behalf of the group.

One region of the world where this dynamic seems intuitively likely is Australasia. Colloquially, in both Australia and New Zealand, the phrase "Tall Poppy Syndrome" is stereotypically used to refer to predict a "chopping down," by the majority in a group, of high individual achievers. Moreover, this tendency, in Australasian society, has been researched empirically, for example in Australia by Feather (1994), and in New Zealand by Harrington & Liu (2002).

2.1. Australia

In his research, Feather has made cross-cultural comparisons with social groups in relatively power-distant settings in Japan – where for example a common adage predicts that, "the nail which sticks out gets pounded down" (1994). Feather found relatively high anti-tall poppy attitudes there, compared to his samples from Australia. Individual attitudes *favoring* the tall poppy, in turn, have been linked to valuing personal achievement, using Schwartz's Value Scale (Chapter 2, this volume). By contrast, an individual's alignment with "traditional" Australian beliefs, for example in egality, have been linked in Feather's research to attitudes favoring *the fall* of a tall poppy (Table 2.2). This finding suggests that power-distant positions are not the only values likely to interact with *n* Ach. Belief in egality will conceivably interact with it, too (Buick Bar & Grill, Chapter 1, this volume). Supporting that idea, Feather's research has also revealed that tall poppy syndrome is both negative and positive, for example when a low achiever is given a "hand up" to return to the middle of the group's achievement spectrum (Feather, 1994). In this way, tall poppy syndrome may be more about centripetal values than about mere base envy.

2.2. New Zealand

The ways in which cultural values and positions underlie tall poppy syndromes are explored still further in research from New Zealand/Aotearoa.

Intuitively, for example, we might be tempted to equate tall poppy syndromes more with collectivism than with individualism. Yet Harrington and Liu found that relatively group-oriented Māori participants were *more* in favor of rewarding a tall poppy from within their group, than were their reportedly less collectivistic Pākeha counterparts (2002). Findings like this remind us not to over-equate collectivism, or its power distance counterpart (above), with tall poppy syndromes. In fact, Harrington and Liu's finding could be due to any combination of (1) adopted individualistic values; (2) traditional values stressing personal māna; and/or (3) "standing tall against" a non-Indigenous "mainstream." In this way, individual achievement often blends with social achievement. But the research also reminds us that "culture" refuses to be mapped simplistically onto reactions to *n* Ach. Instead, how groups react to *n* Ach is more often an issue of cultural and political climate combined.

If cultural and political contexts influence reactions to *n* Ach, then so, too, do economic settings. As regards the distribution of material resources, for instance, the literature in social science contains discussions on the emotions of jealousy and envy. Psychologists, as one example, have focused on individual differences in the extent to which each of us is capable of being envious (e.g., Salovey, 1991). Similarly, and not surprisingly perhaps, anthropologists and sociologists have tended to focus more on propensities and capacities for groups in society to feel envy toward each other (e.g., Berke, 1998; Kohnert, 1996). Thus, reactions to *n* Ach are partly economic, and reflective of economic contingencies, and these contingencies affect both individuals and groups alike (Adkins & Naumann, 2001).

3. *n* Ach in Work Context

What happens in groups in society has repercussions at work, and for this reason alone we would expect envy to spill over, periodically, into relations at work (Templer et al. 1992). Anecdotally, for instance, workplace envy has been alleged to stifle innovation within organizations in Australia (Anderson & Alexander, 1995; Brewer, 1995; Robbins, Waters-Marsh, Cacioppe & Millett, 1994) and New Zealand (Ceramalus, 1994). Envy is also anecdotally reported from Ghana and Malaysia, where in both settings the phrase, "PhD", is an acronym for "Pull Him Down." Included as well in anecdotal observations of envy at work are reports of "Red Eye disease" (from Hong Kong); "Shoe-sock man" (from Papua New Guinea); and (from Scandinavia) "Royal Swedish Envy" (Schneider, 1991). (For further examples of such reports, see Carr & MacLachlan, 1997).

3.1. Envy at work

In a key critique of workplace envy, envious feelings have been explicitly linked to workplace dynamics (Bedeian, 1995). Bedeian in fact suggests that, "envy is especially common in business," and that "the assignment of limited organizational resources – promotions, travel money, salary increases, windowed offices, company cars, secretarial support, prime sales terms, and the like … any situation in which one colleague gains advantage at the expense of others will inevitably evoke envy" (1995: 50). Not surprisingly then, Bedeian links sentiments of envy to globalization, even suggesting that it is "a central aspect of consumer-oriented economies worldwide." The global economy, Bedeian argues, deliberately encourages us to envy our neighbors, in order to motivate us to consume more, and so reduce the feeling of envy! To the extent that promotions - and other forms of contested achievement at work - provide a means to consume more, envy at work is logically fuelled by consumerism too.

3.2. Envy and personality

Over and above these global spurs to envy, Bedeian argues, some individuals will be more prone to feeling envy, at work, than others. Key individual differences, that research has identified as being associated with destructive feelings of envy at work, include: Type A personality; emotional instability and insecurity; and equity-sensitivity to the point of feeling "entitled" to one's share of just desserts (Bedeian, 1995). When resources are limited in fact, entire groups can become *more* equity-sensitive toward each other than they otherwise are (Morris & Leung, 2000). Overall therefore, we can expect group backlashes against *n* Ach, at levels that range from individual differences in personal identity through to group differences in social identity.

3.3. Organizational structure

In the workplace, unlike much of wider society, behavior takes place within the constraints of an organizational hierarchy (for a notable exception, Semler, 2002). It would be strange indeed if such structures did not, somehow, impact on *n* Ach! For example, even within today's relatively "flat" organizational structures, we still have supervisors and bosses who have a certain amount of legitimated power over what is done, and thereby achieved, at work (Chapter 5, this volume). Having status like this inevitably creates the potential not only for subordinates and co-worker peers to envy individual achievers, but also for their *supervisors* to have specific feelings, too. As Bedeian indicates, co-worker envy at work should be distinguished conceptually, and carefully, from supervisor *jealousy* at work. Whilst envy means coveting what we do not have, e.g., wanting the promotion that the other worker has, jealousy means literally the opposite of this – being overprotective of what we "have," for fear that we might "lose" it to someone else.

3.4. Jealousy at work

A prime example of what those in power can lose to high achievers at work, particularly in today's relatively flat, lean and internally competitive organizations, is power itself. 'Empowerment for all' means *dis*empowerment for *some*. This is partly why perhaps one of the largest obstacles to successfully implementing workplace teams is supervisor resistance (Chapter 5, this volume). Even the supervisor's *job* is not risk-free in the current zeitgeist. Since the late 1980s, interest in job insecurity has been steadily growing (Ashford, Lee & Bobko, 1989). Accompanying this trend, survey research has indicated that feelings of job security in general have been steadily declining (Cooper, 2000). This decline in job security is now being linked, explicitly, with the wider process of globalization (Sparks, Faragher & Cooper, 2001). Thus, globalization may be partly fuelling backlashes of job insecurity amongst superiors, against *n* Ach at work.

3.5. Abuse of power

One of the key workplace consequences of an enhanced feeling of job insecurity is workplace bullying (Bassman & London, 1993). Much of the impetus for studying bullying at work has come from the Scandinavian countries of North Western Europe (Einarsen et al., 2003). In Scandinavia, for instance, workplace bullying has been given the evocative term "mobbing" (Leymann, 1990). For the mobbed themselves, mobbing has subsequently been linked to organizational outcomes such as work stress (Lee, 2000), and intention to leave an organization/employer (Quine, 2001). As the metaphor of mobbing vividly connotes, bullying at work can assume both within-group, inter-individual dynamics, as well as relations between groups, i.e., inter-group dynamics (respectively, Rayner, 1997; Terav & Keltikangas-Jaervinen, 1998). These groups encompass and entwine, for instance, gender relations at work, and racial discrimination within occupational professions (respectively, Daroesman & Daroesman, 1992; Grey & Pratt, 1995). Once again, therefore, we can expect a range of local reactions against *n* Ach.

3.6. Two key forms of backlash

So far, we have identified at least two basic senses in which there will be local backlashes against individual achievement will move. Firstly, they may take place as a form of "pulling down" action from below, for example through envy; and, secondly, they may take place as a form of "pushing down" action from above, for example through jealousy. These potentials have been termed, respectively, the Pull Down and the Push Down (Carr & MacLachlan, 1997). Logically, too, of course, the same negative possibilities also imply some *positive* potential. The semantic antonyms to Pull Down and Push Down are, Push Up from below, and Pull Up from above (in an organizational hierarchy). Thus, by starting to think more glocally about individual achievement (n Ach), i.e., placing it in a context of work groups, we have been able to conceive of at least two dimensions of resistance to its individualization.

3.7. A visual schema

These two dimensions now enable us to being modeling the glocality of achievement. The two dimensions, one more horizontal and the other more vertical, are portrayed for us in Figure 3.1. This depicts what is termed a *motivational gravity grid.* From Figure 3.1, co-worker peers and subordinates are pictured in the horizontal dimension. Faced with an individual who is high in n Ach, they have options before them. These options can be thought of initially as attitudes. Those attitudes range from Pull Down (–) to Push Up (+). Also in Figure 3.1, the polar options, for *supervisors* of a high performer, are pictured in the vertical plane. Their options, too, resemble attitudes. They however range from Push Down (–) to Pull Up (+). From Figure 3.1 therefore, the two dimensions of Pull Down-Push Up and Push Down–Pull Up create a grid. This grid contains quadrants, each of which represents a qualitatively unique combination of Pull Down versus Push Up, and Push Down versus Pull Up. Hence, through the glocality of Figure 3.1, we are able to arrive at four diverse prevailing "climates" of *n* Ach. More importantly, however, in these different climates, the individualization of achievement is predicted to either wither or grow on the proverbial vine.

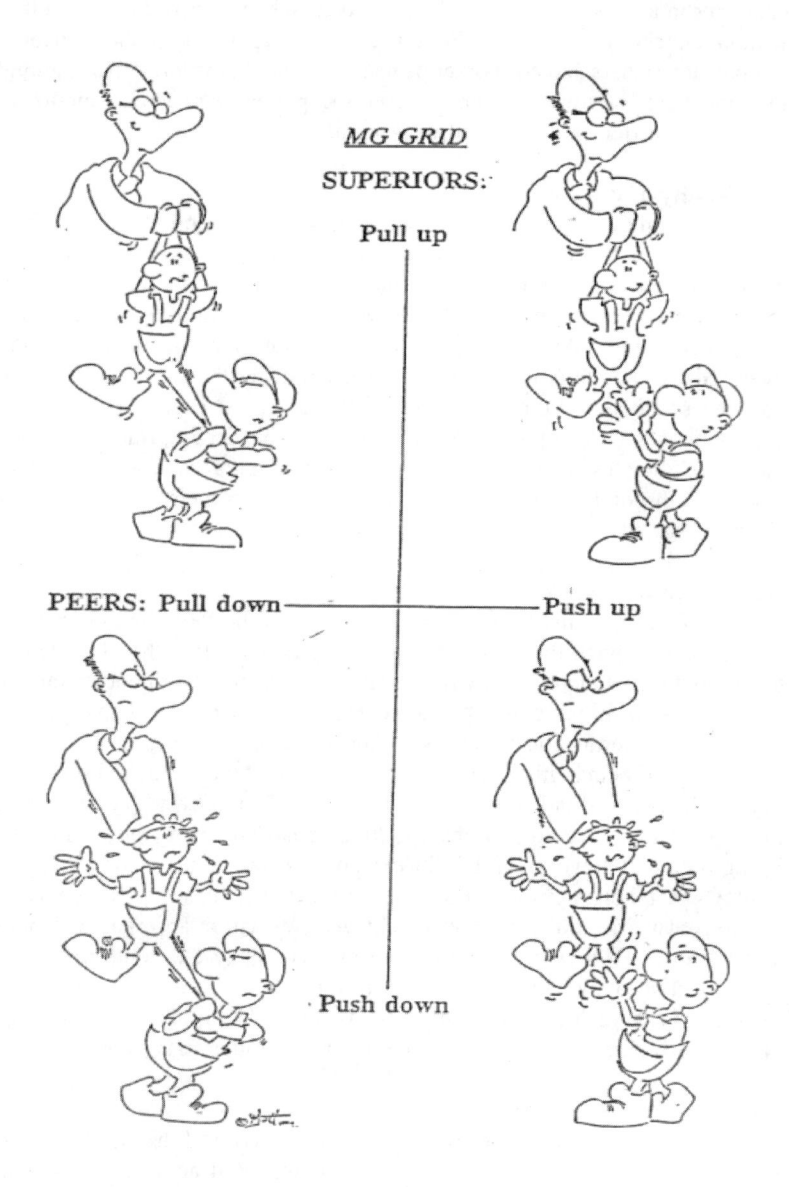

Figure 3.1 The motivational gravity grid

Source: Carr & MacLachlan (1997)

3.8. Characters in the grid

From Figure 3.1, the three characters in the grid, which are deliberately and ironically stereotyped, are meant to caricature the *quality of work life* in each quadrant, for each of the major stakeholders in the groups concerned: managers/supervisors (the character in glasses); co-worker peers/subordinates (the character in a peaked cap); and the individual achiever himself or herself (the figure without either glasses or cap). From Figure 3.1, depending on the motivational intent of both supervisors and co-worker peers/subordinates, the worker-in-the-middle – our individual achiever who is high in n Ach – experiences different emotional climates, and thereby differing qualities of working life.

3.9. Quality of work life

From Figure 3.1, the diverse climates for n Ach range from doubly negative, i.e., Pull Down–Push Down (– –), to doubly positive (+ +), i.e., Push Up–Pull Up. In-between these two extremes of emotional climate, the central character may experience a –/+ work climate of Pull Down–Pull Up, or a +/– work climate of Push Up–Push Down. At face value, these climates may seem as though they are intermediate in emotional meaning, between climates that are – – and + +. But that is not necessarily so. Sometimes, for instance, being caught between one set of expectations and its opposite creates acute role conflict and role stress. To an extent therefore, climates for achievement that are themselves ambivalent can create *more* emotional discomfort for the high achiever than even their "– –" counterparts (also, Chapter 5, this volume, on broken promises).

3.10. A new metaphor

To capture the valences and sensations of the force fields depicted in Figure 3.1, we have coined the term *motivational gravity* (Carr & MacLachlan, 1997). In this term, the metaphor of *gravity* was chosen, like any other good metaphor, because it resonates with pre-existing knowledge and experience. Gravity is a familiar concept. The term reflects our everyday sensations – depending on one's point of reference – of being either "weighed down by", or "drawn towards," a body of mass greater than the individual self. The ideas of "up" or "down" (i.e., Push/Pull Up and Pull/Push Down) are not, strictly speaking, meant to convey any value connotation. Being brought "down to earth," for example, is sometimes a good thing. Instead, a gravity metaphor was chosen so as to reflect the inherent 'verticality' per se of relations at work, in the pursuit of achievement, within an organizational structure. The adjective *motivational* was chosen to accompany the noun gravity in order to capture an idea that the social context for achievement (i.e., gravity) invariably interacts with achievement motivation. Ipso facto, for instance, a positive gravitational climate is more likely to buoy n Ach rather than suppress it.

3.11. The grid as descriptor

In theory, the motivational gravity (or MG) grid in Figure 3.1 can be used, first and foremost, to describe the various climates of achievement found at work. These descriptions can be either qualitative (by quadrant), or quantitative (degrees of Pull Up, etc., within each quadrant). Description is a first step in building theory (Gould, 1994). As well however, the climates of achievement depicted in Figure 3.1 can have different scopes of application. They apply equally to organizational climate as to occupational climate. As regards organizational climate for instance, the grid can be used to help profile reactions to n Ach across different departments, cliques, teams and other forms of affiliation at work. As regards occupational climate, the grid can be used to delineate the various climates for achievement within which professions, and occupational groups generally, feel they are working – for example CEOS, engineers, and operators (Schein, Chapter 2, this volume).

4. Research on Motivational Gravity

The research on gravity stimulated by, and conceptualized from, the MG grid, has evolved in several distinctive strands. A primary strand has concentrated on how to measure motivational gravity in a valid and appropriate manner. A second strand of research has taken more of a functional approach, focusing, for instance, on the influences of motivational gravity in selection, performance management, and occupational wellbeing. A third strand of research, again using the MG grid, has focused explicitly on exploring how to possibly *manage* motivational gravity, both personally and from a group perspective. This, "tertiary" layer of research has suggested ways of both minimizing the consequences of negative motivational gravity, and of avoiding it in the first place. Overlaid on this programmatic research, our studies of motivational gravity have systematically shifted their focus across the principal characters in Figure 3.1. Thus, attention has progressively ranged from the intentions of co-workers and supervisors; to intentions of the character high in n Ach; to, finally, more dynamic – and inherently glocal – interactions between the two.

5. A Primary Strand: Measurement of Motivational Gravity

As Bedeian (1995) points out, gravitational intentions, at least of a negative kind, are likely to be somewhat "slippery" to measure. Firstly, they are probably susceptible to social desirability effects, i.e., respondents will attempt to disguise any negative intentions if we ask about them too directly. Secondly, the concept of organizational learning (Chapter 6, this volume) suggests that respondents may not even know, consciously, that they harbor either envious or jealous intentions toward their colleague. As Bedeian points out, such emotions probably have to be *concealed* from the self in order to "work." Admitting to envying, or being jealous of, a colleague is tantamount to admitting to some inferiority in self; and to that extent would be self-defeating. Thus, according to Bedeian, many features of envious behavior at work – and hence, by implication, motivational gravity, too – are largely implicit.

5.1. Scenario scaling

Considerations like these create obstacles to the valid measurement of negative motivational gravity. The way that we have chosen to circumvent these issues is to rely on relatively indirect forms of questioning, and in particular, on scenario scaling. In scenario scaling, a respondent can be asked to indicate what employees like themselves, not themselves per se, would probably do in a given scenario – such as another individual becoming a high achiever in their workplace. Once everybody's responses are aggregated, it is possible to gain an overall sense of how the majority in the group as a whole might respond to conspicuous "success" by one individual. Scenario-based techniques such as this – as opposed to more direct self-report tests – have been shown to help deflect social desirability effects (Aycan, Kanungo & Sinha, 1999). Such relative impermeability to social desirability effects includes being suited to groups who find direct questioning socio-culturally inappropriate (Sinha, 1989; Table 2.1). Moreover, scenario techniques – particularly when they are framed in the here-and-now – can be just as valid for measuring emotions, both positive and negative, as actual "online" measures taking place in "real time" (Robinson & Clore, 2001).

5.2. Motivational gravity scenario scaling

In an early empirical study focused explicitly on motivational gravity, a set of experienced managers and less experienced but future managers, located in Malaŵi, East Africa, were asked to predict the probable reactions of a local work group to a high-achieving individual worker (Carr, MacLachlan, Zimba & Bowa, 1995a). This hypothetical worker repeatedly earned a bonus; or was awarded a conference trip overseas; or was promoted to a higher rank than the work group as a whole. Participants in the study, which included persons from a range of organizational and occupational settings, were given options of predicting either encouragement or discouragement, on a sliding scale from 7 to 1, respectively.

The study revealed a tendency to predict both Push Down and Pull Down. Figuring significantly in this equation was *n* Ach: When asked whether "Malaŵians in general want to do better than others," almost all participants responded, "Yes." This response suggests a certain amount of tension, interaction, and contradiction, between predicted group responses (Push Down–Pull Down, – –) and personal motivation to actually "do" the achieving at work, in the role of someone like the central character in Figure 3.1. Such dynamics, according to Chapter 1 (this volume) are inherently glocal. Specifically, and as Carr et al. (1995a) illustrate in their report, these dynamics embody interactions between (1) the *globality* of individualization (e.g., "Everyone wants to be number one;" and counteracting "threat to own position"), and (2) the *locality* of collectivist traditions ("reserve encouragement for family and friends").

5.3. Scale properties
5.3.1. *Social desirability?*

The more experienced managers in our sample reported more negative motivational gravity than their inexperienced counterparts (future managers). The fact that *more* experience on the job was equated with *less* socially desirable answers gives the responses in this study as a whole an air of candor. Candor in turn suggests too, of course, that the responses were relatively free from social desirability effects. That possibility was explored relatively directly in Carr, Powell, Knezovic, Munro and MacLachlan (1996). In their research, conducted with employed participants and students in Australia, Carr et al.'s (1995a) 7-point scale (above) was modified. On the new scale, respondents could predict levels of encouragement *and* levels of discouragement, first amongst co-workers and then, as well, amongst supervisors. This plurality was allowed by asking the respondents to indicate the proportions of characters (first co-workers, and then supervisors) who would be supportive, and discouraging, or neither of these. By subtracting the proportion of co-workers or supervisors who would *dis*courage the high achiever, from those who would *en*courage the high achiever (as distinct from just ignoring them), a "net encouragement score" was calculated. This score was then tested for any correlation with scores on a measure of socially desirable responding. The net encouragement scores did not correlate with social desirability – indicating that the scenario measure was comparatively free of desirability bias.

5.3.2. Acceptability.
As well as checking empirically for any social desirability effects, we also gauged the face validity of the scenario instrument, compared to the more conventional, i.e., self-report, Likert scales. In organizational settings, and especially in contexts of cultural diversity, the face validity of scales and measures is often a necessary condition to prevent litigation, boost acceptability, and foster validity generally (MacLachlan, Mapundi, Zimba & Carr, 1995). In our comparison of face validity between scenario measure versus a Likert scale, the experienced employees in our sample, unlike their less experienced student counterparts, significantly preferred the scenario instrument (Carr et al., 1996, Study II). That preference was due in part to the explicitly "workplace" focus of the scenario scale. As well however, the Likert scale – unlike its scenario-scale counterpart – was not free of social desirability effects among some employees (Study I). In general therefore, the scenario scale may have been relatively free of constraints in work settings.

5.3.3. Discriminant validity
One of the first lessons Carr et al. report learning from the grid-based scenarios just described is that organizational climates were extremely variable, even within a single "national" setting (Chapter 2, this volume). In Carr et al. (1996) for instance, geographically proximal organizations ranged in climate from Push Up–Pull Up (+ +) to Pull Down–Push Down (– –), all within the same national setting (Eastern Central Australia). In one sense, variability like this is broadly consistent with the idea that prevailing climates, like their cultural underpinnings, are found across a variety of levels, from societal groups through to small teams at work. In another sense however, the data also contain a profound warning – a warning that has been sounded from the beginning of this book: There is often as much, if not more variation within countries as there is between them. Hence, just as it would be a mistake to assume that motivational gravity in, say, Australia or Malaŵi is relatively "uniform," so, too, it would a mistake to position the climate for n Ach, in those national settings, uniformly in one or other of the quadrants in Figure 3.1.

6. A Secondary Strand: Influences of Gravity on Work Behavior
In an early study of job applicants' communication styles, and hiring decisions made by selection panels, it was found that candidates can be both under-assertive *and* too assertive for their own good (Gallois, Callan, & Palmer, 1992). Also, high achievers exert more of a positive impression when they display a modicum of human imperfections (Aronson, Willerman & Floyd, 1966; Helmreich, Aronson, & LeFan, 1970). Findings like these suggest that overachievement can (in some cases) be its own worst enemy. Hence job candidates for example may *over-*impression-manage themselves (Baron, 1986). Baron's studies of over-impression-management, what he terms "too much of a good thing," focused on the use of scent and hyperbolic power dressing. But the focus nonetheless raises an important question for us, of whether achievements themselves, beyond a certain point or limit, can become a liability. Theoretically, for instance, impression ratings for a job

candidate, by a selection panel, may show a motivational gravity dip. That is to say, ratings may lose impact beyond a certain level of self-professed achievements. We already have at least two possible reasons for expecting such a dip: Baron's "too much of a good thing (to be true)" effect; *plus* motivational gravity.

6.1. Job selection

During selection for jobs, predicting a motivational gravity dip runs counter to, or at least stretches, several eminent and enduring theories of impression formation. The principle of averaging (and weighted averaging), for instance, suggests that, provided the achievements themselves remain equally positive, earning more of them will keep overall impression constant (Anderson, 1974). This is partly because there are no "weak" elements to "pull the average down" (Anderson, 1981). Another potentially relevant principle is that of addition (or, "more equals better"). This principle of addition is arguably part of the global zeitgeist today. Addition suggests that any achievement, provided it is positive, will add to overall impression rating garnered by the candidate (Carr, 2003b). These theoretical possibilities are depicted, schematically, in Figure 3.2. Figure 3.2 also however adds new elements to the mix - motivational gravity and the glocality for achievement. Specifically, and in clear contrast to its predecessors, Motivational Gravity Theory predicts a "motivational gravity dip."

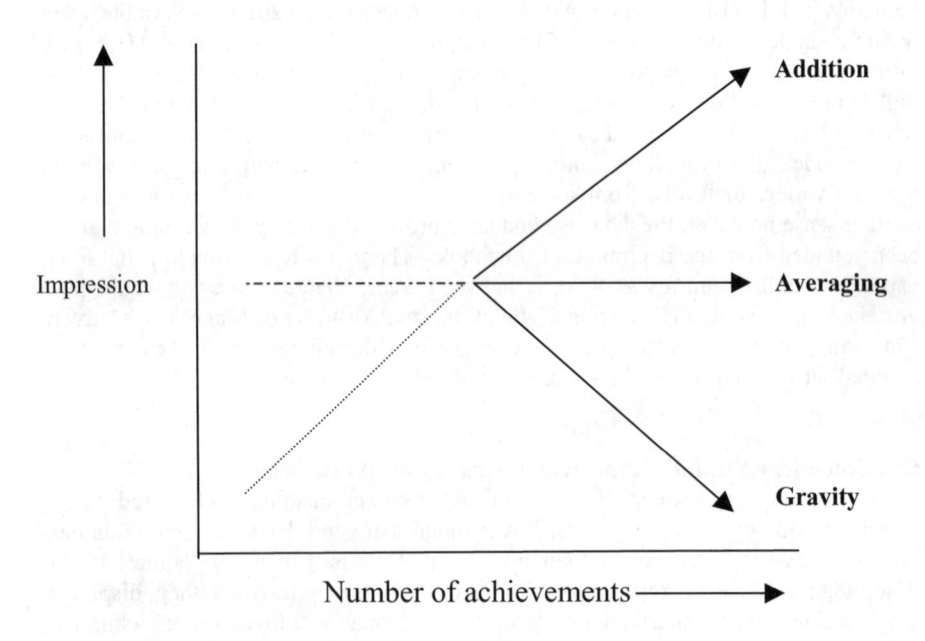

Figure 3.2 Three competing models of impression formation and impression management

Source: Carr (2003b)

Thus, according to Figure 3.2, as the number of achievements on a job application increases, all else being equal, we will see one of *three* possible curves emerging – depending on whether *averaging, addition,* or *gravity* gives the best approximation to selection decisions.

6.2. A critical test

A test of these three models has been conducted in Australia (Smith & Carr, 2002). Job-experienced students were given a job selection scenario containing a list of candidates' qualities, as they might be presented on an actual job application. These qualities included (a) personality traits, which are often presented on job applications as if they were "achievements" in themselves; and (b) actual achievements, such as educational attainments and awards. Each participant viewed a unique, but equally positive list of these achievements, which had been randomly selected for example (a) from a linguistic database. Between them, the only factor that varied systematically was the *number* of achievements, which ranged from five to 20, in increments of five. These varying numbers of achievements were then plotted against the resulting levels of liking for the candidate, and as well the overall impression formed about them.

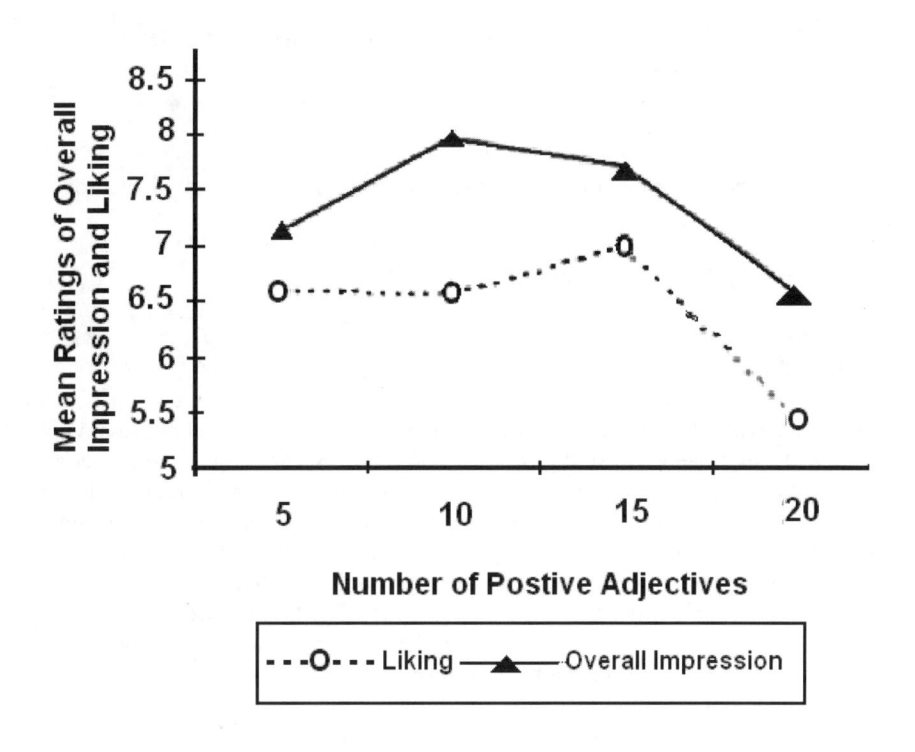

Figure 3.3 Number of positive trait descriptors and impression formation

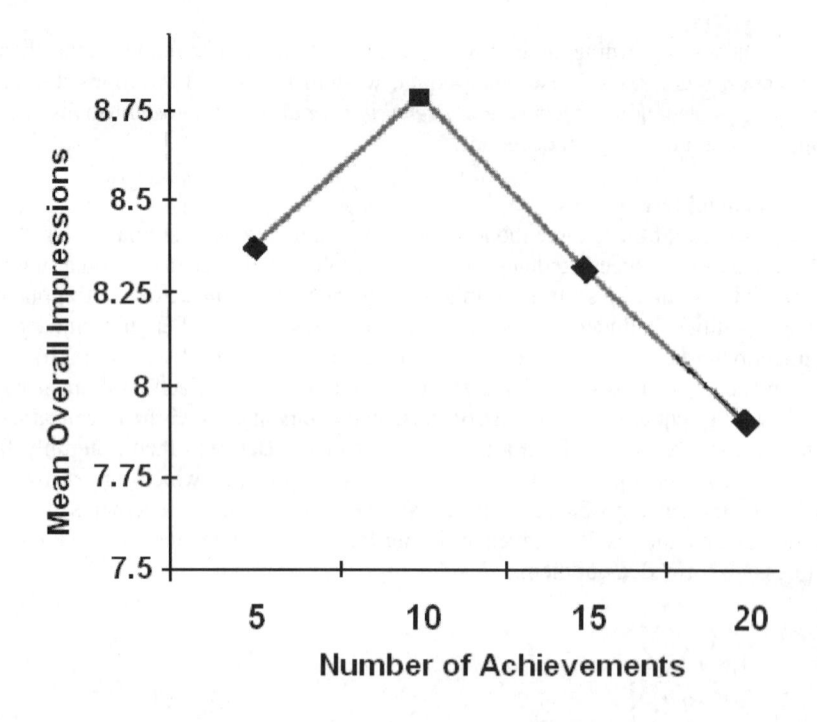

Figure 3.4 Number of positive achievements and impression formation

Source (for both figures): Smith & Carr (2002)

6.3. A dip emerges

From Figures 3.3 and 3.4, it is evident that, beyond a certain number of achievements listed on the job application, both liking and overall impression ratings dropped, significantly (Smith & Carr, 2002). In each figure, we see a clear motivational gravity dip. In order to check whether this dip is genuinely attributable to motivational gravity, rather than to, say, simply "too much of a good thing," we administered an attitude scale about tall poppies (Feather, 1994). We already knew that the population from which our sample was drawn found this particular scale reasonably face valid (Carr et al., 1996, Study II). The findings from this measure are presented in Figure 3.5. From Figure 3.5, the participants who were more in favor of seeing a tall poppy fall were also more likely to have a lower impression of the job candidate in our selection scenario. The inflected function in Figure 3.5 is supported, also, by added qualitative measures. Specifically, respondents explained their attitude scale ratings using a combination of both "too much of a good thing" *and* motivational gravity. For example, the candidate was described as a "tall poppy" who did indeed "deserve to be cut down to size."

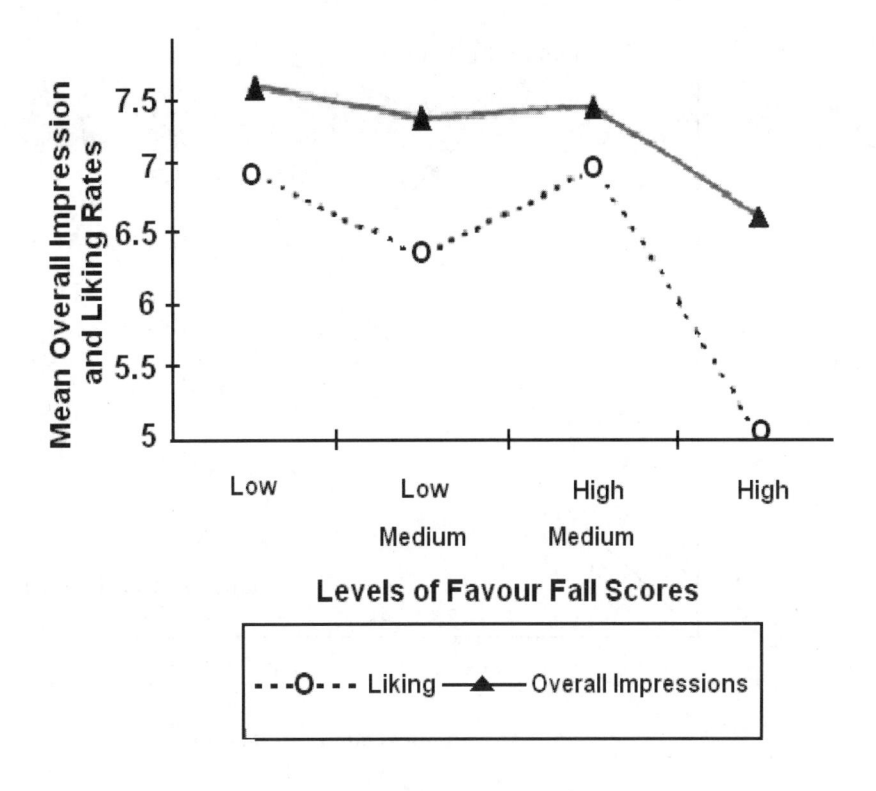

Figure 3.5 Impression factors as a function of gravitational attitudes by quartile

Source: Smith & Carr (2002)

6.4. *n* Ach reconceptualized

The data that are summarized in Figures 3.3 to 3.5 mark a first explicit charting of motivational gravity at work in selection. In terms of *n* Ach itself, the early research, by McClelland and associates, implied that there is a linear relationship between levels of *n* Ach and levels of successful personal "performance" that we can expect at work. Figures 3.3 to 3.5, and the grid, suggest, however, that unqualified expectations like this are organizationally naïve. A more realistic way of thinking about the link between *n* Ach and success is *glocal*. That glocal model of *n* Ach is schematized for us in Figure 3.6. The essence of Figure 3.6 is that links between achievement and success are often moderated by the local climate of motivational gravity, negative or positive, surrounding an individual achiever at the time. Here, then, are the "social restraints" described in our opening quotation, and we can term them motives toward *social achievement,* or *s* Ach. Figure 3.6 encapsulates the way that groups will act to bridle *n* Ach, and thereby balance the individual with the social (*s* x *n* Ach).

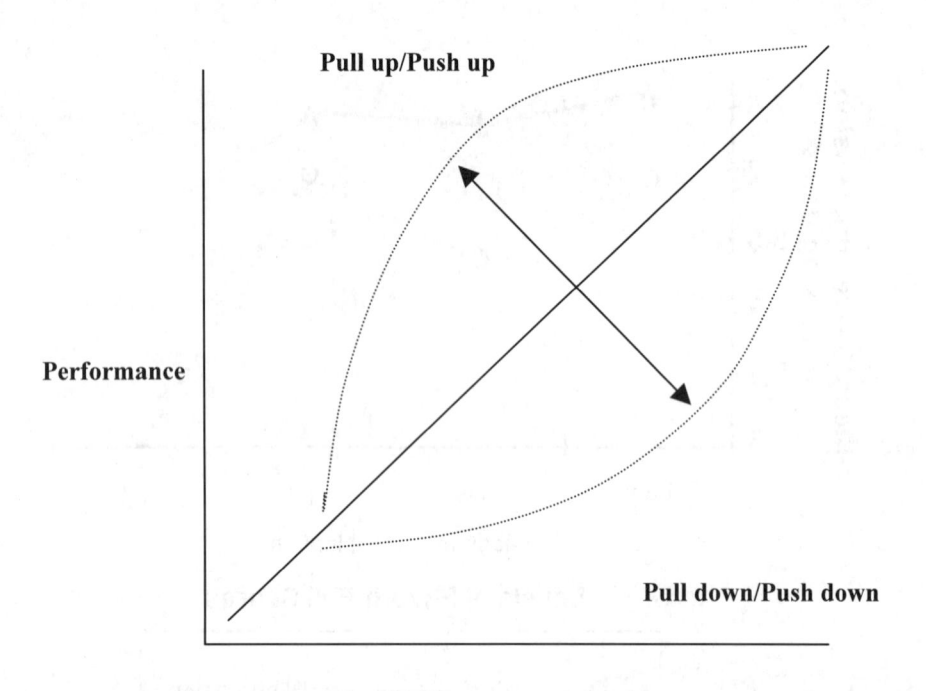

Figure 3.6. The social psychology of achievement ($fs \times n$ Ach)

Source: Adapted from Carr (2003)

6.5. Selection biases between groups

The influences of motivational gravity dips are likely to extend beyond interactions between selection panels and individual applicants. They will also include, of course, relations between groups. In Figure 3.7 for instance, we have plotted the relationship between number of achievements and overall impression separately for applicants of different genders, corrected for the gender of the respondent (Smith & Carr, 2002). The (statistically significant) interaction of trends in Figure 3.7 begins to suggest that the perceptual thresholds for motivational gravity dips are sometimes lower for high-achieving females than for high-achieving males (Smith & Carr, 2002). To that extent, motivational gravity dips may be linked, in theoretical and practical terms, to managing the implicit prejudices of the proverbial "glass ceiling" (Melamed, 1995).

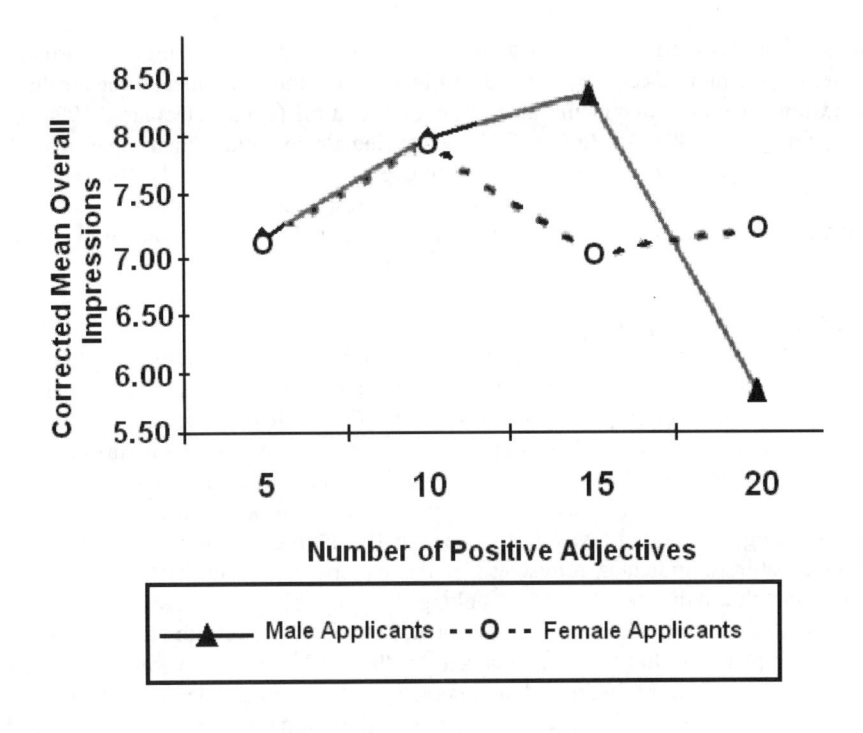

Figure 3.7 Motivational gravity and gender of candidate

Source: Smith & Carr (2003)

6.6. Critical appraisal

A weakness in Smith and Carr's (2002) study of gender and achievement is that we do not know whether the influence being exerted in Figures 3.3–3.4 and Figure 3.7 is (a) Push Down or (b) Pull Down or (c) a combination of both. In the study scenarios themselves, we neglected to overtly steer our would-be panelists into a specific role, either as future supervisors (Push Down) or as future co-worker peers/subordinates to the job candidate who was being selected (Pull Down). That particular theoretical oversight is addressed, however, in a recent and ongoing series of studies on gender and achievement (e.g., The Afro-centric Alliance, 2003). These newer studies have focused in turn on performance appraisal and management, and to that extent internal selection, i.e., placement.

6.7. Performance management

In our principal theoretical statement of motivational gravity (Carr & MacLachlan, 1997), it was proposed that women high in n Ach may experience at least two major types of gravitational climate. In climate "1", a high female achiever experiences support from other women (Push Up), alongside implicit prejudice and discrimination from predominantly male supervisors and managers (Push Down).

Supporting this prediction, for instance, is research evidence that high performance by females is more likely (than the same high performance by males) to be attributed to external factors beyond the achievers' own control (e.g., Ashkanasy, 1994; see also, Trudgett, 2000). In climate "2" however, female coworkers themselves may not always be highly supportive of female achievers (e.g., Power, 1994). In Smith and Carr (2002, Figure 3.7) for instance, many of the respondents providing the data were female; and, in Figure 3.7, the interaction remains statistically significant even after correcting, statistically, for gender of the respondent.

6.8. Gender gaps in gravity

As part of their research exploring gendered aspects of motivational gravity, the Afro-centric Alliance has given achievement scenarios to a sample of workers from Ghana and future managers in Tanzania (The Afro-centric Alliance, 2003). This Alliance has deliberately refrained from testing for cross-cultural "differences." Instead, they preferred to look for any recurring patterns of *similarity* across the two very diverse contexts, in which the samples happened to be located. One rationale for choosing this strategy was that independently finding a common pattern, across diverse settings, indicates robustness in the pattern itself (Strohschneider, 1999). However, the Alliance was also looking for possible differences between the perceptual outlooks, on female achievement, between male and female respondents in the samples. In that sense, and stirred by the kind of pattern witnessed through Figure 3.7, they were interested in interactions between gender of achiever and gender of perceiver, and especially in perceptions, amongst *male* versus *female* respondents, about how *female* achievers are likely to be rewarded.

The data from these studies highlighted a number of significant gaps. In the Ghanaian sample for instance, the male participants predicted an all-negative, Push Down–Pull Down environment for an all-female scenario (female achiever, female bosses and peers), but an all-positive, Push Up–Pull Up force field when the central character in Figure 3.1 was female but the rest (bosses and co-worker peers) were all male. The *female* participants in the Ghanaian sample however took a different view. In *their* view, male co-workers would exert not Push *Up* but Pull *Down*. Nonetheless, like their male counterparts, the female respondents from Ghana also predicted that an all-female work group would exert both Pull Down and Push Down. In Tanzania, the same pattern, of "– –" for a female work group but "+ –" (Pull Up–Pull Down) for a female achiever in an otherwise all-male group, was also predicted by the respondents who were male. The female participants in the Tanzanian sample predicted a "+ +" climate in an all-female work group, versus Push Down—Pull Down from males towards a female achiever, but unfortunately the female sample in Tanzania was also too small and inexperienced to infer any firm trend.

Despite this limitation, and overall, the available evidence is consistent with a pattern in both locations. In predicting male reactions to *n* Ach in females, male predictions were comparatively self-serving, on at least two counts. Firstly, the males participating in our studies predicted more support for female achievers, from workplace males, than the females did. Secondly, the male participants in our studies also predicted more support for female achievers from workplace males than they predicted would be forthcoming from workplace females. Overall therefore, the male participants may have been viewing female achievement through lenses that are somewhat rose-tinted.

Plotting the coordinates of motivational gravity in a descriptive grid is one thing, but deciphering what those coordinates mean to people, at work, is another. Perceived Push Down from female leaders, for instance, may simply reflect the fact that female leaders "lean" more heavily on their female subordinates, in order to inure them to the barriers of male prejudice that they are likely to face in the future. In the Alliance's (2003) study, we examined the respondents' reasons for predicting that males, especially supervisors, would show positive gravity (encouragement) toward female achievers. Salient among their reasons was what A. Eagly has termed "women are wonderful" (1999). According to Eagly, such "warm and fuzzy" sentiments often mask an implicit assumption, that women are not cut out for the "masculine" role of becoming senior managers (for a complementary analysis invoking perceived fit with occupational cultures, Hill & Augoustinos, 1997). Thus, *quant*ifying gravitational fields using the MG grid is only ever a first step toward more fully *qual*ifying them, with crucially significant forms of meaning.

Regarding women as "wonderful" and so not well suited to the rigors of "leadership," is a group bias. Biases like this, though, are not restricted to relations between groups. An individual's performance, too, can become a subject of gravity. In one study, for instance, a negative correlation was found between individuals' psychometric test entry scores (to Defence Forces) and later performance appraisal scores (Bau & Dyck, 2002). A possible interpretation of this negative correlation is that the psychometric tests themselves, or the criteria used to attempt to validate them, are faulty. An alternative interpretation, more "gravitational" in ethos, focuses instead on the performance appraisal process. Through this more glocal lens, the candidates who showed signs of being high in n Ach at entry, through their test scores, later experienced a Push Down from supervisors (in this case, superior officers) who may have been made to feel insecure by their upwardly mobile new recruits. Thus, motivational gravity dips can happen in the vertical as well as horizontal (Push Up-Pull Down) plane of the grid.

6.9. The perspective of achiever

The research described above, by being focused primarily on the behavior of supervisor and peer, reminds us by omission that an individual achiever's own perspective, too, is a key element in the grid (Figure 3.1). In the literature on gender and achievement, for instance, levels of achievement motivation itself have been linked to overcoming sensitivity to rejection, and being low on *need for affiliation* (or n Aff) (Kaur & Ward, 1992). Such needs signal the possibility of differential thresholds, in this case not toward achievements in others (Bau & Dyck, above), but instead to *gravity from* them.

Those thresholds for reacting to motivational gravity have been explored in a range of empirical studies.

6.10. Fear of success

One possible reaction to gravity is fear. Fear of Pull Down, for instance, has been reported in a variety of settings, both social (e.g., Wikan, 1989) and, more latterly, organizational (e.g., Duffy, Ganster & Pagon, 2002). Fears such as these can influence organizational and vocational behavior in surprising ways. With regard to promotions, for instance, "Royal Swedish Envy" (fear of being envied) may actually make promotions themselves less desirable (Schneider, 1991). This kind of tension, i.e., the anticipation of serious "problems" from others in the workplace, on being publicly rewarded at work, can even tip the balance toward refusing a promotion in the first place (Bowa & MacLachlan, 1994). That is to say, people are actually declining promotion for fear of the consequences (McLoughlin & Carr, 1994). Thus, in cases where personal success is publicly recognized, apprehension about being a target of "threatening upward comparison" increases levels of work-related stress (Exline & Lobel, 1999).

6.11. Gravity and mental health

In a powerful illustration of the potential consequences of this kind of strain, admissions to a major psychiatric facility (in Malaŵi, East Africa), and their guardians, were asked to attribute the primary source of their admission to hospital (MacLachlan, Nyirenda & Nyando, 1995). Content analysis of those attributions revealed that a predominant theme was perceived group reactions, both jealousy and envy – Push Down and Pull Down respectively – to personal successes and achievements. As MacLachlan et al. report, many of these successes and achievements were made at work, in the context of individualistic personal achievement. Research of this kind complements the growing body of evidence that bullying at work has negative consequences for the wellbeing of its victims (e.g., Vartia, 2001). However, the research is also a poignant reminder that work-related stress, like "personal" achievement, is an inherently social and interactive phenomenon (Invernizzi, 2001). That inherent dynamism can be brought to life by theorizing about how the characters in a grid will interact with each other in developmental time – through a systems-based approach.

7. Systems Approach

In grid terms, we can envisage the development of a climate in which the players as an ensemble progressively position themselves into a Pull Down–Push Down glocality. That glocality begins with a globality – the introduction, by management, of a heavily competitive work ethos, to an otherwise cohesive work group. Before long, as in the Buick Bar & Grill case (Chapter 1, this volume), a minority of individuals within the group is singled out for rewards and promotions. Now, the less "successful" individuals – who constitute the majority – feel slightly envious. At the same time, the successful individuals, as the minority faction, feel slightly jealous about their position of privilege. According to systems theory, those two positions will, now, begin to interact with each other.

7.1. A systems dynamic

From Figure 3.8, the *"Unsuccessful"* 'failures' actually began with an *Expectation* that they might succeed (McLoughlin & Carr, 1994). When this expectation was not met, creating a sense of failure among the majority, that majority felt let down. There was a sense of *Broken Promise* (Chapter 5, this volume). The disappointed majority then reacted to this perceived breach of promise with some equity-restorative *Pull Down,* for example backbiting or gossip (*Envy*). If and when the *"Successful"* individual, or group, got to hear about this, or sensed it, they started to perceive a little *Threatening upward comparison.* This in turn created a climate and *Sense of insecuritystrain.* That downturn then prompted a little *Push Down* behavior, designed (whether consciously or not) to help protect their position of relative privilege *(Jealousy)*. That localized Push Down, however, then fuelled another round of *Pull Down*, again on the part of the relatively deprived *("Unsuccessful")* individual or group; which reinforced the sense of job insecurity on the part of the *"Successful";* and so the cycles continue. If left unmanaged, a twin cycle such as this one will escalate until it reaches a point of no return – and the kinds of breakdown, turnover and possibly even violence, which that watershed can bring.

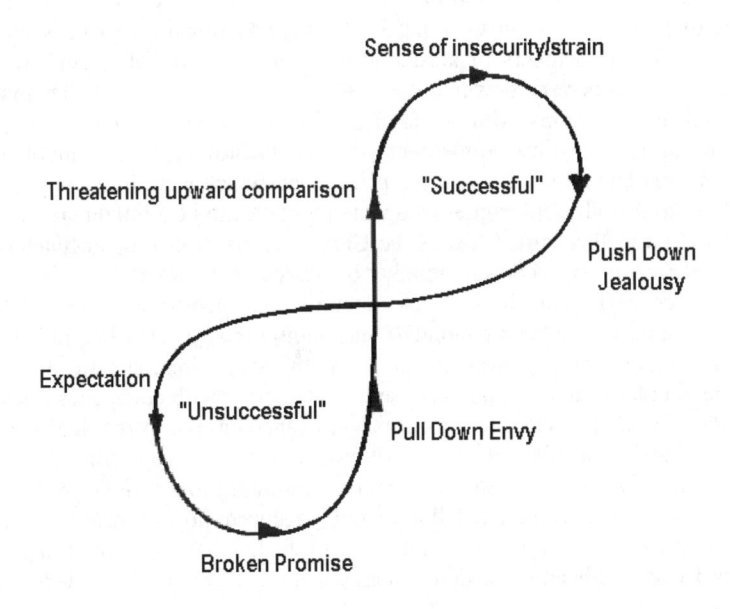

Figure 3.8 A cycle of envy and jealousy

7.2. An example of escalating self-destruction

The example of motivational gravity climate given below is unashamedly subjective in its focus. This overt subjectivity is entirely appropriate however, insofar as motivational gravity is by definition a subjective phenomenon (above). When, for example, does strong leadership become perceived bullying? The case itself also lacks an overall "measure" of the extent to which its perceptions existed at an organizational level. This might in principle have been furnished using a survey instrument like the Motivational Gravity Scenario Scale (Carr et al., 1996). But, perceived practical and political barriers in this particular case study aside, it is precisely the emotional ethos of subjectivity that arguably offers us the most dynamic and realistic glimpse of the dynamics of motivational gravity "force fields." In the flesh after all, these are played out between perspectives and positions that are fundamentally *contested*.

7.3. A dysfunctional workplace

The sociology lecturer had joined her new department after having been led to believe, during an upbeat recruitment and selection process, that the University and the Department were in expansion mode. All that was now required, they told her, was a "quiet achiever" who would work collegially with colleagues to expand and develop the offerings to more and more students. But from the moment of arriving in this new job, she had been dismayed to discover that the culture of the workplace was completely opposite to each and every initial expectation.

In this department, school, and even across much of the faculty as a whole, academic staff often "survived" in their job by forming factional allegiances with other co-workers, senior members of academic and administrative staff, and even students. The culture was very power distant, and the only way "up" rather than "out" was to find senior patrons, who would crush their acolyte subordinate's rivals in exchange for upward loyalty. Sometimes, this downward protection involved taking a favored complainant's side in formal grievances, which were frequently laid as tactical devices to dislodge colleagues who were perceived to be a job threat. This insecurity was not altogether unrealistic, as the University claimed to be in financial jeopardy, and had recently stood down a number of academic employees.

In the three years that this sociology lecturer managed to stay in her job, there was never a time without some cloud of suspicion, through formal complaints of one kind or another, hanging over her head. At the same time, she steadfastly refused to descend to keeping notes on every social interaction with colleagues (these notes were widely used as "evidence" in formal grievance cases), in the vain hope that the initial promises of a collegial work environment might one day "come good." But instead, her moral stand only seemed to incite and incur more trouble from the system, and eventually the lecturer left this incredible imbroglio of corruption and nepotism for a much safer work environment. In fact, of the seven academic members of staff who had been in the department when this lecturer first arrived, she was, after just three years, *the only one left*.

Source: Extracted from Bolitho & Carr (2003).

7.4. Case synthesis

Events and their interactions in the above workplace can be synthesized with the aid of Figure 3.8. During the recruitment phase to this organization, new employees were sometimes oversold about the extent to which achievement motivation would actually be regarded, interpreted and treated, from junior to senior colleagues alike, as being pro-social. This "oversell" created unrealistic job *expectation*. Once the new recruits realized that perceived upward mobility threatened, unsettled and provoked others, they experienced a sense of *broken promise*. Disappointments like this can fuel *Pull Down* among the disappointed (*envy*), or, alternatively, when seen from the perspective of the existing "elite," can create the perception that Pull Down is being exerted by the new staff member. Such perceptions could create, or indeed stem from, feelings of *"threatening upward comparisons."* This in turn creates a sense of *job insecurity/strain*, which then prompts *Push Down*, i.e., *Jealousy*. Such jealousy then reinforces any existing sense of broken promise among the majority, thus prompting another round of perceived

Pull Down; and so on. Thus, we arrive at an escalating and essentially vicious cycle of envy and jealousy.

8. Managing Motivational Gravity

8.1. Personal solutions

The kind of climate depicted above has been envisaged in Bedeian (1995), where he also suggests a number of potential remedies. These include, for instance, not boasting; being humble; keeping one's salary a secret; and being secretive generally. Such recommendations are focused on individual impression management. When this fails, as they are likely to do in the case above, Bedeian recommends leaving the organization voluntarily and permanently. A corollary to this advice, introduced in the opening chapter of this book, would be to select one's employer more carefully at the outset. In either case however, such recommendations for managing negative gravity remain relatively individualized and, to that extent, more individualistic and reactive, instead of collectivist and preventative.

8.2. Group solutions

Alternative ways of managing the kinds of escalation depicted in our case study would focus on organizational intervention, rather than simply personal and essentially palliative 'damage control.' These alternative measures by definition would be partly structural and systemic, and to that extent, group-based rather than individualistic. In addition, and consistent with the ethos of "groups," the measures could focus on recognizing both *n* Ach *and s* Ach. Thus, the suggestions we are about to consider each attempt to manage *n* Ach and s Ach by joining individual with group goals, in a socially appropriate way (Bedeian, 1995).

8.2.1 Better metaphors.

A first possible tactic for preventing negative gravity is to give greater respect to traditional mental models for working. These can be captured, for example, through traditional local metaphors (Chapter 1, this volume). In a preliminary study of such metaphors, middle managers in Japan were surveyed, using scenario scaling, about their experienced perceptions of motivational gravity at their workplace (Carr, 1994). In terms of Figure 3.1, the climates sampled emerged to be clearly, on average, inside the "+ +" quadrant of the grid. The predicted *s* Ach climate for *n* Ach was Pull Up–Push Up. Interestingly, popular Japanese adages, such as "the nail that sticks out gets pounded down" (Feather, 1994), suggest that motivational gravity was not unknown in the wider context in which these managers worked. Compared to *out*side of work, that is, Japanese work groups may have been doing something to manage gravity *in*side of it.

That possibility was explored by listening to managers' explanations for their predictions.

8.2.2. Traditional metaphors.

When asked to explain the *reasons* for their predictions about a "+ +" climate at work, the Japanese managers in Carr (1994) reported, often, that their work group felt and functioned like an extended family. The traditional family metaphor, which includes cooperative family relations, had been successfully adopted in their organization (see also, Kashima & Callan, 1994). As Kashima and Callan point out, metaphors like this are locally, not just globally, constituted. They are glocalities. In Japan, they were a form of social capital directly relevant to engaging – post-World War II – with a new, more globally integrated economy. Contextual ideas like this imply that mental models for working will vary with the local context. In Australia for example, a metaphor of sport, rather than an extended family, might be a more appropriate glocal metaphor to help manage negative gravity (Chidgey, 1995): Individual achievement in sport is well tolerated, and even supported, provided it is perceived to be well earned (Grove & Paccagnella, 1995). In other settings, the appropriate metaphors might be military, or communal, or any combination of these with family, or sporting life (Gibson & Zellmer-Bruhn, 2001). The more general point however, is that traditional metaphors that emphasize cooperation or admiration for a tall poppy may help "constrain" negative motivational gravity, whilst at the same time enabling individual achievement to happen. Thus, for any given glocality, it is possible that traditional metaphors are able to facilitate a "sublimation" of *n* Ach into socially acceptable forms.

8.3. Workplace socialization and training

Even with a relatively encouraging climate for achievement at work, new recruits to a work group may still need to be socialized into that climate, if the nurturance of achievement is to be sustained. A promising vehicle for socializing new recruits, into a positive gravitational climate, is to overtly encourage "achievement" to be a topic for discussion and discourse, during induction and socialization. Discussion like this has been shown, for multiple reasons, to be an effective vehicle for nurturing group leanings (Carr, 2003b). In one research study, for example, discussing the issue of personal achievement, in work-related situations, enhanced groups' pre-existing tendencies, from favoring only *slightly* the reward of tall poppies to favoring it *more* (Carr, Purcell, Bolitho, Moss & Brew, 1999). This augmentation, of initially only mildly positive gravity, was maintained even after the discussion was over. Post-discussion, on measures of private opinion, clearly positive attitudes, toward tall poppies, were partially sustained.

Based on these changes, Carr et al. (1999) argued that group discussion might be an effective way for work groups to (a) engage new recruits into work climates and cultures where the pre-existing ethos already partly encourages *n* Ach; and, in addition, to (b) nurture that ethos itself socially. Through the group empowering its members to socialize and ease *themselves* into tolerably individual achievement, *n* and *s* Ach are encouraged at the same time *(*see also, Sokolova & Akkuratov, 1995). Group polarization is therefore an inherently glocal way of managing motivational gravity.

9. Conclusion

This has been a very brief foray into the glocality of achievement, and how to negotiate that glocality more intelligently and sensitively than many of us do at present. The cursory nature of our foray is not an issue for concern at this stage. The main point of the chapter is simply to provide a conceptual platform, and vista, for the remainder of the book. In the chapters about to follow, and through the lens of glocality, we will be looking more closely at motivational gravity, and how to manage it, across a range of settings and contexts. That discussion begins with the context of "pay diversity," and how this particular bastion of globalization sometimes leads to envy and jealousy, between both individuals and groups.

Chapter 4

Pay

> The motive was a pretty familiar one – money. You know, there's nothing much worse in life than people doing the same job and getting paid at different rates. It happens in every office, in every profession in the land. Anger ... jealousy ... bitterness ... usually controllable but potentially dynamite.
>
> *Source*: C. Dexter, 1999, p. 274.

In the previous chapter, we examined the social costs, at work, of individual achievement. One of the major ways in which work achievement is recognized is through enhanced pay relative to others, i.e., through pay diversity. This diversity is sponsored by globalization in a number of ways. Key drivers of pay diversity include the individualization of work discussed in Chapter 1 (this volume); the culture of individuality and individualism that accompanies this change (Chapter 2, this volume); and a "performance" management, of "achievement," that the latter has spawned (Chapter 3, this volume). It should also be noted that pay diversity is not just found between individuals, it is also found between groups. Examples of this inter-group diversity in pay include enterprise bargains; and international assignments, where the assignees are paid from a different economy than their hosts. Whether pay diversity is inter-individual or inter-group however, the dominant discourses about pay diversity implicitly endorse the idea that variety in pay is good. This chapter adopts a different position. From a behavioral perspective, pay diversity implies pay discrepancy. Furthermore, this discrepancy takes place in a glocality. In that glocality, pay diversity promotes gravity and endangers health. A primary conduit through which these possibilities are fostered – as Dexter observes above – is through perceived pay injustice.

1. A Theoretical Foundation

For employers and employees alike, compensation systems are among the most salient features of work life. Although these systems are multi-modal, including, for example benefits and other forms of reward such as travel and promotions, the primary form of reward at work is still money, i.e., pay. This pay itself, however, takes increasingly diverse forms. Over and above base pay, for example, work performance can be rewarded by pay-for-performance (e.g., piecework); by merit pay (based on performance appraisals); by profit sharing (percentages of the profit margin); and by gain sharing (bonuses for enhanced profit). Not surprisingly perhaps, the study of pay diversity owes a strong debt to disciplines like Labor Economics (Heneman, Fay & Wang, 2001). Yet disproportionately less room has been accorded to the ways that pay systems are perceived at ground level, in the kind of microclimate observed by Dexter's Inspector Morse.

2. Behavioral Theories of Work Motivation

Comparatively localized perspectives like those above can be fleshed out with the aid of motivation theory – which, fortunately, we have in abundance. Roughly speaking, theories of motivation at work can be split into two primary categories. One category is more closely aligned with the global view of pay diversity. It focuses on the performance of task. Its supporting theories include, for example Scientific Management (Taylor, 1912), Expectancy Theory (Vroom, 1964), and Goal Setting Theory (Locke, 1991). A second major category of theories on work motivation stress more the human-relations side of pay diversity. They examine, for example, the social consequences of differences in pay, for individuals and groups who perceive no fundamental differences in the jobs they perform. These theories include the Meaning of Work (Morse & Weiss, 1955), Cognitive Evaluation Theory (Deci & Ryan, 1990), and Work Justice Theory (e.g., Adams, 1965). The latter theory in particular is actually concerned with perceptions of *in*justice in the workplace. Strictly speaking therefore, Work Justice Theory examines how perceived justice in pay is a necessary condition for maintaining motivation at work, i.e., how perceived *in*justices create work *de*-motivation.

3. Task-focused Theories of Motivation
3.1. Scientific Management

Despite today's rhetoric of "empowerment at work", Taylor's philosophy is still very much with us. From a motivational point of view, the essence of Scientific Management, as regards work motivation, is that work behavior is shaped by its consequences. Also known as Stimulus–Response Theory, and Reinforcement Theory, Scientific Management Theory holds that when good work performance is perceptibly followed by a reward in the form of pay, then the same behavior *(response)* is more likely to occur *(reinforcement)* the next time a similar situation *(stimulus)* arises. The basic process enabling work behavior to be motivated in this way is *association*. Hard or good work becomes "associated" with job stimuli via the repeated co-occurrence of stimuli, response, and reward. For this linkage to be established, there must be sufficient temporal proximity, or contiguity, between the events for the link to be noticed. In organizational terms, this contiguity is appropriately termed *line of sight* (Heneman, Ledford & Gresham, 2000).

There is no doubt that conditioning by pay, and payment, does actually motivate work behavior in certain conditions. In one study, for example, set against a control of base pay rates only, the introduction of daily (i.e., contiguous) feedback about work performance, coupled with weekly monetary reinforcers (and time off) were linked to labor cost savings (and work safety behavior too) (Austin, Kessler, Riccobono & Bailey, 1996). Other studies however, have outlined limiting conditions for Scientific Management systems. For example, these systems are more likely to work, in the longer term, if there is a safety net, or base pay, below which pay cannot dip, no matter how "poor" a performance becomes in any given period (Brown & Huber, 1992). In another study, once the workers themselves actually participated in the pay policy's development, an apparent "ceiling" for satisfaction, with merit pay, was raised (Gilchrist & White, 1991). As an ensemble, studies like these begin to suggest that, whilst pay-for-performance sometimes works, reinforcement technologies per se are not always the most sustainable way of motivating work behavior (Capelli & Chauvin, 1982). Social concerns, it seems, matter too.

3.2. Expectancy Theory

Appropriately enough, given our brief critique of Scientific Management, Expectancy Theory extends Taylor's model by incorporating the way that individuals perceive the groups in which they work. Key social elements in this social perceptual field, according to Vroom, are effort expectancy ("*Can* I improve my performance?"); Instrumentality ("Will the group actually *notice*?"); and valence ("Will the reward that I get *matter* to me?"). The more a system allows its employees to answer "Yes" to each of these questions, the higher – in theory – their work motivation becomes. Clearly therefore, the central tenets of Expectancy Theory are not only aligned with Taylorism. They are also aligned with today's globalizing ethos to make pay contingent on performance.

Meta-reviews of Expectancy Theory have been moderately favorable (e.g., Donovan, 2001). In one study, for example, Expectancy Theory was as good as Cognitive Evaluation Theory (below) in predicting long-term attitudes toward voluntary work (Singer & Coffin, 1996). In addition, however, there are wide individual differences in how *well* the theory predicts work motivation (Muchinsky, 2002). According to Muchinsky, Expectancy Theory is better at predicting work behavior amongst individuals who are high on "internal locus of control," because these individuals more spontaneously stress expectancy and instrumentality in their schemata for "work." Other individuals, however, are more responsive to social expectation, social norms, and, in general, those forms of reward that are non-material. Thus, a key weakness in Expectancy Theory, like its Scientific Management predecessor, is a relative lack of attention to social values.

3.3. Goal Setting Theory

Although goal setting itself is not restricted to the workplace, much of the research on Goal Setting Theory – since its beginnings – has been anchored there (Latham & Blades, 1975). Goal setting, for instance, resembles Management By Objectives (or MbO), which was originally proposed explicitly for workplaces by P. Drucker (1954; 1988). The essence of both models is that work performance will improve if it is guided by concrete and attainable goals. According to Locke (1991), when such goals are consciously formulated and articulated, they help to energize behavior more effectively than implicit and more vague goals, e.g., effusively vowing to "work harder." As the energizing process initiated by more specific goals continues, workers are kept on course by concrete and rewarding feedback, e.g., from their workplace supervisor or mentor. In this way, the "line of sight" from Scientific Management, and the key principles of Expectancy Theory, are each incorporated into goal-setting processes.

At the same time, Goal Setting Theory differentiates itself from these two predecessors. Theoretically, more control is ceded to worker participation (Locke & Latham, 2002). As such, the theory begins to resonate not only with performance management, but also with the more relationship-oriented zeitgeist of "empowerment" (Chapter 5, this volume). Concepts such as "empowerment," "supervision," and "mentoring," each presuppose a human relationship, and to that extent Goal Setting Theory is more attentive to social factors than either of its two predecessors.

Goal-setting techniques have performed well at predicting increases in work-related performance (Locke & Latham, 2002). Certainly, the theory has been criticized for focusing too much on short-term improvements in behavior, and on single concrete goals (Donovan, 2001). Yet this criticism seems a little unfair, since goal setting applies well to the longer term career planning that lies at the heart of Becker's (1975) Human Capital Theory (Mento, Locke & Klein, 1992). In addition, Goal Setting Theory has been applied to groups as well as individuals, suggesting that it comes closer to incorporating social factors than either Scientific Management or Expectancy Theory (Larson & Schaumann, 1993; see also, Punnett, 1986). Nonetheless, MbO, and by implication goal setting generally, has been criticized for being too "global" in its outlook (Hofstede, 1997). Several aspects of the process, for instance, ignore the possibility that belief in hierarchy, and power distance, is a salient, local norm. Thus, even this relatively relationship-conscious theory still seems to be insufficiently attuned to local social matrix.

3.4. Brief summary of task-focused theories of motivation

Undoubtedly, there is much in the task-focused theories we have just reviewed to support current, and already globalized pay-performance reforms. Our critique of those theories suggests however that social factors matter too. Insofar as these "human relationship" factors are salient in pay reforms, and still their influence is not directly addressed in the task-focused theories of work motivation, there remains a potential for group and individual backlash. As Morse suggests, pay awards may foster ambivalence, not only toward the reforms themselves, but also toward the actors who are distributing and receiving the rewards under the new system.

4. Relationship-focused Theories of Motivation
4.1. Meaning of Work Theory

The essence of this theory is that work behavior needs to be meaningful in order to be motivational. Whilst pay is *a* motivator of work behavior, it is not the *only* motivator. For work performance to reach its natural peak, various non-financial motivators should be considered and managed by work groups, too. A primary way in which this non-financial motivation has been articulated in the research literature is through people's answers to the "lottery question" (Morse & Weiss, 1955). The lottery question asks employees whether they would still continue to work even if the financial necessity to do so was removed – specifically, if they had just won a very large sum of money in a major lottery. Such questions approach the non-financial aspects of work motivation indirectly (Carr, 2003b). To that extent, Carr argues, they are less prone to unwanted social desirability effects than their more directly worded counterparts ("Why do you work?"). These unwanted social desirability effects include, for instance, giving incomplete, stereotypical answers, and using "discounting heuristics," that seize on the most obvious (and mentally available) answer (e.g., "money!"), but disregard the rest.

In the original lottery question study, Morse and Weiss found that 80 percent of their sample estimated that they would continue to work, even in the absence of financial necessity. Since this original Meaning of Work study, the finding that a majority of workers would continue to work has proved remarkably robust, emerging across a range of "developed" and "developing" economies (e.g., Adigun, 1997; Harpaz, 1989; Meaning of Work, 1987). Figures like 80 percent do not mean that eight out of 10 workers would literally continue to work even if they did not need to financially. Rather, they indicate that the salient features of work, for most people, are both extrinsic (e.g., pay) and intrinsic (e.g., preserving dignity). For instance, "Yes" answers to the lottery question have been linked, following redundancy, to elevated job-hunting behavior, and to lowered mental health (Warr, 1982). Outcomes like these indicate that work is very often just as much about social dignity as it is about pay, and that making pay fully functional is about – somehow – balancing the two.

Potentially key ingredients for striking versus losing the balance between task and relationships have been explored in the literature. In Morse and Weiss's original study for example, the participants were asked to indicate why they would continue to work. Among the reasons that people gave for wanting to continue to work was a range of non-financial factors, from "keeping occupied" to "warding off the dangers of loneliness and isolation" (1955, p. 44). In our own research conducted in Africa, we have found that a majority of workers wanted to continue to work – not just because of perpetual financial turbulence, but also to help preserve a sense of dignity, or "face," in their own wider community (Carr & MacLachlan, 1999). In a further study, participants from Australasia and Southeast Asia estimated the meaning that work had for *others*, both inside and outside their own cultural groups (Carr & Jones, 2002). Despite rating themselves as motivated by a balance of pay and relationship factors, each of these groups also by comparison discounted the non-financial side of work in *others*. To that extent therefore, and in common perhaps with those who champion pay for "performance," they got the balance wrong.

4.2. Cognitive Evaluation Theory

The core point made by Meaning of Work Theory is that there is far more to work than pay alone. Dignity matters too. Cognitive Evaluation Theory explores how this dignity can be eroded by pay. Specifically, Cognitive Evaluation Theory argues that an over-reliance on money undermines intrinsic motivation; that it transforms organizational citizenship into behavior that is more "transactional," and "calculative." As a result, work quality often suffers. The "cognitive evaluation" component in Cognitive Evaluation processes centers on self-perception and re-appraisal. Too much commodification of work, through overemphasizing pay, primes employees to rethink and re-evaluate their role. In this insidious process, "I work for the fun of it," unintentionally becomes instead, "I work for the money" (Deci & Ryan, 1990).

The most detailed, and best account of how this process works is still to be found in the early experimental work conducted by E. L. Deci (1975). In Deci's experimental paradigm, participants were paid to work on interesting and engaging work tasks, on which they would normally have worked for free. After introducing payment, it was possible to check how long people worked on the task during a free choice period, compared to no payment controls. The more they stayed behind and worked for free, the greater their intrinsic motivation. By the same token, the less they stayed behind, the more *de*-motivated they had become. Counter-intuitively perhaps, the core finding was that people stayed *less* once pay was introduced. Pay, therefore, did more harm than good.

Findings like those derived from Deci's paradigm have been criticized for a lack of external validity beyond the laboratory (Donovan, 2001). Yet field studies have replicated the de-motivation effects (Jordan, 1986). In settings as demanding and intense as international aid projects for instance, it has been shown that payment for intrinsically valuable work actually undermines community motivation for a project in the mid- to longer term (see, for example, Carr, MacLachlan, Zimba & Bowa, 1995b). In business settings, a sympathetic advocate for Cognitive Evaluation Theory has been A. Kohn. Kohn argues against pay for performance, stating that, "no controlled scientific study has ever found a long-term enhancement of the quality of work as a result of any reward system" (1998, p. 3 of 7). Kohn's arguments, though, have been criticized for being a little "all-or-none" (e.g., O'Neill, 1995). As O'Neill points out, pay *can* be motivation-enhancing, and even intrinsically rewarding, provided a sub-text is still conveyed to the employee that they themselves are inherently valued as a person. In Deci's language, both feedback and rewards can be either "controlling" (constraining, de-motivating) or "informational," and to that extent potentially motivating (Deci, Koestner & Ryan, 1999). Overall therefore, a key to understanding pay diversity is to study how pay can transit from one form of meaning to the next, i.e., from "empowering" to "controlling," and vice-versa.

4.3. Work Justice Theory

According to this theory, a key way in which pay diversity may degenerate from being empowering to being controlling is through perceived injustice. Theorizing about injustice at work has taken major strides in recent years (Gilliland & Chan, 2001). Today, the issue is becoming the focus of more and more interest from organizational studies generally (Ambrose, Seabright & Schminke, 2002). A prime example of this interest centers on the construct of a "psychological contract," i.e., the implicit set of understandings for work relations (Schalk & Rousseau, 2001). Of particular interest are perceived breaches of the contract, and any sense of injustice these perceived breaches promote. Such breaches, it is increasingly recognized, happen through three basic pathways: (1) via the way people are treated; (2) through the way procedures are implemented; and (3) because of the way resources are distributed. These domains of workplace injustice are termed, respectively, (1) *interactional justice,* (2) *procedural justice,* and (3) *distributive justice.* According to the literature, perceived breaches of justice, in each of (1)–(3), lead to "counter-productive behaviors" at work, and thence to the undermining of pay diversity at work (Sackett & DeVore, 2001).

4.3.1. Interactional injustice.

Of the three key forms of work injustice, interactional breaches are perhaps the least directly relevant to pay-performance systems. Breaches of interactional justice occur primarily on an interpersonal plane, for example in cases of workplace bullying and the Push Down (Chapter 3, this volume). Of course, pay diversity is partly an interpersonal issue. Performance appraisals (a basis for merit pay) are all too easily made in a relatively brusque and disrespectful way, or in a manner that signals that the feedback is not informational but controlling. In cases like this, however, the problem is not so much with pay diversity itself – it rests more with managing workplace bullying (Chapter 3, this volume).

4.3.2. Procedural injustice.

Interactional injustices are a special example of a wider class of injustices related to organizational procedures and their implementation. Procedural justice is the perception that the procedure through which a pay decision is reached is itself fair; and that standardized procedures in themselves have been followed in a fair manner (Brockner, Mannix, Leung & Skarlicki, 2000). When egalitarian values are salient, for instance, procedural justice is linked to having a "voice" in how pay systems are designed and implemented – a "fair process effect" (Van den Bos & Spruijt, 2002). As this concept of a "fair process" implies, procedural fairness is contingent, also, on a degree of trust existing between employees and employers, for instance with respect to merit pay (Printz & Waldman, 1985). Again however, building trust is not an issue directly related to pay diversity itself (see instead, Chapter 5, this volume).

4.3.3. Distributive injustice.

The question of distribution is clearly central to pay and pay diversity. Issues of distributive justice are not primarily about how resources are distributed in a procedural, administrative sense. Instead, questions of distributive justice are focused more directly on pay diversity itself. They concentrate, specifically, on what rewards should be distributed, and to whom, as a proportion of the overall pool of resources available to the group(s). Pay-diversity systems can be undermined by the perception that resources have not been "distributed" justly. Especially relevant in these regards are the guiding moral principles adhered to in distributing the resources. Those principles are primarily three in number: belief in need; belief in equality, (or egality); and belief in equity (after, Deutsch, 1975).

Belief in need. Examples of believing in need, when distributing pay, include: positive discrimination; the creation of family-friendly policies; and supporting a salary rise for an employee partly on the basis that his or her family needs are larger than others'. It should be noted, however, that much of the literature on belief in need is found in the research on cross-cultural management. In that research, belief in need has often been attributed to "collectivistic" cultures, in countries that are "developing" (e.g., Marin, 1985; to Giacobbe-Miller, Miller & Victorov, 1998). To the extent that cultural norms are a response to economic necessity, such findings do make some sense (Carr, 2003b). Yet it follows from the same findings, also, that pay policies based less on need, and more on performance, will provoke backlashes *wherever* "need" is salient, i.e., more generally. The examples of belief in need given at the beginning of this paragraph are thereby poignant examples of how belief in need can undermine pay diversity systems anywhere, and at any time.

Belief in egality. Egality is all about not granting any 'special' privileges to any single individual within a group. Like belief in need, the credo of "egality for all" has been researched primarily in a cross-cultural sense. Beliefs in egality, for example, have been linked, in this literature, to cultural groups that are relatively low on power distance (Chapter 2, this volume). When group norms emphasize mateship for instance, as they do stereotypically in Australasia, workers may also endorse egality more often than their counterparts in, say, the USA (Mann, 1988; Shubik, 1986). That mateship extends to egality in pay (Headay, 1991), where it can encourage, under conditions of pay *in*egality, negative motivational gravity (Chapters 3 & 1, this volume). Furthermore, since belief in egality is not restricted to socio-cultural groups, we can logically expect backlashes against pay diversity too in, say, "organizational" and "occupational" cultures (Chapter 2, this volume). Essentially therefore, we can expect backlashes against pay diversity whenever the dominant sense of identity, at any one time, stresses belief in egality.

Belief in equity. Equity is a more particularistic concept than egality. A key facet of belief in equity is that diverse outcomes (e.g., in pay) should be proportional to particular inputs. This principle of proportionality has been formally stated in Equity Theory (Adams, 1965). According to Adams, people at work often think about injustice in ratio terms. These ratios are inherently social. Specifically, the ratio of self's outcomes (e.g., salary) to inputs (e.g., effort, or hard-earned qualifications) should equal the ratio of outcomes-to-inputs perceived for a salient comparison *other*. The relationship between perceived outcomes and perceived inputs, of both self and other, can be expressed algebraically, in the following equation:

$$O_a/I_a = O_b/I_b$$

In this equation, O_a and O_b are the outcomes obtained by person A and person B respectively; I_a and I_b are the inputs of person A and person B, respectively (Klein & Azzi, 2001). Putting these elements and the formula into real-life terms, it would be fair, for example, if a colleague at work (B) was receiving twice one's own pay, provided the colleague was also perceived to have invested twice as much effort, or input, into the job as self (A). Alternatively, and under the same maxim, it would be *un*fair for the co-worker (B) to receive any more pay than self (A), if it was perceived that A had worked equally hard as B. In practice at work, the formula above is more metaphorical than real. Adams' formula is only an approximation to mental function, not a literal algebraic one (Carr, 2003b). The crucial prediction that Equity Theory makes is that, once a pay inequity is detected with B, B's ratio will become salient to A, who is then motivated to restore a sense of balance between the two (approximate) ratios. In that sense, pay discrepancy is its own salience. Thus, whilst pay diversity does not *automatically* equate to pay discrepancy, it does mean that there is more chance of a discrepancy *with* pay diversity than there is without.

4.4. A key process

The above process of "equity restoration" can take different forms, depending on one of two elementary, complementary, and often by definition co-occurring events: (1) whether A's ratio is *lower* than B's ratio – in this event, A is said to feel "underpaid" compared to B; and (2) whether A's ratio is *higher* than B's ratio – in this event, person A is said to feel "overpaid." In event (1), for example, A may attempt to avoid the source of inequity altogether, or, since this is not always possible, to lower B's outcome to bring B's ratio into balance with A's (e.g., via motivational gravity). Most likely of all perhaps, A is likely to reduce her own inputs to reflect her already-lowered outcomes relative to B. In event (2) of overpayment, A's possible reactions include not only (again) avoiding B, but also increasing inputs to reflect enhanced outcomes (i.e., working harder to justify a higher pay). Over the course of time however, A may, too, progressively attribute her higher pay to a differential, between herself and B, in underlying ability.

4.5 An early study

In a classic research study stimulating development of the theory, student interviewees on placement work were either underpaid or overpaid compared to the norm, on a fixed or piecework basis (Adams & Rosenbaum, 1962). In the underpaid conditions, the interviewers (1) lifted their output when paid on a piecework basis and (2) reduced their own workload when paid at a fixed rate. In the overpaid condition, the interviewers (1) lowered their outputs when paid by the interview conducted and (2) raised their work output to reflect their reward outcomes when paid on a fixed rate. In each scenario therefore, and as predicted by Equity Theory, the participants in this study worked to restore pay equity, compared to others who were perceived as performing the same job.

4.6. Underpayment in focus

Much of the subsequent research on Equity Theory has focused on the effects of perceived underpayment. In one study, for example, the best predictor of satisfaction with pay was the extent to which workers felt underpaid relative to others (Berkowitz, Fraser, Treasure & Cochran, 1987). Results like this have prompted one observer to comment that, "satisfaction with wages is more dependent on *relative* than on absolute pay, on comparisons with *others*" (Argyle, 1989, p. 99, emphases added). Further studies have explored the possible consequences of underpayment. These include, for example, retaliatory behaviors such as organizational theft (Greenberg, 1993). Counterproductive behaviors like theft are consistent with Equity Theory, which predicts, from the formula above, that perceived underpayment can be compensated for by raising A's outcomes, specifically at the expense of salient and relevant others (here, B = "my employer"). Such behaviors are also - of course - consistent with the broader concept of (relatively localized) backlash.

4.7. Overpayment in focus

The research on overpayment has been more counter-intuitive. It reveals, for example, that the effects of overpayment are not always positive. After an initial burst of energy designed to compensate for the overpayment relative to others, work performance may, in time, start to slow (e.g., Lawler, Koplin & Young, 1968; to Vecchio, 1981). Such decrements are particularly likely when the pay rise has no clear foundation – when, ironically, it actually fosters a sense of relative deprivation, i.e., *under*payment (Greenberg & Ornstein 1983). One interpretation of these kinds of finding is that overpayment leads to a rationalization of injustice, in which higher pay fosters self-serving-ness (Harrod, 1980). By a "reverse process," or "backward inference," people who are paid more than others eventually work backwards from that observation, and any accompanying feelings about it, to infer that they more than deserve their superior pay (Stewart & Moore, 1992). In one study for instance, overpaid participants began to report that "their" job required "more" skills than the *same* job being performed by others who were paid more equitably for it (Stepina & Perrewe, 1987). Self-serving sentiments like these arguably reflect not only a backward-looking inference, but also a downward-looking sense of superiority (Leventhal & Michaels, 1969). As "superior" talent requires less effort than its more "ordinary" counterpart to reach the same goal, it follows therefore that overpayment will produce, in the mid- to longer-term, a work decrement, i.e., work de-motivation.

4.8. Equity Theory across groups

A potential criticism of Equity Theory is that it is inherently individualistic (Chapter 2, this volume). In his original formulation of the theory, for instance, Adams portrayed equity restoration, and the social comparison processes that mediate it, as essentially inter-individual in kind (1965). Recently, however, Equity Theory has been applied to relations between individuals and groups (Kalimo, Taris & Schaufeli, 2003; see also, Carrell & Dittrich, 1978). Equity Theory has also been increasingly applied to relations between *group* and group, for example through inter-group comparisons with pay groups outside of a working ingroup (e.g., Hegtvedt, 1989; to Roberts & Chonko, 1996). 'Expats,' for example, are often a psychological group by definition of their situation, e.g., being far from home, and/or through a subjectively shared sense of relative individualism (Jetten et al, 2002). So too of course are their hosts. According to Social Equity Theory (or SET), self-identifying work groups like these will compare their outcomes-for-inputs, relative to each other's *group* (Carr, 2003a).

Equity restoration may be more salient for groups than for individuals. A pithy example of how, as regards pay, is found in Leung and Bond (1984). Leung and Bond's study was conducted with relatively collectivistic participants in Hong Kong. To these participants, egality was a salient concern for distributing resources *within* a group. However, when resources were being distributed *between* groups, egality's place was taken by *equity* – or, more accurately, *social equity* (for a fuller review, Morris & Leung, 2000). Similarly, and as predicted by SIT (Chapter 1, this volume), when operators change from operating amongst themselves to dealing with engineers, or the salaries of their CEOs, equity may become salient too (Cowherd & Levine, 1992). Dynamics like these are further examples of cultural repositioning (Chapter 2, this volume). More to the point however, when employees compare their pay on an inter-group as distinct from inter-individual basis, belief in equity may gain in salience, and thus relevance.

4.9. Synthesis of motivation theories and pay

Research on the Meaning of Work suggests that the social aspect of pay diversity is important. Cognitive Evaluation processes illustrate this meaning, by suggesting that pay diversity "washes back" into self-perception. Principles of distributive justice fuel the emotions behind that process. In perception, pay diversity produces two fundamental types of injustice: (a) being paid less than comparison others; and (b) being paid more than the same comparison other. For each of (a) and (b), at least three principles of distributive justice are salient: (1) belief in need, (2) belief in egality, and (3) belief in equity. In event (a), whichever is salient between (1), (2), or (3), we can expect local (and perhaps gravitational) backlashes. Those who perceive themselves to be underpaid and relatively deprived (Kennedy, 1995) will strive to have their needs and beliefs recognized (Tajfel, 1978). In event (b), and again, whichever is salient from (1), (2), and (3), we can expect both individuals and groups to feel some guilt and awkwardness. To the extent that guilt is intrinsically aversive and unpleasant, it will motivate attempts to resolve the guilt. Self-inflation ("I deserve more pay"), for example, has been found across a wide variety of social, political, and organizational settings involving relative status (for a review, Carr, 2003b). Generality like this implies that "internalizing superiority" is a form of sense making that arises to a degree in response to all three forms of subjective over-reward, i.e., by perceived inequity, inegality, and need. In situations of inter-group comparison however, or if individualization is well established, the sharpest of these spurs to sense-making may be perceived inequity.

4.10. A glocal hypothesis

Summing up, the available theories of work motivation converge on a particular, and to that extent unavoidable, predicted pattern. As pay diversity globalizes it will also localize, fuelling widespread local backlash. Through these backlashes, each of which is essentially reactive and focused on resolving issues about social justice, pay diversity will de-motivate the underpaid, and the overpaid, alike. In short therefore, we can hypothesize that pay diversity will produce a double de-motivation (for the original statements of this hypothesis, Carr & MacLachlan, 1993/4; MacLachlan & Carr, 1993).

5. Research on Double De-motivation
5.1. Pay satisfaction

Some early research relevant to this double de-motivation prediction was conducted under controlled laboratory conditions. In one study, for example, US participants received differing levels of reward relative to another participant ($2 against $1.50 [overpayment]; $2 against $2.50 [underpayment]; or equal pay [$2 each]) (Austin, McGinn & Susmilch, 1980, Experiment 1). Underpaid individuals were, as expected, dissatisfied compared to their equally/equitably paid counterparts. As well however, the overpaid participants were not more satisfied than their equitably paid controls. Later studies painted a glibber picture. In one study conducted in the Netherlands, for example, the participants were more satisfied with their outcomes when they had received equal outcomes than when they had received either lower *or higher* rewards (Van den Bos, Lind, Vermunt & Wilke, 1997; Experiment I). According to some evidence therefore, both under- *and* overpayment can lead to actual reductions in satisfaction with pay.

5.2. Work behavior

A retrospective weakness in the above research is that the studies did not assess the impact of pay diversity on actual task, i.e., work behavior. That kind of influence on double de-motivation has been investigated in Carr, McLoughlin, Hodgson and MacLachlan (1996). In this Australia-based research (Study I, by McLoughlin), we adapted the experimental paradigm first devised by Deci et al. through Cognitive Evaluation Theory (above). In Deci et al.'s paradigm (above, p. 81), participants were paid varying amounts for working on an intrinsically interesting task, and their performance – i.e., work behavior – during free time was subsequently observed and timed. However, the participants were not explicitly informed about the existence of pay differences - which largely omits the "social" dimension. In Carr et al.'s method therefore, two new conditions were added to the original paradigm. Payments of $1 or $2 were randomly accompanied by information that another participant was receiving, respectively, $2 or $1. In this way, the paradigm represented respectively both absolute and relative pay differences, plus it enabled their effects to be teased apart (below).

5.3. Consequences of relative pay

The key findings from Carr et al.'s (1996) Study I are captured in Figure 4.1. The baseline for these data, i.e., from a no-payment control condition, was nearly five minutes, or 300 seconds. Against that baseline, from Figure 4.1, the introduction of payment *without* explicit knowledge that others are receiving different levels of pay reduces work motivation to approximately 90 seconds (Carr et al., 1996). This first drop, relative to the no-payment control, replicates Deci's original findings. Against that 90-second backdrop, where there is no pay diversity, making pay diversity explicit and known, as it often is in workplaces themselves, brings motivation significantly down. From Figure 4.1, independently of being "underpaid" ("other individuals have been receiving $2") or "overpaid" ("other participants have been receiving $1"), the time spent interacting with a task, during the free choice period, drops – sharply. Thus, the experimental analogue depicted in Figure 4.1 demonstrates an effect, from pay diversity, of double de-motivation.

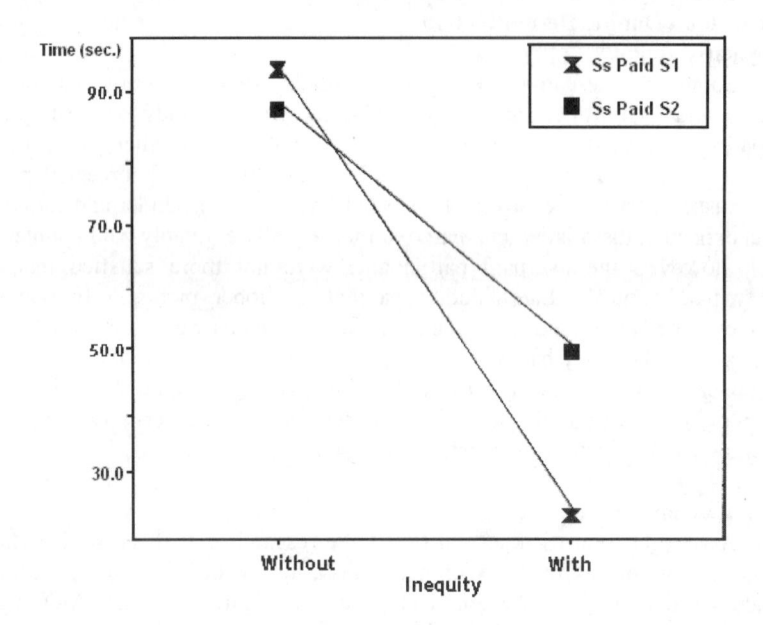

Figure 4.1. Intrinsic motivation (time in seconds) as a function of *Without* versus *With* knowledge of pay diversity

Source: Carr et al. (1996)

5.4. Double de-motivation in the field

The Achilles' heel of some laboratory studies is the extent to which their findings generalize beyond the laboratory. In order to assess the external validity of our laboratory-based findings, we designed a test of the double de-motivation hypothesis for field settings (Carr et al., 1996, Study II, by Hodgson). The participants in this study were Australian workers, from a variety of industries and service sectors. Many of these respondents had recently moved to different forms of pay diversity, for example through individual contracts and enterprise bargaining. As part of a field survey on this change, we first asked the workers whether they felt higher paid, lower paid, or paid the same, compared to others who were doing the same job. We then carefully matched the respondents who gave each type of answer (higher, lower, same), according to their occupational categories. Thus, we derived three groups of workers, who differed systematically only in terms of their relative pay.

The methodology chosen for this study was built around the lottery question (above, p. 80). Based on previous findings using that question (reviewed above), we expected to find (and did) that a clear majority of workers would think about continuing to work even after becoming financially secure (77 percent). This level of non-financial work motivation cleared the way for us to ask a second component to the lottery question: "Would you continue in the same job, or change jobs?" (Morse & Weiss, 1955). According to our theoretical analysis, double de-motivation is more about motivation *at* work than undermining the meaning *of* work. Hence pay diversity should de-motivate workers in their current job only. On this basis therefore, and in conjunction with the literature on lottery questions, we expected to find that both under- and overpaid individuals, compared to their counterparts receiving the same pay, would be more likely to report that they would *change jobs*.

The findings of this tailored field survey are presented in Table 4.1. The data in Table 4.1 focus on the numbers of participants who would remain working even if they won the lottery. These numbers are furthermore broken down into those workers who would "stay on" in the same job versus those who would "change jobs," i.e., move either within or between occupations. From Table 4.1, there is a statistically significant interaction between, on the one hand, "staying on" versus "changing jobs;" and, on the other hand, whether the respondents felt either (a) paid the same, or (b) paid differently. Whilst the equivalently paid participants were more likely to stay on than change jobs, the participants perceiving more pay diversity, whether under- or over-paid, were more likely to do the reverse – i.e., to change jobs. Converging with this pattern, the same tendency was observed with levels of job satisfaction. We found in our study that these dropped significantly amongst the under- and overpaid individuals, compared to their equivalently paid counterparts (Carr et al., 1996). Thus, evidence of double de-motivation is found not only in the laboratory but also – consistently – in the field.

Table 4.1 Pay diversity and occupational turnover

Stay versus leave job/occupation

Pay perception	Stay on	Change job	n
Equivalence	25	10	35
Underpaid	9	18	27
Overpaid	14	21	35
Total	**48**	**49**	**97**

Source: Extracted and adapted from Carr et al. (1996, Study II)

5.5. Reasons for leaving

As well as the quantitative data presented in Table 4.1, we also asked the differentially paid respondents to explain *why* they felt they would leave. Among the lower paid, the chief reason for leaving was angry frustration ("Pissed off," 46 percent of lower paid respondents). Among the higher paid, the modal feeling was relative gratification ("Feel good," 35 percent of higher paid respondents). This latter group also however reported pity ("Feel sorry for them," 22 percent of higher paid respondents) and perplexity ("Can't see why," 21 percent). Compared to their lower paid counterparts therefore, reactions among the higher paid respondents are less uniform, indicating a certain awkwardness that could, potentially, disrupt relationships (and thereby performance) at work (Carr et al., 1996).

5.6. Links to the wider literature

The overarching pattern in Carr et al.'s data, i.e., both lower and higher paid individuals reporting that they are more likely to quit than their less diversely paid counterparts, is broadly consistent with other research findings in the pay-performance domain (Greenberg & Ornstein, 1983; Harrod, 1980). In one study of voluntary turnover, for instance, turnover was more of an issue among both low and high performers, than it was for average performers (Trevor, Gerhart & Boudreau, 1997). An interpretation of findings such as these is that higher paid individuals become relatively ready to quit because they regard themselves as more "marketable" than their lower (and as well their equivalently) paid counterparts (Stepina & Perrewe, 1987). In that sense, they may also see themselves as being "above" their current job, and its level of pay (Stewart & Moore, 1992). Because of this, they may find their relations at work being partly soured and strained by negative motivational gravity, i.e., Pull Down and Push Down (Manning & Avolio, 1985). In an overall sense therefore, pay diversity is hardly conducive to motivation and commitment at work.

5.7. Pay diversity and mental health

Implicit in much of the above review is an idea that pay diversity can impact on occupational health and wellbeing. In fact – and reflecting our own qualitative observations in Carr et al. (1996, Study II) – perceived overpayment has been linked in the wider literature as frequently with social guilt (e.g., Levine, 1993) as with bravado (e.g., Perry, 1993). The former indicates that pay diversity is a work stressor, which creates mental strain. This potentially disturbing possibility has been investigated in several research studies.

5.7.1. Under-reward and occupational wellbeing.

Some of the studies of under-reward, with a focus on job burnout, have involved the participation of health and mental healthcare professionals, (Guerts, Schaufeli & De Jonge, 1998; Van Dierendonck, Schaufeli & Buunk, 2001). In Guerts et al.'s study, perceived negative inequity in regard to the employment relationship was linked, in the longer term, to both (a) emotional exhaustion and (b) intention to leave the organization/employer. Van Dierendonck et al.'s study extended this finding to relationships with clients. Healthcare workers who felt that they "gave" of themselves socially and professionally more than they "received" back from their clients as a group, later experienced higher levels of emotional exhaustion, compared to their colleagues who reported that they felt socially rewarded more equitably.

5.7.2 Over-reward and occupational wellbeing.

Interestingly, in Van Dierendonck et al.'s study, health professionals who reported giving *less* than they received felt even *more* emotional exhaustion than their relatively deprived healthcare colleagues. In fact, the possibility of emotional backlashes like these has been indicated for some time in business organizations. An early indication that over-reward helps create decrements in wellbeing is contained in research on Equity Theory (e.g., Gergen, Morse & Bode, 1974; Middlemist & Peterson, 1976). In Middlemist and Peterson's study, over-rewarded workers raised their input (to reflect their raised outcome) only if they were able to *maintain* a superior effort. Such difficulties imply strain and exertion. In Gergen et al.'s study, the net result of such strain was that participants began to upgrade their rating of task *difficulty*, and what constituted a fair return for undertaking it, compared to their more equitably rewarded counterparts (also above, on self-inflation effects). Instead of sustainable increments in task performance, therefore, research suggests that overpayment actually either fuels job strain or reduces job effort, or – in the longer term – promotes both.

5.8. Double de-moralization?

Neither of the studies above focused explicitly and exclusively on pay. One recent study however, has done so (Marai, 2002/3). Marai's study was conducted in Indonesia, where teachers, like many educators working in the "developing" world, experience relatively wide pay differentials. Principally, these differences are found between (a) expatriate instructors, who are paid from their comparatively prosperous home economies, and (b) their host counterparts, doing essentially the same job, who instead are paid from inside the ("developing") home economy. These pay differences, between foreign expatriate and local host, can become acute (see, MacLachlan, 1993a). In Marai's study, where the ratio was comparatively mild, the mental health of both pay groups was compared against that of instructors who perceived their pay to be more equitable (e.g., expatriates working for a local salary). Marai found that both underpaid and overpaid groups, alike, had lower levels of mental wellbeing. Specifically, they each had higher levels of (a) anxiety, (b) depression, and (c) hopelessness, compared to their more equitably paid counterparts working in the same or similar job.

5.9. Double de-motivation across groups: Theory

Studies like Marai's remind us that, in a global economy, pay diversity is often aligned with visible and readily identifiable groups. A study that focuses on these forms of identification is reported in Carr, Chipande, and MacLachlan (1998). The study takes up two interrelated implications in the research on reward and occupational mental health – (1) that the social consequences of pay diversity are inherently longitudinal, and (2) that they are socially interactive.

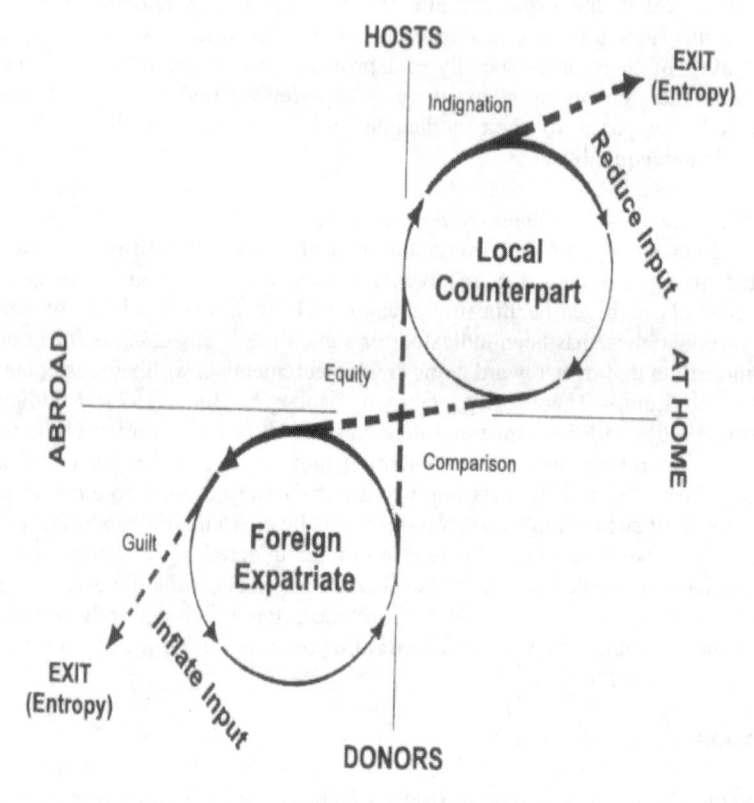

Figure 4.2 Escalating double de-motivation

Source: Carr, Chipande & MacLachlan (1998, p. 136)

From Figure 4.1, Carr et al.'s study takes a Systems Theory perspective on double de-motivation, utilizing the systems template *escalation* (Chapter 2, this volume, p. 40). Figure 4.1 is set within the context of an expatriate assignment (or EA) in a "developing" economy. Both individuals and groups within such settings make pay comparisons which frequently reveal double-figure discrepancies. Thus, Figure 4.1 casts the dynamics of double de-motivation in relatively high resolution (Carr, McAuliffe & MacLachlan, 1998).

5.9.1. *De-motivation No. 1.*

From Figure 4.2, pay comparisons will cause some expatriates to feel guilt (Carr et al., 1998). This is particularly understandable given that many expatriates who go to work in a "developing" economy are partially motivated to do so by sensitivity to social inequity (MacLachlan & Carr, 1999). Both Work Justice and Social Equity theories (above) suggest this guilt will initially put pressure on the expatriate to either work harder or leave. The research described above also suggests however that the strain will be short-lived. Pragmatics – and the sheer magnitude of pay discrepancy – guarantees it. Nobody can sustain working 10 or 20 times harder or better than others doing the same job. Under such circumstances, in the mid- to longer-term, some expatriates will begin to resolve their discomfort psychologically. They will surreptitiously elevate the importance of "their" role and "their" work - inflating their own input - and to that extent, in the process, reduce the effort they apply to their own work goals (MacLachlan, 1993b).

5.9.2. *De-motivation No. 2.*

Amongst the lower paid counterparts in this relationship, pay comparisons will have been producing collective feelings of indignation. These may have been fuelled, for example, by traditional beliefs in need (Giacobbe-Miller et al., 1998); and in equity between groups (Morris & Leung, 2000); plus globalizing norms of entitlement to pay based on work contribution not "country-of-origin" (Carr, 2003b). From either or all of these perspectives jointly, the differential in pay, between the host workers and their expatriate counterparts, will smack of neo-colonialism – of hegemony. Feelings of injustice and indignation are liable to be reinforced in fact, as the expatriate's own sense of superiority begins to leak out, either verbally or non-verbally, as stereotype threat, to his or her pay "subordinates" (Carr, 2003b; see also, Leventhal & Michaels, 1969). Social Equity Theory (above) predicts that this Push Down will nudge the lower paid to either leave or reduce their input, or at least to withdraw their good will, in order to match their comparatively deflated outcomes. From Figure 4.2 however, this reduced input will reinforce the expatriate's working hypothesis that his or her inputs are indeed "superior." That sense of superiority will then further leak out, so re-reinforcing, again, the indignation felt by the host workers – and so on.

5.9.3. *Predictions.*

Overall, according to Figure 4.2's Systems Theory analysis, pay diversity will lead progressively, in the course of developmental time, to an escalating double de-motivation. By deduction, visible and measurable signs that a double de-motivation process is actually in train, from Figure 4.2, will be certain specifiable feelings: (1) feelings of guilt and superiority (among the higher paid group); and (2) feelings of unfairness and indignation (among the lower paid group).

5.10 Double de-motivation across groups: Research

Whether these indicative feelings actually eventuate, in a real situation of pay diversity, was tested in Carr et al. (1998). The study took place with the participation and cooperation of a sample of University instructors. All of these instructors were at the time working at the National University of Malaŵi in Southern East Africa. A proportion of them worked for international salaries, whilst others worked for local salaries (this kind of division in pay, in EAs generally, is known as the "dual pay system"). In monetary terms, expatriate salaries, at the time of the study in this particular context, were between ten and 20 times greater than that received by host instructors. To approach these rather sharp inequities, we chose to ask a series of scenario-type questions, about the dual pay system and the feelings it evoked (for a discussion of the merits of scenario questions in such situations, Chapter 3, this volume). Our questions were posed during the course of an organizational survey. Some of the pertinent items in this questionnaire, along with mean responses to them from the two main pay groups, are presented in Table 4.2.

Table 4.2 Items on which pay groups differed

	Expatriates	**Malaŵians**
Items about foreign expatriates		
Some expatriates on large salaries feel guilty because they earn much more than local workers	3.4	2.0
Expatriates are better employees than their local counterparts	2.7	1.6
Items about host instructors		
Expatriates who work abroad should work under the same terms and conditions as local people	2.2	4.1
Most companies are unfair to their local employees	3.3	4.6
Local people are de-motivated by the large salaries that some expatriates earn	2.9	4.2

Scale ranged from 1 – 5, with higher ratings indicating stronger agreement.
All pairs of comparison were statistically significant, after Bonferroni corrections to protect against Type I error.

Source: Extracted and adapted from Carr et al. (1998)

5.11. Some revealing glimpses
5.11.1. *De-motivation No. 1.*

From Table 4.2, among the internationally salaried counterparts there was a relative tendency to admit to feeling somewhat guilty about the large salary differential between the group and their local counterparts. Also from Table 4.2, and despite their reports of relative guilt, many in the expatriate sample reported seeing themselves as significantly "better" at their jobs than their local counterparts. Any social desirability effects on this question will have acted to suppress the true value of the response, not to inflate it. To that extent, the mean estimate of inflation of input, reported by expatriates in Table 4.2, is possibly a conservative figure.

5.11.2. *De-motivation No. 2.*

From Table 4.2, it is abundantly clear that the underpaid group did indeed feel indignant and unfairly treated by the dual pay system. Specifically, for instance, more than their internationally salaried expatriate counterparts, they were insistent that expatriates *should* have been working under a more equitable system. In addition, they felt strongly that the dual pay system, operated by companies in Malaŵi at the time, was unfair to its local employees. Thus, it is no surprise, from Table 4.2, that local employees agreed that local employees were de-motivated "by the large salaries that some expatriates earn."

5.12. Double de-motivation in Process

Overall therefore, the research from field settings, focused on pay differences between groups, provides evidence to suggest that, in the area of educational development, pay diversity is producing decrements, not only in occupational wellbeing (Marai, 2002/3) but also in work motivation (Carr et al., 1998). In Table 4.2, it is arguably the global-local gaps in pay, and thence conflicting outlooks, that are the core problem. From Figure 4.2, gaps of this kind will interact with each other in their glocality, negatively influencing cooperation and work behavior as each side strives to achieve some restored sense of justice (Carr, 2003a). The interactions may even, in time undermine the mission of entire projects - or organizations. In one poignant and telling case, for example, the University of Papua New Guinea was reportedly closed as the result of an industrial dispute, precisely centered on the dual pay system which operated there (Australian Broadcasting Corporation, 1998). In another case, encapsulated for us directly below, a mining organization in Tanzania experienced significant disruption, both to its personnel and its overall mining mission, as a direct result of pay diversity (and resulting perceived injustices).

6. The Case

Zeffe is a Tanzanian national who was granted an aid scholarship from a Scandinavian donor country to study Geology in Europe. During the course of his studies, he befriended a classmate from Sweden, named Bjorn. Throughout their studies and many group projects, they worked well together. Nonetheless, Bjorn tended to rely quite heavily on Zeffe, who was more senior and had much more actual field experience. Each friend eventually completed their studies and returned home. In accordance with his scholarship contract, Zeffe returned home and joined the State Mining Corporation in Tanzania as a geologist, on a salary of 36,000 Tanzanian shillings. This was during the late 1980s, when 250 shillings were equivalent to US$1. In US dollar terms therefore, Zeffe was earning approximately $144 per annum.

Soon after commencing work in Tanzania, Zeffe was told that an "expert" was being recruited from overseas, someone who would head the Geological Mining and Surveys Department. This new Head of Department would, Zeffe was told, provide new and innovative ways of conducting business operations. The position was being funded and created by a Scandinavian aid agency. It would therefore be filled with an expatriate from the donor country.

Because the expatriate had to be recruited from the labor pool in a relatively wealthy economy, pay and conditions would need to be quite good, especially by Tanzanian standards. The salary would be US$24,000 per annum tax free, plus company car, housing, and several other fringe benefits. These included private schooling for dependent children, furlough (paid home leave), free electricity, and security guards.

Three months later, Zeffe was instructed to join the entourage sent to meet his new Head of Department at the airport. When the newcomer finally emerged from the Customs Hall, both he and Zeffe were visibly shaken. The new "boss" was none other than Bjorn, Zeffe's long-time friend and (less competent) fellow student.

It was not long before Zeffe began to feel increasingly hurt and bitter about the rift that had been created between him and his former friend. His work suffered, and he complained to his employers in the State Mining Corporation. They in turn protested to the aid organization, but to no avail. Zeffe soon felt compelled to resign his position, and he was promptly joined by several of his Tanzanian colleagues. Within three months of his arrival, Bjorn, too, had quit his job and returned home.

Source: Rugimbana (1998).

6.1. A widened scope for double de-motivation

The case above implies that double de-motivation is likely to be found not just in educational, not-for-profit organizations. It is possible, also, in industrial and multinational organizations, geared toward making profit. In any expatriate situation where pay discrepancies are acute, we can expect to find processes not radically dissimilar from those depicted in Figure 4.2. Expatriates continue, for example, to be located in economies that are "developing" (Sinangil & Ones, 2001), and the literature on EAs is now starting to acknowledge the importance of perceived pay justice in those settings (Chen, Choi & Chi, 2002; Toh & Denisi, 2003). In one study of hotels in China, for instance, perceived fairness in salaries – in comparison with expatriate managers – determined a significant proportion of the variance in attitudes toward the job (Leung, Wang & Smith, 2001).

6.2. Beyond "developing" economies

Double de-motivation is probably not restricted to glocalities that are "developing." Outside of "developing" economies, for example in cross-community work, or within organizations that are pay diverse generally, we can expect to see not dissimilar dynamics to those depicted in Figure 4.2. In Figure 4.2 for instance, expatriate "guilt," which is more likely perhaps in not-for-profit work, might be replaced by a more emotionally "neutral" kind of backward inference. Reverse effects, after all, are not necessarily "hot," i.e., driven by emotions such as guilt. As Cognitive Evaluation Theory implies, they can also be relatively "cooler", somewhat detachedly "inferring" attitudes from behavior via "self-perception" (Ferrin, 2003). The key point about self-perception, however, is that pay diversity will not necessarily require huge, double-figure discrepancies before it has the potential to become insidiously double de-motivating. Double de-motivation processes may be far more subtle than that, and present across a range of work settings globally.

6.3. Summary of double de-motivation research

As we have seen, there is now a growing body of evidence to challenge the received wisdom of pay diversity. Whilst there are clearly circumstances where pay incentives do work (at least in the short term), their mid- to longer term social dynamics have been largely neglected. The crux of these neglected social dynamics is the fact that pay incentives advocated, designed, and dictated by the markets "out there," in the wider global sense, have social psychological and motivational ramifications "in here," at a local level. Once that inherently glocal perspective is envisaged – as we have done in this chapter – it becomes increasingly difficult *not* to see the range of work behavior "challenges" that pay diversity, today, presents.

7. Managing Pay Justice

Recognizing a problem is a first step toward managing it. But how do we actually begin to manage it? Perhaps the most basic way of curbing any potential double de-motivation is through improved job selection. Personality traits, for example, have been used, on occasion with clear promise, as part of job selection for expatriate assignments (for a prime example, Kealey, 1989; for a review, Sinangil & Ones, 2001; for a policy-related study, Ones & Viswesvaran, 1999). In the case of double de-motivation, we have already identified three core characteristics that are relevant to pay discrepancies: belief in need; belief in egality; and belief in equity. Of these three, the belief that has received the most attention, to date, is beliefs about equity. Specifically, individual differences in beliefs about equity have been operationally defined, in the management literature, as *equity sensitivity* (Huseman, Hatfield & Miles, 1985; 1987). Importantly, the literature has linked equity sensitivity to tolerance thresholds for both under-reward and over-reward (King, Miles & Day, 1993). Thus, equity sensitivity is potentially relevant to managing double de-motivation during job selection.

7.1. Equity sensitivity

A scale for measuring equity sensitivity can be found in King and Miles (1994). This instrument has been used to assess individual differences, in equity sensitivity, during a replication of the original double de-motivation experiment (in Carr et al., 1996, Study I). In our extended replication, we found effects for both double de-motivation and equity sensitivity (McLouglin & Carr, 1997): The double de-motivation effect was replicated; plus it was replicated particularly clearly for individuals who were more equity-sensitive. Thus, the effect size for knowledge of pay inequity was 37 percent of the time spent working for free during a free choice period; whilst for equity sensitivity, it was an additional 17 percent of that time. In the applied domain of testing for selection, percentages like these normally have test utility.

The findings outlined above link double de-motivation directly to beliefs about distributive justice. Counter-intuitively, the most "socialistic" and the most "capitalistic" individuals alike, either through a "hotter" or through a "cooler" form of backward inference, are likely to experience double de-motivation. Because of that risk, sensitivity to equity could be a potentially useful construct for managing job selection (amongst, of course, other elements in the selection process). In particular, equity sensitivity could be a useful construct in selecting candidates for jobs in which people are expected to (a) work in pay diverse settings, and (b) form partnerships with people earning pay that is very different from their own. This point would apply equally to over- and under-paid positions, relative to each other. Logically too, an analogous point could also be made about the degree to which individuals choose to espouse the Belief in a Just World (see, Lerner, 1980).

7.2. Realistic job previews

From the point of view of employees themselves, it may not be a good idea for individuals who are equity-sensitive to select organizations or projects where their pay is acutely low, or high, compared to their colleagues. In that regard, the research reviewed so far could be useful as a way of empowering individuals, and groups, to make better selection decisions – for themselves (Chapter 5, this volume). A step in that direction has already been taken, for instance, in the research on realistic job previews (Werner & Ones, 2001). Using a scenario-based format, Werner and Ones found that the expected deleterious effects of pay diversity could be reduced, by overtly explaining the principles on which the pay is based. Findings like these clearly suggest that realistic job previews can help prevent double de-motivation from happening in the first place.

7.3. Social equity sensitivity

Like realistic job previews, equity sensitivity has largely been thought about in individualistic terms (Sauley & Bedeian, 2000). Equity sensitivity has been linked, for example, with outcomes such as personal job satisfaction (O'Neill & Morne, 1995), and personal withdrawal behaviors (Kickul & Lester, 2001). Recently however, equity sensitivity has also been linked with inequities between work groups, i.e., to social inequity. In one of these studies, a comparison was made of levels in equity sensitivity, among business students studying in the USA versus those studying in Central and Eastern Europe countries (Mueller & Clarke, 1998). In Mueller and Clarke's research, attitudes of "entitlement" (equity sensitivity = high) were more prevalent within the sampled "transition" economies of the former Soviet Bloc. Findings like this arguably reflect unrealistically high expectations, within newly liberalized economies, about upward mobility when joining the "global economy" (also, Chapter 5, on broken promises). More to the point however, Mueller and Clarke's findings also imply that equity sensitivity is a selection concept that applies alike to both individuals and groups.

7.4. Social justice

Accepting that justice beliefs vary across group locality, as well as individuality, has implications for how we research pay. First and foremost perhaps, if sensitivity to social equity is relevant, then sensitivity to social need and social egality can and will be salient, too. In a study conducted, for instance, in Japan and the USA, Japanese workers as a group were more likely, if overpaid compared to others in their plant, to experience feelings of discomfort (Levine, 1993). To the extent that Japanese work groups self-identify as "one family" (Chapter 3, this volume), they are comparatively likely to believe in a principle of egality, as a way of distributing resources internally to their group (Morris & Leung, 2000). Secondly, the research extending justice beliefs, toward relations between groups, implies that justice beliefs are practical considerations when designing pay systems through which self-identifying "groups" are expected to work together. In the cases above for example, realistic forewarning about the prevailing sensitivities (and potential insensitivities) in each cultural and historical group could well have been useful. It might for instance have enabled the mining company, and sponsoring aid agency alike, to anticipate, and to that extent monitor and micro-manage, the emotions their goodwill gesture could stir.

7.5. Social Identity Theory

A central proposal of Social Identity Theory (or SIT) is that groups will derive self-esteem by achieving positive differentiation from a salient out-group. To that extent, pay diversity which is partly founded on group identity may bolster the esteem of a higher paid group, and perhaps even galvanize a lower paid group to raise its performance (Chapter 1, this volume). On the surface, a similar point could be made with respect to pay diversity between individuals, but groups are also, often, more competitive than individuals (Insko, Schopler, Graetz & Drigotas, 1994). There are a variety of reasons for this relative competitiveness. Those reasons include, for instance, the notion that any pay-induced guilt, or alternatively inflated sense of self, will be diluted, or "diffused" in a group setting (Carr, 2003b). To that extent, and on the basis of a priori theory and research evidence, double de-motivation may be reduced, especially for the overpaid, if pay is distributed on an inter-group, as distinct from a purely inter-individual basis.

A preliminary test of this prediction has been conducted (Carr, Hodgson, Vent & Purcell, 2001 Study I; based on an experiment by Hodgson). In the study, we created a new laboratory paradigm, by combining the procedures utilized in Carr et al. (1996, Study I) with the Minimal Group Paradigm described in Chapter 2 (this volume, p. 43). Each participant was paid either $1 or $2 for working on an intrinsically interesting task, but half were paid on an individual basis whilst the rest were paid as a group. The latter manipulation was "minimal" in the sense that all participants were informed that they were being paid simply on the basis of whether their work period fell during a morning or an afternoon session. Whereas half the participants (inter-individual condition) were informed that their pay was different from an *individual* counterpart who was coming in the alternative (morning or afternoon) session, the remaining participants (inter-group condition) were informed that their pay, as part of a morning or afternoon *group*, was different from the pay of another group, who were coming in the alternative session (afternoon or morning).

7.5.1. Preliminary findings.

The participants who experienced their overpayment in groups, as predicted, spent significantly more of their free time interacting with the task than their over-rewarded counterparts, who were paid instead as individuals. To that degree, the effects of over-payment were attenuated (in the short-term, during an experimental session) by the introduction of group-based rather than individual-based pay. In field settings, not dissimilar end-outcomes were observed in Perry (1993). Perry found that African-Americans who were "overpaid," compared to market norms for their job, derived job satisfaction from the feeling of reparation that it gave them – for social wrongs committed against African-Americans, as a group, in the past. Findings like these, experimental and field alike, raise more questions than they answer, for example, "Is pay diversity *necessarily* pernicious, socially, at the inter-group level? And, if not, is pay diversity *invariably* beneficial in the longer term?" Such questions are clearly germane to the sustainability of pay diversity.

7.6. A lateral thought

In the research just described, pride is at stake between competing groups. This competitiveness is often appropriate since groups (like individuals) are regularly required to "compete" at work. Yet competitiveness at work is not always an appropriate mentality (Dunphy & Dick, 1987). Cooperation may be the overarching goal (Cowherd & Levine, 1992). What does Equity Theory say about this reality? Beneath its surface, the theory does indeed offer some indirect guidance on how to minimize the risk of inappropriate competition. Equity theorists have suggested that people can rely on multiple referents for inter-individual, individual-group, and inter-group comparison; and that these work referents may combine to form over-arching composites (Carrell & Dittrich, 1978; see also for example, Chen et al., 2002; and Toh & Denisi, 2003). Such views and findings are broadly consistent with the arguments about multiple identities advanced in our own earlier chapters (this volume). Perhaps, then, a way to enhance the workability of pay diversity is to encourage a sense, not that pay is "minimally" diverse, but instead that it is abundantly and amorphously so (Kennedy, 1995)?

7.7. A metaphor

Capturing nicely the idea above is the metaphor of an oasis (finite resource = water, instead of money). To the extent that *more* people, metaphorically, seek to drink from a single source/resource, it is inherently more difficult to enter into conflict with just *one* of them. Hence an oasis metaphor suggests, in a situation of "variegated" pay, that any potential for conflict will become diluted or "diffused." The foundation for this metaphor already exists within pay systems themselves, because pay is normally distributed over a pay scale in which there are not just two but instead multiple gradations. Thus, the image of an oasis fulfils the basic requirement for a good metaphor – it resonates in multiple ways with pre-existing experiences (Chapter 1, this volume). Even in aid situations, there is often a range of agencies operating, with a range of economic backgrounds, so that the "dual" pay system is actually overlaid with finer gradations of pay diversity generally. Whilst these gradations, as in other work settings, do not prevent pay being stereotyped as "dual" faceted, they do create a *potential* to think about them differently – and in particular, perhaps, as an encircled oasis.

To begin studying the social utility of this pay "variegation" metaphor, we have modified the double de-motivation one step further (Carr et al., 2001, Study II, based on an experiment by Vent). In this procedure, a $1/$2 pay discrepancy is visually pegged for the participants to group-based pay scales. One such scale is written on a card adjacent to the physical surface on which the participants are working. In one condition, there is written a simple pay dichotomy – a dual pay system ("$1 versus $2" condition). In a second condition, the same $1/$2 pay rates are visibly placed at the ends (or poles) of a multi-runged pay ladder. In a third condition, the $1/$2 amounts are positioned at the bottom and top of the third and first quartiles of an extended pay ladder. Thus, whilst participants work at their task, they each become aware, to differing degrees, of how their pay is structured and/or imbedded in the pay being earned by other groups.

7.7.1. Preliminary findings.
In this initial study, the impact of variegating the pay scale, on lower paid groups, was relatively negligible. There was little variation, across the under-paid conditions, in intrinsic motivation, which was consistently low. Amongst the higher paid group however, motivation levels were on average higher. This was especially so, not surprisingly perhaps, for the 'elite' group, whose members believed that their pay was at the 'top rung' of a multi-runged pay ladder. The clear exception, however, was when the same ($2) overpayment happened to be imbedded in an extended pay ladder, i.e., the in-group was not *quite* at the top pay rung. In this condition, and like a student who receives a "distinction" grade but not a "*high* distinction," there was a relative deprivation effect (Stouffer et al., 1949). Motivation was again low. This kind of outcome has been pithily summarized as "having a little, wanting a little bit more" (Alinsky, 1972). According to Alinksy, the groups at risk of disaffection are the ones who have done relatively well out of a system. It is they who have developed raised expectations of continuing upward momentum. When this momentum starts to slow up, there is inevitably a sense of "broken promise," emotional disappointment, and often anger at coming a disappointing second place (Lee & Martin, 1996).

7.8. Some new directions
To sum up, an oasis metaphor warrants further testing. Especially relevant would be research that included more mid-range pay positions – which have not been critically studied, to-date, as much as pay extremes. Middle-of-the-range pay positions, after all, are where the majority of people's pay positions, by definition, will be located. These shortfalls in our understanding apart, the effects of pay diversity, in groups, may depend crucially on managing raised expectations of entitlement amongst the upwardly mobile. These people are metaphorically the most "thirsty" in the system. Previous research and theorizing suggests that such effects may be more acute for individuals who are equity-sensitive, and for groups that are more social-equity-sensitive. In fact, more salient beliefs in all three key types of justice (equity, egality, and need), and belief in a just world generally, can be expected to amplify prospects of a felt relative deprivation, and hence de-motivation.

7.9. Melded incentives
One area where an oasis metaphor seems intrinsically germane is in teamwork. Team dynamics, and pay dynamics, are inherently close-up and "in the face," and to that extent will require careful balancing of both group and individual needs (Chapter 3, this volume). In such situations, the image of an oasis suggests a

fusion, or meld, of both group and individual incentives, into one overall pay performance system. An example of this fusion in practice, in work team situations, is the "pay-performance matrix." A schematized illustration of how pay-performance matrices are designed is presented below. The matrix in Table 4.3 strives to balance individual and group rewards. Thus, individual rewards, for good individual acts, are balanced and counterbalanced by social rewards, for good team acts by the group (Chapter 3, this volume, on balancing individual and social achievement).

Table 4.3 A pay performance matrix

Percentage increments in pay (units)

The	Exceeds target	3	4	5
	Achieves target	2	3	4
TEAM	Misses target	1	2	3
		Misses target	Achieves target	Exceeds target

The INDIVIDUAL

7.10. Some evidence

In a leading study of team-based incentives, the factors differentiating successful teams from less successful teams were identified empirically (Wageman, 1997). Amongst Wageman's critical factors was the way that pay diversity was structured. Pay-performance matrices succeeded in this particular company when the bulk of rewards (at least 80 percent) were allocated to group rather individual rewards. Results like this begin to suggest, perhaps, that the precise content of a pay-performance matrix – how much of the "oasis" water can or should be distributed to individuals, and how much to the team – will vary with the local context (Scott & Einstein, 2001). In that way, the concept of a pay-performance matrix is broadly consistent with the concept of glocality.

7.11. A case in point

Pay-performance matrices are relevant to relations between groups as well as to relations within them. An example of "inter-group" systems of pay is clearly visible in the Case (above). In the Tanzanian mine's everyday activities, as in the daily activities of many other real organizations, different self-identifying and remunerated groups are required to work together. Theoretically, the pay matrix depicted in Table 4.3 speaks to such needs. Its TEAM axis is based on a concept of "superordinate goals," which aimed originally to bring mutually disaffected groups together, through shared tasks and interconnected roles (for a review, Carr, 2003b).

Those superordinate (or shared) goals later proved to be effective, when arranged as a series of challenging but attainable ends. Extending this parent concept through Table 4.3, it is conceivable to design pay-performance matrices that not only reward multiple GROUPS (in place of the INDIVIDUAL in Table 4.3), but also redistribute some of the available resources to a combined *PROJECT* TEAM. Configurations like this might help to bring work groups together instead of forcing them apart, and to that extent would combat de-motivation in dual pay glocalities.

8. Conclusion

At a more general level, our consideration of pay-performance matrices is a reminder that pay diversity is clearly not *necessarily* a social evil; nor is it necessarily a precursor to double de-motivation. Various theories and processes do already exist for managing it. These range, as we saw, from selecting a better "fit" to the inequities and inequalities of a project; to realistic job previewing of the project and its relative pay levels; to using group incentives in competitive situations; to creating an expanded scale of diversity where cooperation is required; and, finally, to designing and testing multidimensional pay-performance systems, that explicitly incorporate shared team pay-scapes. This concept of developing shared landscapes for team functioning is where our discussion heads to next.

Chapter 5

Power

> Creating a climate of teamwork and openness is a common goal nowadays, but it is the rare company that figures out how cultural assumptions about individualism, about managerial prerogatives, and about respect for authority based on past success may make teamwork...virtually impossible ... . Recall how quality circles failed in the United States – not because workers don't care about quality, but because workers did not want to sit around in groups to talk about it.
>
> *Source*: Schein (2000, pp. xxiii/xxiv).
>
> Diversity in teams ... is a subjective experience of social categories to which members "feel" they belong. These categories, or social identities, may become more or less salient in different contexts and at different times ... . This dynamic view of diversity provides us with a better understanding of ... the cognitive and affective processes that may help to explain behavior and subsequently team performance.
>
> *Source*: Garcia-Prieto, Bellard & Schneider (2003, p. 413).

Power is often supposed to be about empowerment, either through individualization or through teamwork. Having discussed individualization in previous chapters, this chapter focuses on teams. Toward these, Schein adopts a relatively localized attitude. He is reacting to the globalistic rhetoric of teamlife, or "one size fits all," with some cultural contingencies. Groups vary in their inherent receptivity to teamwork. Garcia-Prieto et al.'s perspective is more glocalized. Receptivity to teamwork, and the cultural positions it presupposes, constantly changes. That variability in receptivity stems from plural forms of identity – individualistic or collectivistic, egalitarian or power distant, and societal, occupational or organisational – that become by turns salient through changing work situations. This chapter surveys the evidence for each perspective - one more local the other more glocal - and to that extent the glocality of power, and empowerment, at work.

1. The Concept of Empowerment

One of the clearest definitions of empowerment is to be found articulated in Spreitzer (1995). According to Spreitzer, empowerment is behaviorally constituted from four core elements: caring about the job being done (meaning); feeling confident in the job itself (competence); having autonomy at work (self-determination); and perceiving that one can make a difference in the workplace (impact). Autonomy at work, for instance, includes having self-determination in choosing work methods, in scheduling of tasks, and in setting performance evaluation criteria (Sadler-Smith, El-Kot & Leat, 2003). Taken together at face value, these elements of empowerment imply the individualization of work already discussed throughout Chapters 1 to 4 (this volume). It is therefore ironic, and even perhaps a little ominous, that empowerment has become almost synonymous, in much work behavior literature, with self-managed teams (Randolph, 2000; Robbins & Fredenhall, 1995).

2. Defining Teamwork

A first step in any conceptual analysis is often the development of a descriptive taxonomy (Gould, 1994). According to Devine (2002), teams can be categorized on the basis of their context (e.g., temporal duration) and their balance of thinking versus doing (e.g., executive planning versus sports performance). Teams can also be conceptualized in terms of demographic features, such as their level of diversity, or their optimal numerical size (e.g., Orpen, 1986; to Karotkin & Paroush, 2003). More fundamentally than this however, teams can be analyzed, as we do now, from a perspective that is historical (West, 2001).

2.1. Historical steps toward teams

People have been working in self-managing teams for eons of human history and pre-history (West, 2001). During the twentieth century, the industrialized nations began a "re-discovery" of this ancient form of organizing work (Tubbs, 2002). Landmark steps in this process of re-discovery, at work, include the Hawthorne Studies (Mayo, 1933), Channel Theory (Lewin, 1947), Socio-Technical Systems Theory (Trist & Bamforth, 1951), Job Characteristics Theory (Hackman & Oldham, 1976), and – a penultimate development prior to self-managed teams themselves – Quality Circles (Argyle, 1989). Today, empowerment in self-managed teams has for example been linked to benefits in task performance and quality of working life (Cohen, Ledford & Spreitzer, 1996). Thus teams and teamwork theoretically have the potential to knit together both halves of the "motivation factor" – task and relations – discussed in the previous chapter (4, this volume).

2.2. A trend in empowerment

At each of the above overlapping phases of thought, various barriers to sustainability have been identified. These have ranged, respectively, from external economic conditions (Snodgrass, Levy-Berger & Haydon, 1985), and occupational culture (Marrow, 1964), to political resistance (Trist, Susman & Brown, 1977), individual differences (Fried & Ferris, 1987), and cultural values (Schein, 2000). Through a lens of their history, therefore, it is possible to view the advent of teams as a progressive "cranking up" in levels of participation, in the possibly vain hope that once empowerment was enhanced to a high enough level, these would be followed by sustainable increments in production (Hallier & Butts, 1999).

2.3. Do self-managed teams work?

Clearly, there are cases where team implementation works. In purely "doing" terms for instance, cooperation often has the edge, in performance terms, over competition (Stanne, Johnson & Johnson, 1999). Similarly, even in relatively individualist organizational settings, the implementation of self-managing teams can be successful (Wageman, 1997). Across a range of different team types, self-managed teams have shown that they can be more effective than more traditionally managed work groups (Cohen & Ledford, 1994). Key structural features of workplace teams, for example like distributed leadership, have shown that they can make a difference over leadership that is more centralized (Taggar, Hackett & Saha, 1999). At the same time, however, it is possible to find instances where team interventions did not work (Kirkman, Jones & Shapiro, 2000). One meta-analysis for instance could find no significant effect of team building on performance, and even a slight tendency for team building to *de*crease objective levels of performance (Salas, Rozell, Mullen & Driskell, 1999). Team interventions that fail outright may be even less likely to appear in journals in the first place (Gergen, 1994b). Thus, the available evidence prompts us to wonder why some team interventions succeed whilst many others possibly fail.

"Why" questions bring us directly to Team Theory.

2.4. Theoretical developments in team studies

Again, an historical perspective is useful for our analysis. How have we arrived at a point where conference proceedings today are arguably dominated by research on teams and teamwork (Reddy, Langan-Fox & Code, 2003)? Until the 1970s, the ideas about teams were conveniently contained within the literature on, and theory of, small group dynamics (Tindale et al, 1998). Thereafter, however, according to Tindale et al, "the literature" began to burst out of the small groups domain, and its basic social science journals, into a range of often uncoupled, applied specialist areas (e.g., business, sports, military, educational groups). As a result of this development, the applied research on teamwork has not only outgrown but also, arguably, come adrift from its previous points of anchorage in classical group theory (Levine & Moreland, 1990; see also, Edmondson, 2000). Such slippage is why, today, we are witnessing calls to bring the strands back together, both at organizational levels (Weinberg & McDermott, 2002) and at micro behavioral levels generally (Jones, 2002). Thus, the literature on teams is now very much in need of theories that span diverse human performance settings (Carr, Fletcher, Atkins & Clarke, 2002).

3. The Mantra of Diversity

In the wake of the proliferation of applied research on teams, much hope, in theoretical terms, has been pinned on the concept of "diversity." On the face of it, the logic in this maneuver is impeccable. It is simply a reflection of the fundamental logic of organizing work into groups in the first place: Since nobody possesses all of the skills, aptitudes and attitudes to conduct all tasks, combining diverse individuals into groups and dividing labor according to their respective talents will increase capacity to achieve complex organizational missions (Frandsen, 1969).

3.1. Levels of diversity

Diversity can be defined as surface-level (demographic) or psychological (Harrison, Price & Bell, 1998). Much research however has focused on the latter, and in particular on diversity in personality (Belbin, 1997). This research has been heavily psychological. Belbin's central thesis, for example, is a logical extension of R. Bales' classic work on emergent leadership (1956). For a team to be successful, Belbin argues, a ninefold range of key behavioral roles, from "creative ideas person" to "resource gatherer" to "completer," must be represented, to the best possible degree, within the team's various individual personality profiles (for an example, Fisher, Macrosson & Wong, 1998).

3.2. Evidence on diversity in personality

Generally speaking, the empirical evidence about impact of team diversity, on team performance, has been equivocal (Fisher et al., 1998). In particular cases, variety has been shown to be conducive to group performance (e.g., Lieberman, 1990). In other cases, it has not (Partington & Harris, 1999). In meta-reviews, the combined effect sizes for the effects of diversity are either non-existent (Webber & Donahue, 2001), or positive but minimal (Bowers, Pharmer, & Salas, 2000). With the benefit of hindsight, this equivocalness makes logical sense. For example, in circumstances requiring rapid responses, heterogeneity in views will be a disadvantage (Hambrick & Cho, 1996); surface diversity can encourage stereotyping (Shaw & Barrett-Power, 1998); and diversity in feelings can foster intra-team conflict (Barsade, Ward, Turner & Sonnenfeld, 2000). This conflict can become magnified by the fact that teams are small in number (Carr, 2003b). To that extent, diversity may be something that is best tolerated, in smaller groups, in smaller doses, for example when the group's shelf life is short rather than long (Schippers, Den Hartog, Koopman & Wienk, 2003). Findings like these remind us that there are just as many aspects of diversity that can work against effective team functioning as there are those that can work in its favor. To that extent, and within those limits, team success is an issue of contingency.

4. Contingency Approaches

These have taken at least three different basic approaches, namely contingency in personality profile for the team as a whole; contingency in behaviors performed by the team; and contingency in shared values within the team, or "cultural" contingency.

4.1. Personality factors

Amongst the so-called "Big Five" of personality traits, one meta-review of team performance highlights a role for agreeableness, which is a significant positive correlate (but not necessarily a cause) of team performance (Kleven & Jenssen, 2001; see also, McCleod, Baron, Marti & Yoon, 1997, on the complementary role of dissenting, and to that extent disagreeable, minorities). In another meta-review, three further elements of the Big Five, in addition to agreeableness, have been found to predict team performance in the statistical sense: conscientiousness; extraversion; and emotional stability – or neuroticism (Barrick, Stewart, Neubert & Mount, 1998). The remaining element in the Big Five, openness (to new experience), has been linked indirectly to performance, through a moderating effect on the link between communication and decision-making (Colquitt, Hollenbeck, Ilgen, LePine & Sheppard, 2002). According to the personality-in-teams literature therefore, and perhaps not too surprisingly, teams that are on average higher on any of the big five characteristics, across their members as a whole, tend on average to be better positioned to perform successfully as an ensemble.

4.2. Behavioral factors

In previous chapters, we have seen that one sign of robustness in a behavioral principle is the extent to which it applies with consistency across diverse situations and settings. In teams research, for instance, it would be difficult to conceive of a more dissimilar pair of situations than the surviving hunter-gatherer activities of the Pygmies of Cameroon (De Vries, 1999) and the ocean-racing activities of Team New Zealand when successfully challenging for the America's Cup (Maani & Benton, 1999). In each of these radically different settings however, ethnographic studies have compared the behavioral factors that seemed, to de Vries, with Maani and Benton, to characterize their functioning teams' ethos. Uncannily in fact, these studies have thrown up a common set of properties. These comprise respect/trust, open dialogue, common goal, selflessness, and distributed leadership. Across the two radically different settings, a near-perfect alignment of these factors is sufficient to make us wonder if they partly reflect a relatively global stereotype for team functioning. Such stereotypes, as we shall see, can themselves moderate the enthusiasm with which teamwork is advocated, received and enacted in organizations.

4.3. Cultural factors

An alternative form of stereotype about teams is more of a dampener than the above. This alternative view is more inherently localized in its point of view. Schein, for example, believes that some cultural settings are inherently more "receptive" to team initiatives, and team working, than others (opening quotation, 2000). According to this view, at an ecological level, employees are inherently more receptive to self-managing teams if they value collectivism more than they value individualism (Kirkman, Gibson & Shapiro, 2001). At a more micro level too, groups in which personal (and culturally related) values are more on the collectivistic rather than the individualistic side, may be more receptive to team-based work initiatives (Lemons, 1997).

Implicit in the quote from Schein is the idea that teams can be provocative. Individualism, at either the ecological or the individual level, may foster resistance to team-based initiatives (Kirkman & Shapiro, 1997). This resistance can range, in principle, from that which is relatively passive resistance, as for example in social loafing (Karau & Williams, 1993), to the more active forms of resistance, as in local backlashes against global faddishness (Sinclair, 1992). Sinclair's critique is noteworthy for arguing that teams and team ideology are often instruments of exploitation and oppression, suppressing individuality in the name of group conformity. Sinclair further suggests that the ideology of teams can deprive a group of its preference, and indeed, right, to choose firm leadership in times of crisis. In that event, teams ride roughshod over transitory preferences for power and hierarchy (Chapter 2, this volume). Added to this, team ideology can also serve as a smokescreen for politically powerful cliques, who seek to gain and retain political capital by instilling organizational groupthink. Overall therefore, Sinclair's antithesis is that teams are frequently instruments of oppression, and they are oppressive in the sense that they create "oppressive stereotypes of what teams should be like and how they should behave" (p. 611, emphasis added).

Yet there is logically another side to this story. Counter-balancing the aforementioned propensities, the sheer potential efficiency of teamwork (p. 107, two heads are better than one), including the potential this creates for personal advancement, may appeal to values that are more individualistic. Thus, the claim that teams are somehow more suited in an indelible way to one particular configuration of values, even values that are relatively fixed, is inherently contestable.

5. A Glocal Analysis
5.1. Globalization

Our brief historical analysis of the development of self-managed teams has identified a globalized rhetoric toward ever-higher levels of empowerment. This progression can be seen, it was suggested, as an implicit attempt to capitalize on the "human-relations" side of work motivation. Specifically, combining a concern for human relations with Scientific Management's emphasis on task efficiency enables firms to boost at the same time both productivity and – conveniently enough – quality of working life. Thus, although teams are not strictly speaking part of the individualization of work that we discussed in the context of globalization in Chapter 1 (this volume), they are, nonetheless, allied with other zeitgeists in globalization as a whole.

5.2. Localization

Throughout the history of teams at work, we found evidence of local backlashes against teams and teamwork. The reasons for these backlashes have ranged from personal and behavioral to political and cultural. But what binds them together is their anti-conformity toward a perceived constraint. Counter-positioning of this kind is neatly encapsulated in Schein's observation that empowerment initiatives, at a micro level, often backfire partly because they conflict with pre-programmed cultural assumptions (2000, p. xxiii). Sinclair's refreshing (1992) analysis too seems approach a not dissimilar kind of stance, for example by rallying against the "*cult* of the 'team player'" (1992, p. 617, emphasis added). In each case, the group itself is portrayed as relatively fixed in its basic predilections, e.g., for working alone versus working together. Hence a second form of positioning in response to team initiatives, equally staunch as the first, is to advocate a kind of cultural mediation in which, in the final analysis, "one size fits some" much better than others.

5.3. Glocalization

A possible objection to the localized perspective just outlined is that it is just as oppressive as its globalized antithesis. Whole groups of individuals, whether as societies or professional groups or organizations, are rigidly positioned into being "hostile" to, and "unreceptive" to, the team variety of empowerment. Against this form of positioning, Spreitzer's enduring definition of empowerment (p. 105) suggests that situations, and organizational context, are more the enablers of empowerment than relatively fixed "cultural dispositions." On her conceptual, a priori grounds, it is possible to begin questioning the kind of position being projected in both Schein (2000) and Sinclair (1992). The essence of this doubt is that the case for localization and potential backlash might be overstated; that people are not so black-and-white in their reactions to teams.

5.4. An alternative conception

The capacity to reject or embrace self-managing teams can be seen as a question of choice, ability, effort, and – most importantly of all perhaps – workplace facilitation. Whilst groups may be relatively unreceptive to empowerment under some conditions, they may become relatively receptive to them under others (Garcia-Prieto et al., 2000). Global and local systems are not necessarily incompatible with each other. This inherently glocalized perspective, on teams, stresses behavioral fluidity and dynamism, and the potential for teams to succeed, versus fail, in any work setting that we care to name. The great challenge of course is explaining precisely 'how' such resonance actually materializes. First however, we need to show 'that' it happens, even under local conditions that appear at first, on the surface, to be absolutely adverse.

6. An Acid Test

Logically, the most difficult kind of test situation for a glocal stance like the above is the domain of virtual or "cyber" teams (Beyerlein, Johnson & Beyerlein, 2001). Cyber teams offer a range of fairly obvious potential benefits to their users, including maximized recruitment pools, minimized response times, and optimized work-life balance (Bell & Kozlowski, 2002). Yet cyber teams are also by definition widely dispersed, both within countries (Kirkman, Gibson & Shapiro, 2001) and – increasingly – between them (Fontaine, 2002). In the latter case, they tend to be particularly diverse (Zigurs, 2003). This includes diversity in language and communication skills (Kayworth & Leidner, 2000). But differences in cultural values are critical, too. These can entail, for instance, diversity in attitudes to time and in levels of belief in power distance (for both, see Chapter 2, this volume).

Apparent differences on cultural dimensions can easily disrupt virtual teams' basic functioning (Montoya-Weiss, Massey, & Song, 2001). In one study for instance, some team members felt that e-mail was too "direct," and in that sense disrespectful, for communicating with a team "leader" (Ook Lee, 2002). Differences like these will replicate and multiply the more culturally diverse the group is. To that extent, global virtual teams represent a supreme test for the idea that we can all become team players, under the right set of circumstances. They are perfect grist for the skeptic's mill, i.e., the position that, "you cannot build network organizations on electronic networks alone" (Nohria & Eccles, 1992: 304–05). A primary reason for this skepticism is that global virtual teams are, on the surface, bound to fall prey to a hydra of localizations: There are simply too many differences, communicative and values-based, for the group to ever coalesce into a coherent and purposeful team. According to a staunch advocate of localization therefore, and his thesis of cultural mediation, global virtual teams are pre-destined to end in a disempowerment of the majority, not in their empowerment.

6.1. The world of practice

Despite all the arguments against global cyber teams, organizations the world over are implementing them, and on an increasing scale (Fontaine, 2002). "To ask *if* trans-national teams exist is unnecessary" (Earley & Mosakowski, 2000: 47, emphasis added). Moreover, global virtual teams do, often, work (from Finholt & Spoull, 1990; to Gibson & Cohen, 2003). In one study for instance, cyber teams that were extremely diverse culturally still managed to develop at least one of the preconditions for successful functioning – trust (Jarvenpaa & Leidner, 1998). Researchers claim that the barriers of time, distance, presence, and culture can be overcome by interacting through multiple communication media (Solomon, 2001). In that process, as Spreitzer's analysis suggests, social and organizational support mechanisms, like structured and collective goal setting, play an important facilitating role (Huang, Wei, Watson & Tan, 2002). Thus even in settings that are stereotypically high on power distance, teamwork can and does work, provided power is socially and organizationally framed as expandable rather than finite (Tjosvold, Coleman & Sun, 2003).

Overall therefore, the available evidence indicates that teamwork can indeed crystallize in the ultra-diverse ether of global virtual reality. To that extent, the "localization" argument advanced by Schein and Sinclair (above) does not hold water. Cultural and local differences do not prevent team entities from forming and functioning. Instead, diverse stakeholders within a group can manage to transcend their differences, transiting and shifting attention to their mutual compatibilities rather than foregrounding simply their differences (Cunha & Da Cunha, 2001). During that process for instance, their very variegation may actually become a similarity, by engendering a sense that the team's constituents are "all minorities together" (Chapter 4, this volume; see also, Earley & Mosakowski, 2000).

What links all of these possibilities together however is the idea that transitions to team-hood, and with it empowerment, are a process of emotional labor through time, and therein hard team 'development.'

7. Teams through Development

The best-known developmental model for group and team development was originally propounded in Tuckman (1965). Tuckman's model includes the stages of forming, storming, norming, and performing, with a fifth stage consisting of group decline and death (Tuckman & Jensen, 1977). Tuckman's model has stood the test of time and place relatively well, and has remained influential in the way that practitioners and theoreticians alike think about, and practice in, groups at work (e.g., Morgan & Salas, 1993; McGrew, Bilotta & Deeney, 1999; to Wallace, 2001). The essential point about the model for us, however, is that "barriers" to team formation are seen as perfectly normal, and to that extent, in principle, surmountable. According to the model for instance, "conflict" is a perfectly normal feature of team development – i.e., it is to be expected as a matter of course during the stage termed by Tuckman storming (Clarke, 2001).

7.1. Implications for practice

From a practical point of view, each of Tuckman's stages can be managed through a variety of well-conceived and tested group techniques (for a review of these, Carr, 2003b). In the early stages of group formation and development, these are often aimed at expanding the base of ideas (Sessa, 1996), and in general, at capitalizing on in-group diversity (e.g., Rogelberg & O'Connor, 1998). In order however to help the group through Tuckman's stages as a whole, general principles too, such as giving and obtaining feedback, are also important (e.g., Pritchard, 1995). In the latter stages of group development, social cohesion, not just diversity, becomes a key factor (Holt & Sparkes, 2001). This cohesion is a double-edged sword. As well as allowing for concerted action, it also brings a risk that the cohesion becomes overly "tight" (Barker, 1993), locking the combined membership into organizational groupthink (Choi & Kim, 1999). Again however, a variety of techniques exist for managing that risk for team development (e.g., Janis, 1982). In general, these techniques tend to focus on amplifying "voice" in the group (LePine & Van Dyne, 1998), and in particular on fostering a norm of reflexivity (Schippers et al., 2003). According to some commentators, this reflexivity – a kind of antithesis to groupthink – is the lifeblood and defining feature of "team-hood" (Neck, Connerley & Manz, 1994). According to Neck et al in fact, reflexivity should be a meta-norm, in which the most sacrosanct idea in the group is to question all other norms. To capture that supposed defining feature of team-hood, Neck et al. have coined the term 'teamthink' (1997).

7.2. Incorporating some theory

In the modern business world, as in other domains such as sports, we can expect that a primary raison d'être for teamthink will be "the competition." Teams are often, for instance, locked into a race with a rival team, to be the first to produce a new health product, or piece of software, or to produce the best of these products and services. Thus in teams of all kinds, the level at which a team is functioning is contingent not only on its internal dynamics, but also on how it performs against its rivals, and even its own previous performance (e.g., Vargo, 1976 to Feltz & Lirgg, 1998). This focus on team competition brings us squarely back to Social Identity Theory (SIT), and in particular to the development of a team identity (Chapter 1, this volume).

7.3. Social identity processes

According to SIT, behavior in groups is a continual, competitive quest for an identity that is both positive and distinctive (Hogg & Williams, 2000). Specifically, people are seen as being driven by two key motives – to be alike and to be different from others – and, as a consequence of this, striking a good balance between the two (Brewer, 1993). Workplace teams, in theory, are the perfect vehicle for such balances to be struck – through affiliation with a team in-group, whilst at the same time out-performing a rival out-group (Brown & Williams, 1984). Either of those twin processes can also, of course, "get in the way" of effective functioning – for example when cooperation is required within multi-team systems (Mathieu, Marks, & Zaccaro, 2001). One of the primary reasons for becoming inappropriately competitive like this is that the group's sense of identity is, at the time, insecure (Klein & Azzi, 2001). Thus, SIT suggests some underlying reasons "why" teams sometimes behave inappropriately, or alternatively appropriately, and in that sense may help empower a team to manage its own development better.

Most importantly of all however, SIT suggests that behavior in teams is inherently flexible and fluid (Garcia-Prieto et al., 2003). At any one time, people are a blended matrix of individual and social identities, both explicit and implicit (Glynn & Carr, 1999). Developing towards versus away from team-hood thereby becomes an issue of choice. Different latent identities, ranging in receptivity to teamwork, can be primed, and made explicit (externalized) by different organizational and work situations (Hertel & Kerr, 2001). In Hertel and Kerr's research for instance groups were merely asked to think about concepts related to either loyalty or equality, and this minimal form of priming changed the way they later, in a group, behaved toward an out-group: groups changed the forms of identity that they adopted at any one moment, from competitive to cooperative, and from a relatively insecure mode of functioning to one that was arguably more mature. Thus, as far as teams are concerned, it is fundamentally incorrect to position groups into any one fixed locality, or indeed globality.

7.4. A glocality of teams

Findings like Hertel and Kerr's are now leading some thinkers to conclude that SIT has direct implications for practitioners. Diversity of identity is not an obstacle to teamwork, but rather an asset to be actively sought and managed in order for teamthink to happen. Thus, according to Garcia-Prieto et al, the potential benefits of diversity exist in all work teams, even those that are "visibly homogeneous" (2003: 433). To this point about surface and underlying identities, we could add a complementary point, which follows from exactly the same basic premises: The benefits of homogeneity (common identity) exist in all work teams; even in those that are, on a surface level, heterogeneous. Taken thus, teams become possible glocalities par excellence.

7.5. Enacting the glocality of teams

The idea that every person is a repository of different possible selves begs an obvious question: What perspectives? According to Hertel and Kerr (2001), the different forms of personal and social identity that reside in each of us are like behavioral scripts. Dramaturgical metaphors like this suggest that we need to begin to describe not just the priming mechanisms for identity transitions (Chapter 2, this volume). We also – more basically – need to articulate some of the scripts themselves. In the literature on teams, those precursors for identity transition are termed "team mental models."

8. Mental Models

A "mental model" is a shared understanding, in this case about team functioning, that either predates or emerges during the course of an actual team's development (e.g., Klimoski & Mohammed, 1994; to Fiore, Salas, & Cannon-Bowers, 2001). Defined like this, team mental models are the nuts-and-bolts of team social identity. As the very phrase "nuts-and-bolts" implies, these mental models most readily become visible to us through everyday language, and in particular via metaphors (Chapter 1, this volume). Team work has been described for example as the conducting of, and performance by, an orchestra (Fryer-Keene & Simpson, 1997). This particular mental model captures nicely the ideas of leadership, distributed leadership, working collaboratively, and in general "working from the same sheet of music" (Hall, 2001). Shared understandings like this have, in turn, been linked to successful team performance, first in sport (Prapavessis & Carron, 1997) and, more recently, in business organizational settings (Ensley & Pearce, 2001). Team metaphors generally have also been linked to societal and organizational cultures, and thereby to preferred modes of team behavior (Gibson & Zellmer-Bruhn, 2001). Finally, having a clear mental model, within a team, has been linked to workplace health and wellbeing (Carter, 2002). Hence, a growing body of research suggests that shared mental models influence both team behavior and team wellbeing (Druskak & Pescosolido, 2002).

8.1. But what about groups?

The literature on team mental models, like much of the literature on teams generally, implies that teams have something "special," over-and-above their more "ordinary" counterparts, groups. This implication has partly arisen perhaps because groups have in the past been demonized (Gergen, 1994a). The implied dichotomy between teams and groups - one implicitly good and the other implicitly bad - is captured neatly, at a theoretical level, in the distinction between team-think (Neck et al., above) and groupthink (Janis, 1982). Yet that distinction is very questionable – there seems to be little actual evidence to support it in a mental models sense. Before proceeding any further therefore, there is a real need for us to distinguish teams from groups, in a behavioral, mental models sense. Otherwise, we will never know what we are supposed to be aiming at, or how to attain it, or know when it is attained.

8.2. Back to the basics: A fundamental question

The issue of comparing and contrasting the essence of teams and groups is not confined to mental models. The entire literature on workplace teams could in fact be asked the self-same basic question: What, if anything, is the difference between a team and a group? (Carr, Fletcher, Atkins & Clarke, 2002). Of course, at a non-behavioral, purely structural kind of level, this kind of question can be answered relatively easily: A team has organizational properties that a group does not, for instance, its own resources, meeting space and time, and an organizational mission for the team as a whole (Wageman, 1997). But this kind of answer still begs the question about any psychological sense of team- versus group life, i.e., at a behavioral level. The concept of team mental models, and team metaphors, do imply a subjective sense of team that groups will not have. Yet some authors have questioned this implication, claiming that the terms team and group, in a behavioral sense, are actually quite interchangeable. According to Langfred (2000), for instance, the term team is simply preferred in the one (popular management) literature, whilst another literature (more academic) prefers the term group to refer to the same entity. Thus, within the literature on teams itself, there is a good deal of basic confusion about whether teams are in fact any different from groups at all, in a behavioral sense (Carr et al., 2002).

8.2.1. *Significance for theory*

A resolution to this issue of team versus group is of fundamental concern to theory, especially the theory of empowerment. On the one hand, if there is no difference between a group and a team, at the behavioral level, then our behavioral theories of groups are equally applicable to teams – where we have already seen there is a serious need for theorization (above, p. 107). On the other hand, if there is a difference between teams and groups – a special "added ingredient" in the latter – then existing theories such as SIT, which make no special allowances for team psychology as distinct from group psychology, may need some extensions or "restatement" (Carr, 2003b). As we have already seen for instance (p. 114), teams conceivably transcend the need for constant comparisons against out-groups, and in that sense may make redundant some of the principles of SIT itself.

8.2.2. Significance for practice

A resolution to the theory issue just painted is also of crucial significance to practice. On the one hand, if there is no difference between a group and a team, the 'hype' surrounding teams will eventually become, at the local level, a disappointing and demoralizing disempowerment (what is termed below a broken promise). On the other hand, if there is a difference between teams and groups, then making selection, performance management, and other consequential decisions about people, based on either outmoded theory, or lack of any theory at all, are ethically and legally questionable (Fletcher & Atkins, 2002).

9. An Approach to the Fundamental Question

A first clue on how to approach the question, "Is a group any different from a team?" is contained in the literature itself. That literature, as we have seen, adopts contradictory positions on the question. There is disagreement about what exactly constitutes a team versus a group, in behavioral terms (Carr et al., 2002). Group and team, like groupthink and teamthink, are self-evidently social constructs, and to that extent they are inherently fuzzy (Levi, 2001). Hence, to decide whether a "team" is behaviorally any different from a "group," we need a theory that deals directly with fuzziness (Carr, Fletcher, Atkins & Clarke, 2003).

9.1. A conceptual foothold

A guiding literature for locating a theory of relevance to our question about teams versus groups can be found, strangely enough, in the study of love (Fehr & Russell, 1991). Like the question of defining teams versus groups, the definition of love is often contested. The boundary lines between it, and say, lust or, say liking, are open to debate. In that sense, the question, "Is love any different from liking?" is analogous to what we have now pinpointed as our own core question, "Are teams any different from groups?"

9.2. A theory

The theory that Fehr and Russell used in order to help them mark out the differences between love and other relationships, at a behavioral level, is Prototype Theory (Clore & Ortony, 1991). From our perspective in this chapter, the essence of Prototype Theory is that some features of love will be more commonly part of the mental model for love [or "teams"], whilst others will be more commonly represented in the schema for liking [or "groups"]. These commonly mentioned features, if and when located, are said to be "prototypical" of the mental model for each referent. The way to ferret out these prototypical features is to ask people directly – the model is inherently about a process of listening. Thus, by asking people simply to free-associate to the concept of "teams," and as well asking them, in a separate question, to free associate to the concept of "groups," it becomes theoretically possible to measure whether indeed teams have prototypical, pre-existing features that groups in the same glocality do not.

9.3. An innovative study

In a first attempt at this kind of study, 62 work-experienced American Samoans and San Franciscans were asked, "How is a team different from a group?" In their responses to this question, three principal (i.e., prototypical) themes were found. According to Chavez (1997), teams were relatively frequently perceived to have (1) common (versus individual) goals; (2) participative (versus centralised) decision-making; and (3) high (versus low) social cohesion. Methodologically however, there are some shortfalls in the Chavez study. These include, for instance, a relatively modest sample size (N = 62), and the possible one-sidedness of the question itself. For these and other reasons, we have conducted further research (in New Zealand) on this same topic.

9.4. The Teams Project – Study I

In our first study on team prototypes, 250 work-experienced New Zealanders were asked to list the features that came to mind when they thought of groups and the features that came to mind when they though of teams (Carr et al., 2002; and Carr et al., 2003). Among the core findings of the study were four most frequently mentioned themes for each concept, team and group. For each of these eight themes, we calculated two forms of summary statistic, a raw frequency/250 and relative frequency (after Clarke, 2002). Relative frequency indicates how many times more often a feature was mentioned in the context of team (versus group) and group (versus team). Because Prototype Theory makes predictions about both raw frequency and relative frequency, these two statistics – together – will provide a relatively content valid index of the "prototypicality" of any particular given feature, for any given referent (i.e., "team" or "group").

For teams, the top two themes were perceptibly having a "shared goal" (103/250; ratio = 11:1) and "working together" (109/250; ratio = 7:1). These two features (total raw frequency = 212; combined ratio = 9:1) closely resemble Chavez's top theme of common (versus individual) goals. Such resemblance again suggests a role for a global stereotype (mental model) about teams. Also in the top four themes for teams in our glocality were "sport" (a relatively localised feature, perhaps) and "cohesion" (this latter emotional feature converges with the third of Chavez's themes). These were less frequent in raw terms (respectively, 36 and 29/250, although they remain more impressive in relative, ratio terms (36:1 and 29:1, respectively).

For groups, a different, almost antithetical set of features came through in the top four. Being "just a collection of people" and "working as individuals" emerged with relative frequency (59 and 35/250; combined ratio = 65:1). The remaining themes were team size and similarity. These features however were much less salient (or prototypical) in our sample's mental models for a group (on both statistical indices, raw frequency and ratio). Overall therefore, and despite an inherent fuzziness – especially perhaps in mental models for groups – the available data are suggestive of there being some differences, between teams and groups, at a behavioral level.

9.5. Study II - Validation

As an independent check on the validity of the prototype features found in Study I, we have run provisional laboratory tests. How does a new set of participants respond to the same features when they are presented (Carr et al., 2003)? Do they behave in ways that are consistent with them genuinely holding two distinctive mental models, one for teams and the other for groups? The more we can answer "Yes" to this question, the more we can be confident that our initial features validly predict behavior (reactions).

Central to our reasoning in this test of validity is the question of levels of awareness. According to Schein and others (Chapter 2, this volume), team mental models may be found on at least two levels of awareness – explicit and implicit. This distinction raised for us as researchers a question about the data gathered in Study I: Are the prototypes we found mainly functional at an explicit level; or do they apply mainly at the implicit level. Or, do they possibly even apply at both levels simultaneously? Either of these options is possible, given the quasi-implicit nature of free association.

To address the different possibilities, we devised two different recognition tasks.

Firstly, we designed a basic sorting task that would constitute a validation test at a relatively explicit level. We asked participants in the study to consciously sort the prototype features from Study I into the categories, "related to teams" vs. "related to groups." On this task, and if the prototype is explicit, we expected to obtain an above-chance level proportion of trials "correct" for each pile (i.e., proportion of responses in agreement with the team versus group categorization in Study I).

Secondly, we designed a test of whether the features reported in Study I apply mainly at an implicit level. For this test, we used what is termed a priming paradigm (Fazio, Jackson, Dunton & Williams, 1995). "Priming" is simply providing people with a stimulus that provokes an idea, or an image, and then seeing how this affects reactions to other, possibly related words. In this case, we merely primed participants with either the word team or the word group, and then asked them to name the (different) colors in which the features in Study I had been typewritten (on a computer screen). If the mental models for teams are implicit, and actually do include the top four themes in Study I, then it would be expected that the prime, "team," would make the neural "circuitry" for that particular mental model active, and so increase the time taken to perform any additional mental burden, such as naming the color of the word itself, compared to when the same features are preceded instead by the prime "group" (latter event = Team Group). Similarly, when the prime is "group," and the features come from the 'group' question in Study I, reaction time to name the color of the ink should again increase, compared to when exactly the same theoretical features are preceded by the prime "team" (latter event = Group Team). Thus, the signs of an implicit prototype are (1) slower color naming times for an event that is matched (team prime followed by what we think are team features; and group prime followed by what we think are group features); relative to (2) faster color naming times for events that are "unmatched" (respectively, Team Group and Group Team).

9.5.1. *Explicit judgments*

For a clear majority of trials, the participants agreed with us on what features help to constitute groups and teams. Interestingly too (Carr et al, 2003), the overall percentage of responses correct for teams (82%) was higher than its equivalent statistic for groups (74%). This higher proportion of responses correct (for teams) suggests that the mental model for teams, at a relatively explicit level, may be somewhat more easily defined and articulated, with a little more consensus than its more "diffuse," or fuzzy, counterpart (for groups). That interpretation, and the finding that suggests it, is consistent with what we found across the top eight raw and relative frequencies in Study I (above).

9.5.2. Implicit judgments.

The reaction time data bearing on implicit mental models are summarized in Figure 5.1. The most striking and interesting feature in Figure 5.1 is that the matched event Team Team does not in fact produce longer reaction times on average, compared to its respective non-matched counterpart (Team [words] Group [prime]); whereas the matched event "Group Group" visibly does, i.e., compared to its respective non-matched counterpart (in this case, Group [words] Team [prime]). Hence the prime 'team,' unlike the prime 'group,' does not appear to be activating anything in particular. Admittedly, this is arguably only at this stage one interpretation of the data, but it is, nonetheless, based on the rationale for the priming paradigm as a whole. On that basis, we find it interesting that, with regard to teams, we see almost a kind of opposite of what was observed at a more explicit level. There, as we learned above, it was the words for teams that were more readily thought about. Thus, whilst at a relatively explicit level it is the model for team that is more sharply defined, at a relatively more implicit level it is the model for group that appears, at a first glance, to be more substantive.

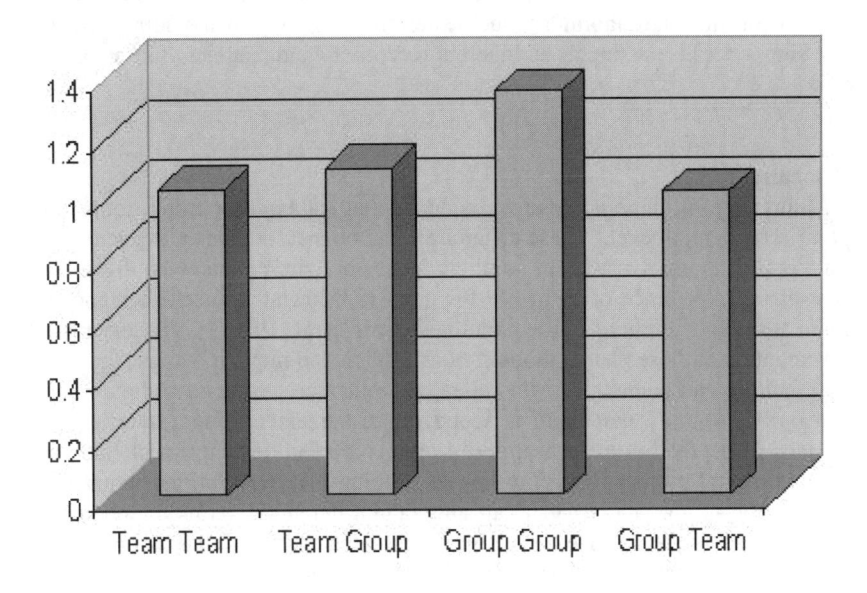

Figure 5.1 Color naming time (in secs) for events (unmatched/matched)

Source: Carr, Fletcher, Atkins & Clarke (2003, July)

9.6. An interpretation

With hindsight, the pattern in the findings makes sense (Carr et al., 2003). All of our lives, as we continue to grow and develop, inside and outside of work, the concept and experience of groups surround us with their omnipresence. We have more than ample opportunity to internalize metaphorical scripts for what groups are – family, cultural, friends, school class, work – and how we expect to function toward each other when we are "in" them. With teams, however, the level of direct, procedural experience is liable to be less extensive. In fact, much of the "experience" we have of team life is probably secondhand and vicarious. It is for instance based on text – i.e., coming through the rhetoric of teams that we have encountered in the media, at work, and in 'the literature' on work behavior.

The above interpretation of the reaction time data in Figure 5.1 is highly tentative at this stage, and still subject to much further investigation (Carr et al., 2003). Nonetheless we can in future check if the interpretation is correct. If we are right, having a sample of highly experienced team players, for example, professional project team leaders or leading sporting athletes, should in the likes of Figure 5.1 increase the length of the bar for a matched event Team Team (Carr et al., 2003). In other words, with experienced team players, we expect their internalized scripts and routines for teamwork to be so well rehearsed and practiced that they have been internalized, into an elaborate and substantive implicit mental model. Once this procedural knowledge about teamwork is primed, or socially facilitated, then team features from the mental model will keep the circuitry active, and to that extent slow down the speed at which people are able to do other experimental tasks – such as naming the color of the ink in which the prototype words for teams have been typed. In the world outside the laboratory, such interference is not an impediment but a welcome sign – because it signals an inherent receptivity and readiness for teams and teamwork.

10. A Glocality?

Summing up, there is tentative evidence that teams differ from groups at a perceptual/ experiential level. These differences can be measured at an explicit level, and may reveal themselves at an implicit level for participants who have had sufficient direct experience of team life for them to have internalized their models into automated (and implicit) skilled routines (Carr et al., 2003). The extents to which the content of these mental models, both explicit and implicit, varies according to precise culture and context, remains open. The fuzziness of team and especially group in our data imply that there is scope for disagreement amongst workplace stakeholders, over precisely what teams and groups are and do. Fuzziness like this, according to mental models theory, means in addition that expectations about what teamwork is and is not, and what it can and cannot deliver in terms of workplace empowerment, will vary. Hence the available research indicates that there may be value in listening to what employees themselves, at a "local" level, understand by the "global" concept of teams, before attempting to implement them, possibly unsuccessfully, according to some hypothetically acceptable template. Listening may for instance suggest workable metaphors that resonate and connect with the stakeholders' salient experiences (Chapter 1, p. 1). Otherwise, there is an elevated risk of local backlashes, and a glocality of disempowerment rather than empowerment.

10.1. A new springboard

As well as indicating directions for future research, and advocating respect for what employees have to say about teamwork, the data from our Prototype studies sounds a behavioral warning. People seemed more able to talk about teams than knowing implicitly, i.e., automatically, what they might actually entail. To that extent, the verbal rhetoric of teams may often be stronger than any actual understanding of how they work at a procedural level. Gaps like this could lead ultimately to an over-promise and an under-delivery on the promise of empowerment. In fact, that idea of an over-promise and an under-delivery brings us directly to our final topic in the domain of teams – the concept of a promise that is broken.

11. The Broken Promise

All of the key elements of broken promises are encapsulated in a case study written about a failed bid to empower a paints factory in New Zealand (Sligo, 1991). The study is set at the stage of Quality Circles – i.e., an early, and to that extent fundamental, form of teamwork.

11.1. The case of Spectrum Paints

The Te Matawai factory of Spectrum Paints Ltd had had the reputation for some years of being an undesirable place to work. The factory was known for its poor morale, low productivity, and an unenviable history of labor-management disputes. Stuart Brand, 58, the former manager, was classic old school (or Theory X) in his personal management style.

Yet his behavior displayed something of a paradox.

On the one hand, he appeared to have favorable opinions about the importance of communicating with staff. He had even been heard to tell his staff about the key role of communication in motivating personnel. When, like all the other managers, he was sent to the company's "Managing Through People" training program, he had no disagreement with the principles stressed there, such as keeping staff well-informed, encouraging upward communication, and MBWA (Management by Walking Around).

On the other hand, Stuart had done little to bring about improved communication. He rarely talked to staff other than the group of most senior personnel. When he did speak to subordinates, it was often in quite critical and blaming terms. The staff was afraid of his biting comments, and preferred to avoid him.

Because this site had been showing significantly worse results than other locations the company decided some six months ago to replace Stuart with one of their most effective young managers, Pat Speirs, with the aim of reversing the factory's declining profitability and productivity. Because the company valued Stuart's long-standing experience, he was left at Te Matawai as Technical Manager, and was given particular responsibility for manufacturing processes.

In her previous jobs within the company, Pat had earned the reputation of being able to boost productivity and staff morale. She was skilled in managing people, and was known as innovative and successful when it came to getting new forms of communication started. Sure enough, Pat soon took steps to improve communication within the factory. One innovation was a team briefing designed to strengthen downward communication. A second was a series of regular small group meetings, based on a Quality Circles model. By this means all staff could talk to their supervisors about anything that was bothering them, and suggest new ideas related to their work.

On the last Friday of every month Pat would organize a "manager's shout" (i.e. the manager buys everyone a round of drinks) for a staff social/get-together. In addition, she required all supervisors to practice MBWA, that is, to regularly spend a few minutes each day just talking to their subordinates so they were aware of current issues within their immediate work group.

All these methods of communication were new to the Te Matawai factory. Pat was aware that both staff and supervisors had found the transition (from Stuart's style to hers) quite a shock. Some of them seemed almost resentful that there were now new expectations of them – that they were expected to think and make suggestions, instead of just taking orders as they had done in the past.

When six months had passed, Pat sat down to review her progress. She felt she had definitely made some good steps toward improving staff morale, but that things had not improved as much as she had hoped. For example, one of the quality circle groups had come up with a suggestion for speeding up a paint-mixing system. After examining it, Pat had found that the costs of the proposal heavily outweighed the benefits. When she pointed this out to the group, she was surprised at their strongly aggrieved reaction. Group members had made comments to the effect that, "Why did she bother consulting people if she didn't intend to use their ideas?"

From other staff, and in particular some supervisors, Pat was hearing the comment that, "We're spending all our time communicating, and we're not getting any work done." Pat was not too concerned by this, because she knew from studying the weekly production figures that in fact profitability and productivity had been steadily increasing over the six months she had been in charge.

Nevertheless, she was starting to realize that not all staff were necessarily in favor of the changes she had introduced. Some personnel appeared to be threatened by the increased amount of activity within the branch. Others welcomed the new style, but seemed to expect that all their ideas would be put into effect, and that the management style of the entire organization would be changed overnight.

While she was thinking these things over, Pat received a phone call from Spectrum's Chief Executive. He told her that the group human resource manager had opted to take early retirement following a heart attack. The CEO went on to tell Pat he particularly wanted her to accept the role of Group Human Resource Manager in Head Office.

"I've been looking at the profit figures for your branch," he said, "and clearly you've got things back on track again. We're really short of people who can manage a branch like yours. I'm not entirely happy about putting Stuart back into the job of branch manager again, but right now we have no choice."

On his first day back in charge of the branch, Stuart confided to a friend that activities such as team briefings, Quality Circles, MBWA, manager's shouts and the like, were all very well and good, but should not be confused with the real work of the branch. He said that he intended to let these new endeavors die out quietly, because a number of personnel did not want them, and he personally felt they were unnecessary.

Within two months of Stuart taking over, the previous problems of the branch had returned, but even more acutely than before. Staff were saying that they felt betrayed by the company promising that people would be listened to, when, clearly, the company had no intention of taking notice of its staff.

Supervisors told each other (but not Stuart) that they had never known the staff to be so disillusioned and dispirited. Productivity had fallen to a 10-year low point, and profitability had declined sharply. Staff were saying that it would have been better not to have introduced measures like the Quality Circle meetings at all, rather than to start, then abandon them.

Source: Extracted from Sligo (1991).

12. Case Analysis
12.1. Supervisors

One of the most interesting and relevant facets of the Spectrum Paints case is the ease with which Stuart Brand is able to profess one philosophy (empowerment, Theory Y) and yet to practice another (Theory X). Stuart is a living embodiment of the discrepancy between what Organizational Learning Theory terms espoused theory and theory-in-use (Argyris, 1998). Stuart is perhaps the kind of supervisor who might say to a workplace team, in an implicitly non-supportive and even sabotaging way, "You're empowered, now go and get on with it!" This contrasts sharply with the theory that team leaders are supposed to be actively "transformational" (Garman, Davis-Lenane, & Corrigan, 2003). In this theory (and admittedly as Garman et al. point out, sometimes in practice too), transformational leaders adopt more expansive schemata for the transformation of power, giving it away to others without losing it themselves (Cox, 2003). In that way, the logical contradiction in asking supervisors to empower others whilst at the same stroke disempowering themselves is, theoretically, avoided. This preferred style seems to be Pat's most characteristic strength, however she was arguably not given enough time to reap its potential returns.

In a more political and personal sense, Stuart is well versed in the 'theory' of empowerment, but chooses to ignore it in his everyday actions. Whether he does this knowingly or implicitly, such divisions between theory and practice - between rhetoric and reality - are neither unusual nor new. In a classical treatise on workplace ethics and politics for instance, organizations are described as "typically elaborate rhetorics of harmony and teamwork" (Jackall, 1988, p. 24). These rhetorics, Jackall is suggesting, will mask managerial and supervisory resistance to teams and team-related change (see also, Manz, Keating, & Donnellon, 1990; and Fisher, 1993). In a broader sense too, the zeitgeist of empowerment generally is arguably just a politically expedient "rhetoric of partnership" (Hallier & Butts, 1998, p. 80). Surface veneers like that are presumably partly why managers value the idea of empowerment, whereas the shop floor expects more team action – i.e., that actions will speak louder than words (Payne, Nielsen, & Kristi, 2002). At the root of this discrepancy may be a certain ambivalence towards the empowerment of others at the expense of self – an ambivalence that will have to be somehow managed.

12.2. Shop floor

Discrepancies like the above, and the sense of pseudo-participation that they can soon engender, have dogged participatory management since its inception (Rosenfeld & Smith, 1967). In its day for instance, Drucker's MbO was criticized for being pseudo-participative (Halpern & Osofsky, 1990). In Spectrum Paints, the same criticism applies to Quality Circles (Sligo, 1991). A core feature of the scenario that unfurls and unravels at this paintworks, from the point of view of the employees themselves, is an over-promise and an under-delivery, on empowerment at work. First of all, there was an unfulfilled promise that the Quality Circles would have their voices heard, and second, after a trial period that was essentially too short, there was a disappointing re-implementation of Stuart's hierarchical style of management. As a result of these twin shortfalls – a double broken promise – the workers at Spectrum Paints experienced an acute sense of disempowerment. Whether or not we partly blame the workers for their own initial sanguineness (Randolph, 2000), their eventual disappointment will nonetheless probably precipitate perceived injustices (Conway & Briner, 2002), organizational withdrawal (Coyle-Shapiro, 2002) and job turnover (Wanous, 1992). Capping these costs, pseudo-participation has also been linked with the development of dislike for those managers and supervisors who are seen to have made the promise in the first place (Mitchell, 1993).

12.3. A glocal collision

Spectrum Paints experienced its broken promise with respect to Quality Circles, but the same points could be made in principle about self-managed teams. In our earlier analysis, it was suggested that the history of teams, in the literature and management practice alike, is one of steadily 'talking up,' and amplifying, the benefits of empowerment. Naturally enough, that strategy will have steadily increased workers' expectations about empowerment, and working in a fully empowered way. This of course raises the risk of disappointment. As well, as the clarion cry of giving power away is sounded louder, it is likely to be experienced, by supervisors and others who have invested in the old system, as inherently threatening, unjust, and disempowering (Adams, 1965). After all, supervisors can feel betrayed and misled, too.

Increments like these, from rising expectations to rising insecurities, can be placed within a broader zeitgeist of globalization. Within the rhetoric of a "global economy," individuals increasingly feel entitled to "their" slice of the empowerment pie (Lawler & Finegold, 2000). Meanwhile, previously privileged individuals and minorities can start to feel threatened by the very same process (Bedeian, 1995). Logically, of course, all forms of empowerment must stop somewhere. Aspiration levels cannot continue to rise indefinitely (Paul, Niehoff & Turnley, 2000). In that sense, and within those limits, empowerment initiatives are bound to disappoint the majority of staff at work, sooner or later (Carr, 2003b). In the case of teams, rotation from one team to another is only a partial solution. Many teams, for instance, have only a limited shelf life, and, even apart from that, rotation can become a form of disempowerment in itself. Whichever way we turn therefore, understanding the dynamics of broken promises becomes a pressing priority.

12.4. Training for teamwork

A relatively unusual example of research on broken promises at work is contained in Baldwin, Magjuka & Loher (1991). Baldwin et al.'s study focused on the preamble to training, and in particular on how much input and voice was promised to the trainees themselves, during the phase of training needs assessment and analysis. Specifically, the trainees in Baldwin et al.'s study were assigned to one of three basic conditions, depending on how much empowerment they had been promised during this training needs analysis phase: (1) no choice in training (no promise condition); (2) employee's preferred training solicited (through an organizational survey), with that choice of training actually being later delivered (fulfilled promise condition); and (3) preferred training solicited but then not delivered (a broken promise condition).

The results of this study are fascinating. They highlight a "frustration effect" (Folger, Rosenfield, Grove, & Corkran, 1979). Frustration effects occurs, according to Folger et al., when rising expectations are not met, hopes are dashed, and mistrust ensues. Despite receiving an identical training module, the trainees in Baldwin et al.'s (3) broken promise condition became significantly less motivated, and learned less from the training itself, than either their counterparts who (2) received the training they had implicitly been promised or – as well – those trainees who (1) had not been promised anything at all! In other words, it transpired that it was better not to have promised any empowerment at all, than to have led employees to expect participation but then to have failed to deliver, in full, on that promise (see also, Mitchell, 1993).

12.5. Communication networks

Right at the heart of the broken promise, and Baldwin et al.'s study, are skills in communication. These skills have been studied through group communication networks. Networks, by definition, are especially relevant to teams and teamwork, since networking is arguably what teamwork is all about (Stevens & Campion, 1999). The classic paradigm for studying communication networks was first developed in Leavitt (1951), and later in Shaw (1964). The literature also experimented, tentatively, with the consequence of ignoring group preferences (Borg, 1957). The communication networks studied themselves ranged from being centralized, as in a structure known as "the wheel," to participative and empowered, as in an "all-channel" network (Carr, 2003b). These structures, and the self-explanatory communication linkages that operationally defined them, are shown in Figure 5.2.

12.6. A brief summary of communication networks research

From Figure 5.2, the literature on communication networks indicates that wheel-like structures tend to be marginally more efficient for lower level tasks, whereas for more complex tasks – i.e., more like the kind of job faced in modern workplaces – the decentralized structures, especially in time, tend to develop a performance advantage (Argote, Turner & Fichman, 1989). Also over time, Argote et al. point out, more centralized structures can produce tension in the majority within the group, leading to a relatively reduced job satisfaction overall (for a review, Wilke & Van Knippenberg, 1990). Thus, on the whole, relatively empowered groups, in the literature, have tended to both out-perform and out-enjoy their less empowered counterparts, working in structures more akin to the classical wheel.

(A) The wheel　　　　　　　　　　　　(B) All-channel

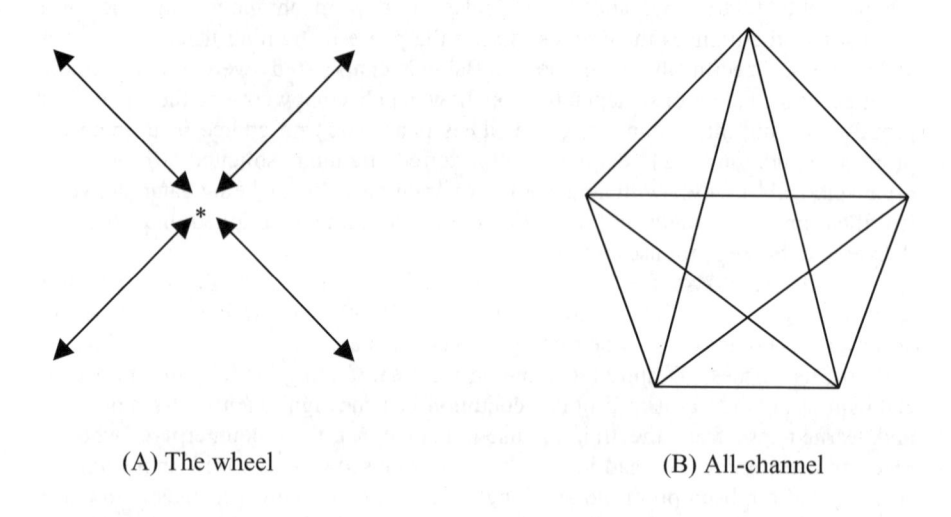

Figure 5.2: Two key forms of communication network

Source: Adapted from Leavitt (1951); and Shaw (1964)

12.7 A prediction

As we have defined it, the broken promise, in workplace teams, is analogous to promising one type of communication system (B) and yet delivering another (A). The study in Baldwin et al. indirectly suggests that promising network (B) but delivering network (A) will lead to lower performance and morale than either (A) or (B) in themselves (Carr, 2003b). This hypothesis was tested recently using Leavitt's original problem-solving tasks (Boggs, Carr, Fletcher, & Clarke, 2003; study by Boggs). The classic task materials were given to groups in three different types of network: (A); (B); and (C), a new condition in which participants first heard a preamble about the advent and key features of team empowerment [as in network (B)]. This preamble constituted an implicit promise about participation and empowerment in what was about to follow. Before the group was given its tasks to perform however, it was also unexpectedly "allocated" a central hub [as in network (A)]. Condition (C) was therefore an experimental representation of the broken promise in team settings.

12.8. Emergent findings

Firstly, individuals allocated to network (A), the wheel, reported the highest incidence of expecting no participation. Individuals allocated to (B), an all-channel structure, reported the highest incidence of participating as much (or more) than they originally expected; and individuals allocated to (C), the broken promise, reported the highest incidence of not being able to participate as much as they had earlier expected. In addition, the groups in this condition reported the lowest incidence of being able to participate more than they had expected (Boggs et al., 2003). Thus, Boggs et al.'s attempt to instill differing degrees of met and unmet expectations, among the participants in different experimental conditions, seems to have been reasonably successful.

Secondly, and more importantly, the results of this preliminary study are consistent with the earlier (but not directly team-related) research reported in Baldwin et al. (1991). Productivity and morale varied systematically across the three conditions (A) to (C). Crucially for example, Boggs et al.'s groups working in condition (C) took significantly longer to complete their problem-solving tasks than either of their two counterparts, i.e., the groups working in networks (A) and (B). In addition, and as regards human relations in the study, the emotional climate of the groups working in network (C) was significantly more negative than in either network (A) or in network (B).

12.9. Conclusion

Although this research vein is still only emerging, the initial evidence is broadly consistent with a hypothesis that it is better not to promise empowerment to teams at all, than to promise it only half-heartedly, illegitimately, or insincerely (also Sligo, above, p. 123). As well however, the research also builds programmatically on Study I and on Study II (above; Carr et al, 2003). This latest research, again from the Teams Project, links teams and groups to the dynamics of power. Specifically, it explores a glocality in which gaps between the rhetoric of 'teams' and the experience of only ever being in groups, or alternatively of not being willing for empowerment to happen for others, may feed broken promises. These promises continue to be perpetrated on would-be empowered teams, who end up as conventional groups, by supervisors and advocates of teamwork, who should, literally, know better (Buckley, Fedor, Veres, Wiese & Carraher, 1998).

13. Managing the Broken Promise

Our analysis of the broken promise suggests that it can be managed in at least two complementary ways. On the one hand, interventions can focus on the expectations of the would-be "empowerees." Logically, this might be achieved by *under*-promising on, and thereby potentially *over*-delivering on, the empowerment issue (Paul et al., 2000). On the other hand, and probably at the same time too, interventions can focus on improving communication skills in the supervisor (Gitel'makher, 1988).

13.1. Preparing empowerees

Ever since the early days of studying industrial change management, it has been known that the way in which change is introduced and explained, at the outset of any planned intervention, is critical for how the change effort will later develop (Marrow, 1948). A latter-day parallel of this maxim is the overly sanguine way in which jobs are often previewed to would-be recruits. This has led (in the literature on job selection) to a call, since Wanous (1973), for more down-to-earth preludes, i.e., more realistic job previews (Buckley, Fedor, Veres, Wiese & Carraher, 1998). In terms of tasks for teams, the literature on realistic job previews suggests that empowerment and teamwork, too, can be realistically, rather than sanguinely previewed (Phillips, 1998). Sanguinity, and over-inflated expectations about the realities of participation, is one of the key reasons why Pat Speirs' initiatives, at Spectrum Paints, failed prematurely.

A first step toward building more realistic expectations about teamwork is to create the equivalent of a job analysis around describing team tasks (Kichuk &Wiesner, 1998; for a first attempt at this, Stevens & Campion, 1999). Thus, a clear direction for future research, directed at managing the broken promise at a team level, is to develop new ways of measuring what teams actually can expect to do (Atkins & Fletcher, 2003). This seems to be absolutely fundamental to managing both team development and broken promises.

13.2. Preparing for supervisory resistance

In order to help us think about ways of preparing for supervisory resistance, we can re-apply Systems Theory (Chapter 1, this volume). Figure 5.3 depicts an interaction between the kinds of assumptions held by Stuart B and by his would-be empowerees on the Spectrum Paints shop floor.

At an implicit level, and in sharp contrast to Pat, Stuart's behavior reflects the assumptions of Theory X. Contextually, this latent belief in Theory X evokes for Stuart the threat of Motivational Gravity – Pull Down. To counteract this threat, Stuart initially espouses the rhetoric of empowerment, whilst at the same time continuing to practise existing habits of using carrot & stick. In short, he practices "pseudo-participation" (Purser & Cabana, 1998).

Through this kind of duplicity, from Figure 5.3, Stuart's Theory X attitudes probably leak out to the workers. They begin to sense some Motivational Gravity – Push Down. That kind of gravity is felt by workers to be a breach of promise in their new psychological contact (Paul et al, 2000). This in turn foments mistrust (Coyle-Shapiro, 2002). Unfortunately, that mistrust is inherited by Pat Speirs. When her reforms are prematurely withdrawn and Stuart's methods reinstated, the promise of empowerment is definitively broken, resulting in outright resistance and disengagement.

The very same resistance and disengagement now reinforce Stuart's sense of motivational gravity – pull down. As well however, they also reinforce Stuart's sense that the rhetoric of empowerment is just that – rhetorical. As a result of such reinforcements, Stuart returns more than ever to his original Theory X practices. He becomes ever more habituated to, reinforced in, and skilled at, practising pseudo-participation.

Overall therefore, one broken promise begets another. Just as supervisors who have invested themselves in a hierarchical system may feel threatened, betrayed and dis-empowered by teams, so too teams themselves can end up feeling betrayed by management. The net result of these twin broken promises, according to Figure 5.3, is likely to be industrial conflict and disruption.

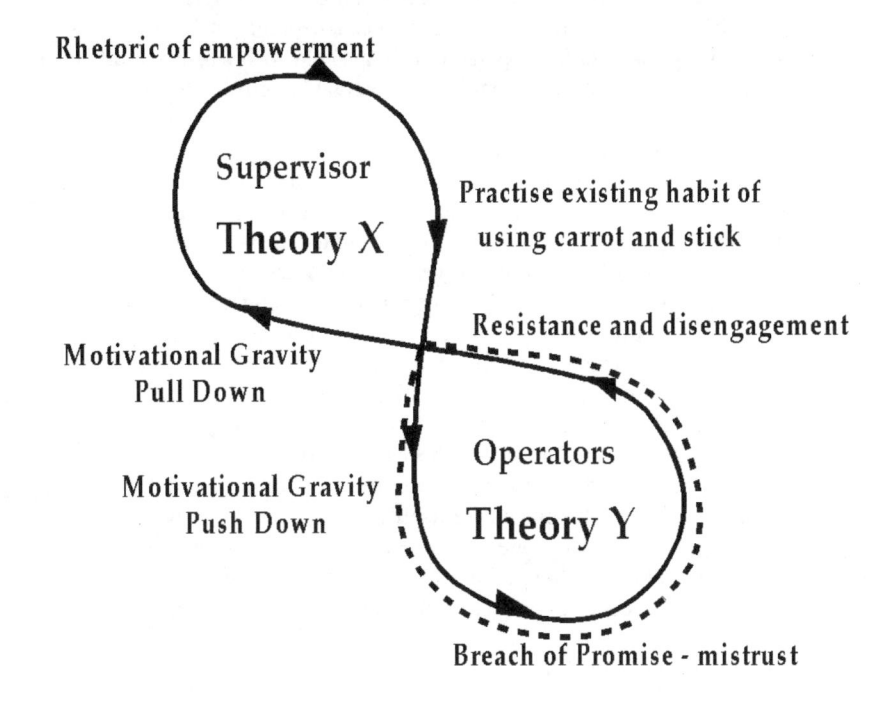

Figure 5.3 The dynamics of a broken promise (and for double loop learning)

Key:-

▬▬▬▬ Single loops (for supervisors and operators in teams alike)

■ ■ ■ ■ Double loop (for supervisors, acquired through experiential training)

13.3. A possible antidote to broken promises

Figure 5.3 suggests a possible intervention to counteract supervisory resistance to teams, thereby neutralizing a major component of the broken promise. Seeing ourselves as others see us, and experiencing the way our ideas impact on others, can be an empowering experience known as perspective taking (Nickerson, 1999). Perspective taking is empowering because it enables us to reflect critically on ourselves and on our behavior. A core feature of over-rehearsed routines for instance, such as the kind of hierarchical management practices that have been practiced by Stuart for decades, is that they undermine any capacity to reflect critically on their usage. Reflexivity is lost. Users become what Argyris terms skilfully unaware and skilfully incompetent (Argyris, 1998). Against this backdrop of being unable to break out of existing loops, Figure 5.3 indicates a theoretical way to reinstate the critical faculty: Enable Stuart to experience directly the *other*'s single loop, and thereby create, literally, an opportunity for *double loop learning*. As Figure 5.3 suggests, such opportunities for double loop learning may help to break the kind of vicious circles of power and disempowerment encountered at Spectrum Paints.

13.4. How, precisely, might it be done?

Our emerging research on communication networks indicates concretely how such double loop learning could be implemented (Boggs et al., 2003). Specifically, supervisors can be prepared for genuine teamwork by allowing them to go beyond the scripted "text" for empowerment – a rhetoric that they already know how to talk anyway – and, instead, experience first-hand the difference between fulfilled and broken promises: A broken promise can be experienced directly by participating as an "ordinary" decision maker in the communication networks exercises described, in Figure 5.2, as combining (A) and (B) into Boggs et al's (2003) condition (C). By experiencing directly condition (C), for example during preparatory training for team work, the comparative impacts of being on the receiving end of each of the three networks, in turn, can be judged directly by the supervisors themselves. This insight in itself is a relatively empowering experience, rather than an un-empowering one. The learning process, from Figure 5.3, would consist of literally adding a double loop to supervisors' procedural knowledge about the dynamics of fake versus genuine empowerment, and of power generally.

13.5. Some potential limitations

Adding a double loop to supervisors' experiences may facilitate reflexivity, and to that extent help to reduce their own implicit resistances to teamwork. Realistically, however, techniques of this nature will probably work better with supervisors who genuinely wish to shrug off their old implicit assumptions. Some supervisors will inevitably continue to believe in Theory X, and to that extent will remain a lost cause for this particular kind of change. In the final analysis therefore, and moving a little beyond Spreitzer's opening definition (p. 105), power and empowerment bring both rights and responsibilities for our own work behavior.

14. Conclusion

Understanding local group dynamics to help manage the globalized change that is teamwork represents an intrinsically glocal approach to managing behavior at work. Such glocality has in fact appeared and re-appeared throughout the chapter. Empowerment, for instance, is both a global idea and a local challenge, depending on the metaphors that people traditionally and spontaneously use to "make sense" of their lives in groups at work. Listening to the local, pre-existing mental models for teamwork the first step in a process of managing team development. Global virtual teams are living examples of how new, shared understandings, and micro-cultures, can arise even out of ultra-diversity. Behavior@work is thereby inherently fluid and flexible, without being overly malleable and manipulable. At a local level, teams are probably different from groups, and this means that theories are lagging behind the practice and talk about teams. The results of the lag include broken promises, which are partly driven by alternative forms of empowerment that stress individual accountability and maintaining the hard-earned privileges of power. Such lags, again, can in principle be managed – by taking the perspectives of all stakeholders more seriously. A reasonable way to do this, and one that is consistent with the general concept of empowerment outlined at the beginning of the chapter, is to share the perspective of others. This can be achieved, for example, by enabling supervisors to experience first-hand what it feels like to be dealt a broken promise. In that way, the cycle of preserving power at the expense of groups can perhaps be transformed from a vicious to a virtuous circle – in which power genuinely keeps its own promise to become expansive.

Acknowledgment

I am immensely grateful for the assistance of Richard Fletcher, Steve Atkins, and Jennifer Stillman, from the Albany Teams Project, for their intellectual assistance, advice, feedback, and moral support during the drafting of this chapter.

Chapter 6

Learning

> The measurement of multiple loyalties, multiple identities, multiple citizenship relating to cities, nations, regions, and ultimately the world, all promise to challenge the prior ways of thinking about immigration, ethno-cultural diversity, and work.
>
> *Source*: A. J. Marsella (1997: 43)
>
> Souls of nations do not change
> Merely stretch their hidden range
> As rivers do not sleep
> Spirit of empire runs deep.
>
> *Source*: B. Okri (poet)

In the previous chapter, we explored the glocality of broken promises in self-managed work teams. In the current, final chapter of the book, that exploration is extended. In the same way that we are free to view organizations as communities (e.g., of self-managed teams), we are free as well to view the wider communities in which they sit as forms of organization. From this extended perspective on work, just as teamwork is sometimes an over-promise to its constituents about empowerment, so too is the promise of a better life and a better job, tendered by some "countries Inc." who wish to capture the talents of skilled migrants for their economies (Atkins & Fletcher, 2003). These migrants' subsequent travel may broaden the migrants' own minds, thereby boosting their countries-of-destinations' levels of latent human capital (Inkson & Myers, 2002). Those potentials may not be fully realized, however, unless the same migration has an equally mind-broadening effect on the community *toward* which the migrants travel. Reducing that risk is the central issue for this chapter, and a crowning glocality for the book as a whole. Our starting point for analyzing that overall glocality is the concept of "boundary-less careers" (Arthur, 1994).

1. Boundary-less Careers

The historical origin of these vocational journeys has been traced to widespread corporate downsizing operations conducted during the 1980s and 1990s (Imel, 2001). According to Imel's overview of those changes, downsizing on a mass scale changed the way that people inhabiting the relatively prosperous economies of the world think about work – shifting it permanently away from "lifetime employment" to, instead, working more as a "free agent." Unlike their more "bounded" *pre*decessors in wealthier countries, and to some extent as well perhaps their contemporaries in poorer economies, those free agents are relatively unattached, cognitively, emotionally, and behaviorally, to any particular organization or employer (Stroh & Reilly, 1997). Instead, and without any specific loyalties to anchor them down, free agents will tend to move, as regards working, to wherever they can best metaphorically invest their own "career capital" (for an excellent review, Inkson & Arthur, 2001).

1.1. The focus of boundary-less careers

Initially, the idea that a career could and should be boundary-less focused not on national boundaries but rather at the level of firms within the same nation (De Fillipi & Arthur, 1994). Even the term *migration,* for example, was reserved predominantly for movement from one national locality to another (see, for example, Kraatz & Moore, 2002). Nonetheless, careers were visualized as knowledge-based, and boundary-less in the sense that knowledge acquisition is neither anchored nor bounded by a particular employment relationship (Bird, 1994). Under that form of psychological contract, a key to vocational and human capital development is being able to cultivate interdependent networks of human relations, and a resulting sense of community (Rousseau & Arthur, 1999). This particular skill is termed *knowing whom,* which implies that the skills apply in a context that is largely intra-communal, -national, and cultural (Eby, Butts & Lockwood, 2003). In Rousseau and Arthur's paper, however, and rather unusually for its time, it is suggested as well that communities can also be *inter*-national in kind, and to that extent, by logical extension, *inter*-communal.

1.2. Thinking beyond national boundaries

Since the new millennia, the meaning of boundary-less careers has, inevitably perhaps, extended outward from its earlier occupational and vocational base, to include as well career expansion that is, literally, geographical (Mahroum, 2000). The migration literature is a case in point. There, for example, it has been explicitly argued that the new worker is less constrained today than ever before by national borders and immigration limits (Naim, 2000). At a relatively micro level too, the literature on vocational development/behavior increasingly features new measures of "geographical barriers" to career progression (e.g., Donohue, 2003). In this theoretically "wide-open" jobs market, skilled migrants cluster not just in their own "local" urban centers, i.e., in a national movement toward the city; they also tend to cluster, from all over the world, in new "global" cities (Beaverstock & Smith, 1996). In that way, the new jobs market, as regards boundary-less careers, increasingly fits the vision of future work life portrayed for us in Marsella (above, 1997).

2. Boundary Conditions

As well as envisioning global cities, Marsella also speaks of competing identities, including the retention of local values and norms. For example, our concept of a broken promise, and of glocality generally, suggests that global migration will spur local backlashes (Chapters 1 & 5, this volume). By definition, these backlashes will be anchored predominantly in the communities in which migrants seek to build their new lives. Yet once again they can also only ever be understood by considering how they interact with the expectations that skilled migrants, themselves, bring with them to the new country and city. Those expectations, and the interactions they nourish, have already been studied, indirectly, through at least two particular overlapping literatures: (a) expatriate assignments (or EAs); and (b) acculturation.

2.1. EA research
2.1.1. *Preparation.*
The first thing we find in the literature on EAs is that pre-departure expectations about the assignment matter to the success of the travel experience. Specifically, adjustment during the assignment itself is related to whether the sojourner's expectations about the job are inflated or realistic (Searle & Ward, 1990). When pre-departure expectations are over-inflated, frustration may develop, hindering the sojourner's adjustment, and possibly the assignment itself (Cushner & Brislin, 1996). Emotional strains like these have been replicated across a variety of commercial and not-for-profit EAs, for example in overseas missionary assignments (Navara & James, 2002), and other "technical assistance" projects (Chapter 4, this volume). Just as we observed in teams therefore, the literature on EAs implies that migration, too, can be jeopardized by a broken promise.

2.1.2. *Adaptation.*
Most of the research on EAs has focused on the psychological and psychosocial characteristics and competencies of expatriates themselves. These characteristics range, for example, from the so-called "Big Five" in personality traits (Van der Zee & Van Oudenhoven, 2001), to the role of political competence in domains of work behavior, and social networking with the host community (Harvey & Novicevic, 2002). What relevance do these findings have for the question of skilled migration? Networking skills such as political competence (or P.Q.) are focused in this literature at the level of forging relations between communities. Skills like that link the literature on EAs directly to the literature on boundary-less careers, i.e., through the touchstone of 'knowing whom' (above, p. 134).

2.1.3. *Re-entry.*
The end of an overseas posting does not signal the end of an EA. This is because the assignee still has to negotiate cultural re-entry, back to their point- and country-of-origin (Ward & Kennedy, 1994). Like the outward, expatriation phase of an EA, cultural re-entry – or repatriation – has also been linked with broken promises. In one study, for instance, repatriates who found re-entry more difficult than expected experienced more distress when the discrepancy between their expectations and experiences was sharper (Rogers & Ward, 1993). More recent research has gone further, linking the anticipation of a difficult re-entry (e.g., due to lost career momentum) to a failure to learn and profit from the intercultural experience itself (Wong, 2001).

2.1.4. *Conclusion on EA research*
Taken together therefore, the literature on EAs warns about the risks of broken promises, both for work performance and career development as well. Outcomes like this have prompted cogent arguments that EAs are a relatively impoverished means of acquiring twenty-first-century career capital (Inkson et al., 1997). According to Inkson et al, a better way to earn career capital is through the 'OE,' for *Overseas Experience*. The OE in turn is a form of travel initiated by the

traveler rather than the employer, and is often undertaken, initially at least, with far less certainty than its OE counterpart (for details, Inkson et al, 1997). The point however is that OEs often resemble migration behavior, which connects it directly to the second of our relevant literatures.

2.2. Migration (and acculturation)

Unlike Inkson et al's work, most of the behavioral literature on migration has a relatively narrowed scope, on immigration rather than emigration; and on how *im*migrants adjust to their new community settings, not on what expectations drove them, as *e*migrants, to relocate in the first place (Carrington & Detragiache, 1999). The dominant perspective in this research has been psychological (Dovidio & Esses, 2001). Under Acculturation Theory, it is proposed that immigrants adopt differing styles of acclimatization, defined by the relative extent to which they identify with their culture-of-origin and/or their culture-of-destination (Berry, 1997). The core acculturation "styles" (*assimilate, segregate, and integrate* – by retaining a balance of both cultures) have been linked in turn to various psychological outcomes. Maintaining an integrated balance of identities, for example, has been linked to experiencing fewer psychological difficulties with resettlement as a whole (Ward & Rana-Deuba, 1999). Thus, successful travel through immigration has been linked to the formation of multiple identities (Marsella, 1997).

2.3. Critique of the acculturation paradigm

A major criticism of the acculturation paradigm is that it has not fully respected the role of social context (Rudmin, 2003). Rudmin's critiques have focused on the inherent circularity of using acculturation styles to "explain" acculturation behavior, rather than referring more directly to the social and community context in which acculturation behavior takes place. In job-hunting, for instance, a crucial factor determining whether the job hunter finds work that befits their talents is how the community of employers and organizations responds to their job-hunting efforts (Feather, 1993). Faced with criticisms like Rudmin's, the field has increasingly borrowed from the concept of vocational fit (Joerin, 2003). Under this model for example, research and theory have begun to look at the degree of fit between immigrant identity and expectations from the community (Bourhis, Moïse, Perreault & Senécal, 1997). Thus, according to an Interactive Acculturation Model (AIM), the style of "integration," on an immigrant's part, will work only if the *community itself* is largely pro-integrationist – rather than being either assimilation-focused or segregationist (Montreuil & Bourhis, 2001).

Models like the AIM are a significant advance on the earlier, and arguably over-psychologized models of acculturation behavior. Inherently too, of course, they respect the glocality of job-hunting processes and outcomes, because these are seen to result from interactions between global emissaries and local hosts. From the point of view of the current chapter this glocality - inhabited by job-seeking immigrants and their hosts together - signals the possibility of a broken promise. On the one hand, the host community may develop expectations about an economic "boon" that immigration "should" bring, only to have those expectations dashed because of perceived threats and insecurities; or because of an insufficient "fit" between their mental models (e.g., *assimilate*) and those held by the immigrants themselves (*integrate*). On the other hand, these very same processes, of fear and disappointment will, logically, fuel a *second* broken promise in the eyes of the immigrants themselves. Thus, and not unlike the escalation dynamics we observed in the field of teamwork (Chapter 5, this volume), we can expect in the field of migration not an unbounded integration, but instead the broken promise.

2.4. Where are migration promises most likely to be broken?

Although the skilled migrant is attracted to live in a new country and society, most of the opportunities to realize these aspirations, as well as those of their intended hosts, will take place in a particular contact zone – the contact zone of work. It is there, for example, that immigrant and host can expect to come into the closest, most proximal contact. It is also likely to be through labor at work, that the material means for a new life are expected to come. And it is at work, from the outset, that the key stakeholders in any migration process – immigrant and host alike – may have the highest expectations of each other. On multiple grounds therefore, the most likely crucible for promises to be met or broken is in the glocality of a workplace.

The behavioral dynamics of that glocality are in turn best illustrated, and brought to life, through a case narrative.

3. Utilizing the Immigrants We Already Have

The government's recent moves toward a better focused immigration policy targeted at skills in demand will be welcomed by most people as a contribution to stimulating economic development through the attraction of human capital. However, attracting good human resources into a country is only one step in the process. Unless there are good mechanisms for ensuring that those resources are properly encouraged, developed, and given the opportunities to contribute, the effort may be wasted.

I came to New Zealand in November 1996 because I wanted to have a better living environment as well as education for my son. I had qualifications and experience in the food industry in my native, prosperous Hong Kong. My English was not perfect, but was reasonably good. I thought I had a contribution to make.

I found it difficult. At first I applied for jobs at my previous, managerial level of employment, but no one seemed interested. Then I tried for clerical and sales jobs. Again, no one was interested.

I thought it might help if I gained some local qualifications. I enrolled for the Master of Management degree at Massey University and gained good grades. But it didn't seem to help my employment prospects.

In the four years since my arrival in Auckland, I have applied for over 100 jobs. Not only have I failed to get a single job, I have failed to get a single interview. It seems that Auckland employers can tell from reading my application that I am not up to working for them.

In view of my job-seeking difficulty, I was curious to find out whether other Asian people shared my experience. How many? And what were the causes? So, as my research project for my degree, I decided, with the help of my supervisor Professor Kerr Inkson, to conduct a survey of Asian immigrants in Auckland.

I contacted respondents through the many Chinese cultural groups in Auckland. Altogether, 226 people completed my survey – all of them were immigrants from Hong Kong, Taiwan, or Mainland China. The detailed results are in my research project report, which is currently under examination by Massey University [since gained]. Here, I can provide no more than a brief summary.

The results show that my experience was far from unusual. Even though 88 percent of my sample had been in New Zealand for three years or more, only 35 percent were in full-time employment. Another 13 percent had part-time employment. Ten percent were in self-employment, though this appeared to be mainly very occasional work. Forty-two percent were, like me, totally unemployed. Many of these will be drawing unemployment benefit, thereby draining rather than invigorating national resources. And yet this was never their intention in coming to New Zealand.

The 42 percent unemployment rate compares with only 6 percent national unemployment at the time of my survey (September, 2000). Great concern should be paid to this issue. Is it because immigrants are inexperienced or unskilled? This is unlikely. Over 80 percent of my sample had tertiary qualifications. Seventy-six percent had been in managerial or professional occupations prior to immigration to New Zealand. Many had worked as information systems professionals in their countries of origin – an area touted in New Zealand as experiencing major labor shortages.

Among those in employment, there was also ample evidence that their skills and experience were not properly recognized. Seventy-six percent of the total sample had held professional or managerial jobs in their countries of origin, but only 25 percent of those employed did so in their first job in New Zealand, and only 44 percent in their current job. Many professionally trained and experienced people were working in clerical and service jobs.

As far as income was concerned, no one in the sample was earning more than $60,000 per year, and nearly all those from Hong Kong and Taiwan were earning substantially less than they had in their own countries (although those from China's low-wage economy were, conversely, better off). More than 60 percent of the entire sample felt their skills were under-utilized in New Zealand.

How do we explain this bleak employment picture for Asian immigrants and the consequent waste of human resources?

When respondents were asked to report the main barriers to employment that they had found in New Zealand, the top-ranked explanation was, "lack of local work experience," followed by "language," "few jobs available," "overseas qualifications not recognized," "lack of market information," "over-qualified for the job market," "race," "cultural difference," "lack of self-confidence," "career transition late in life," "age," and "immigrant status."

Clearly, there are many important barriers, but several of them appear to represent prejudice by New Zealand employers rather than any inherent defect of immigrants. It is hard not to lose self-confidence when these barriers seem to defeat one so often!

Many employers believe that poor English ability and culturally different social skills are good reasons not to employ Asians, particularly as so many jobs these days require constant communication with customers and co-workers.

There is some justice in this argument. Some Asian people could try harder than they do to acquire "European" skill. But little positive encouragement is given to immigrants to upgrade in these areas. It is all too easy for the immigrants, after many rebuffs, to retreat into the comfortable enclave of their compatriots who speak the same language and share the same social norms. I believe that given a chance, many of us would surprise local employers through what we could do.

I believe Chinese people in general have a strong work ethic, stronger perhaps than the average New Zealander. For example, when I asked Hong Kong respondents in employment to report their average weekly hours of work in their own country, compared to their New Zealand job, they typically reported around 50 hours in Hong Kong, but only 30–40 in New Zealand.

According to my results, the main reason Chinese immigrants come to New Zealand is not employment. It is for educational opportunities for their children and a better quality of life. But these objectives are based on the assumption – encouraged by New Zealand authorities and immigration consultants – that gaining employment will not be a problem for skilled, experienced people who are prepared to work hard. Yet, 46 percent of the respondents indicated they had thought of leaving New Zealand to move to other countries or returning to their home countries that could provide them with better employment opportunities.

I have some questions for New Zealand's politicians and employers.

Of the politicians I would ask, why are you increasing the flow of immigrants into New Zealand when New Zealand has shown itself unable to utilize the immigrants it already has?

Of the employers I would ask, what is wrong with us? How can you tell from our applications that we are not up to working for you? What must we do to prove ourselves worthy?

New Zealand's politicians and employers do not owe us a job. They do owe us an explanation.

Source: Chan (2001, parenthesis added).

3.1. Case analysis of vocational broken promises

As the case above makes clear, the experiences of Kam Chan are by no means unusual among skilled migrants to New Zealand from countries within Asia. Nor, in fact, is the prejudice he describes confined to those from Asian countries (Harthill, 1998). In each case, the migrating group has been "sold" an image of a small and needy country "crying out for their skills [but who] then through either perceived language or cultural barriers just don't get a serious look in" (Shaw, 2001: 38, parenthesis added). This kind of barrier to boundary-less careers remains in place despite the fact that, once in a job, the so-called "difficulties" seldom actually materialize (Department of Labour, 2003). Nonetheless, migrants to New Zealand are currently more likely to find employment if they are willing to anglicize their name, minimize their accent, and accept a position with low status, i.e., under-employment (Oliver, 2000: 39).

It would be very unfair indeed to imply that "New Zealand Inc." is the only immigrant-hosting nation that behaves like this – i.e., breaks, however unintentionally, its own immigration promises. In Canada for instance, immigrants are reportedly under-employed, despite their (often) high educational achievements (Aycan & Koc, 1999). In Southern Africa too, there are reportedly attitudes of "suspicion" toward expatriates and immigrants from other African nations (The Economist, 2002). In Western Europe, prejudice is reported to remain against immigrants from the "Third World," despite the fact that, even once all resettlement costs are met, those immigrants bring a significant net economic gain to the host country (Craig, 2003). In the USA, when skilled workers do find work that fits their skills, their salaries can still fall below the market norm (Ruber, 2000). Overall therefore, in local communities around the world, boundary-less careers are, in fact, often blatantly bounded by prejudice and discrimination, creating what is now widely termed *brain waste* (Mahroum, 2000).

3.2. Theories of brain waste

Gathering evidence 'that' brain waste exists is one thing; explaining 'why' it happens, and continues to happen, is another. As the cursory review above indicates, prejudice and discrimination against skilled immigrants is actually quite "discerning:" Not all migrants experience it. Migrants originating from so-called "developing" countries, for instance, will often experience more boundaries than equally (or lesser) skilled counterparts originating from countries-of-origin perceived to be economically "developed" (Montreuil & Bourhis, 2001). Since the terms "developing" and "developed" are themselves discriminatory (all countries are developing!), a substantive question remains to be answered: "Why are some global migrants' careers more locally bounded than others?"

When framed glocally like this, the issue of brain waste starts to be illuminated by a range of behavioral theories.

3.3. Similarity Attraction Theory (or SAT)

SAT is perhaps the most obvious candidate for helping to explain and predict job selection biases against skilled immigrants. The central tenet of this well-known theory is that people are drawn more toward similarity than dissimilarity. SAT implies that migrants will tend to have more bounded careers not just because their country- and culture-of-origin is "developing," but also because their culture- and country-of-origin are felt to be too dissimilar by people in their culture-of-destination. In New Zealand, for example, as well as anglicizing names and minimizing accents, migrants may enhance their job prospects if they also have a European appearance – i.e., a surface identity that signals attitudes and values that are stereotypically close to the perceived (and equally stereotypical) norms of the "mainstream" (Oliver, 2000). In the job selection literature, it has been found that surface identity markers, like names, do influence selection decisions (Carr, Ehiobuche, Rugimbana & Munro, 1996). According to SAT, markers like the ethnicity of name function as they do, not simply because they signal underlying similarity in values and attitudes: Beneath this surface variable of similarity, according to SAT, there is a deeper, natural aversion to dissimilarity – a dissimilarity which renders the candidate more threatening, psychologically, to employers and selectors alike (Byrne, 1971).

3.4. Social Identity Theory (or SIT)

A somewhat different prediction about brain waste can be derived from SIT (Chapters 1 & 2, this volume). Tajfel's model of SIT suggests that in-groups will feel competitive antipathy toward out-groups that are in some sense comparable, i.e., toward groups that are, precisely, *similar* to the in-group (Glynn & Carr, 1999). Such inter-group comparison, motivated by insecure desires to "come out on top," would not make sense if the out-group was vastly different in skills or experience, either in a downward or upward direction. The outcome of competing with such groups is already a foregone conclusion; and in that sense completely uninformative about the abilities of self (Carr, 2003b). Against comparably similar groups, however, a favorable comparison stands to enhance positive differentiation, and to that extent helps boost collective self-esteem (Tajfel, 1978).

Examples of similarity-enabled fractiousness, or "horizontal hostility," are not difficult to find in contemporary societies (White & Langer, 1999). Within the "United" Kingdom for instance, out-group discrimination against other countries, and even especially from "within" the realm, is relatively easy to prime (Rutland & Brown, 2001). Likewise, in Canadian societies, the most salient comparison "other," in terms of out-groups, is often North Americans from the USA (Lalonde, 2002). In fact, even in the original minimal group laboratory studies, outlined previously in Chapter 2 (this volume, p. 43), the participating groups were drawn from the same school (and form), and to that extent were inherently not particularly "different." Instead, they were implicitly (and comparably) *similar* to each other.

Overall therefore, there is support, both theoretically and empirically, for the idea that, between groups, similarity *repels*. In the literature on job selection biases against skilled migrants, and brain waste, this potential effect has been termed *inverse resonance* (Carr et al., 1996). In Applied Mechanics, positive resonance occurs when waves of a similar frequency combine to produce an exaggerated positive amplitude – a whole that is greater, in a positive sense, than the sum of its parts. *Inverse* resonance, therefore, is a metaphor for the exact opposite of this, when groups with similar – and to that extent comparable, competing views – clash with one another to produce cross-group friction.

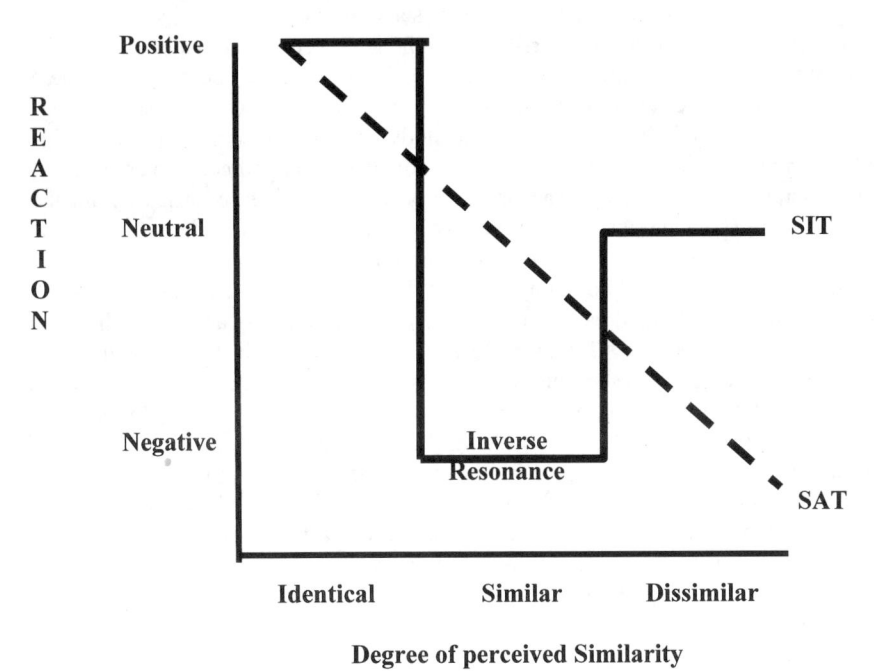

Figure 6.1 Hypothetical links between inter-group similarity and attraction

Source: Adapted from Carr et al. (1996)

The potential friction between similar out-groups is depicted graphically for us in Figure 6.1. As well as helping to visualize the inverse resonance effect, Figure 6.1 also illustrates a predictive contrast between SIT and SAT. SIT, through inverse resonance, predicts a positive preference for the most similar, i.e., socially identical home job candidate; a neutrality toward candidates from countries-of-origin that are radically dissimilar, and to that extent non-comparable; and a relatively easily aroused antipathy, or inverse resonance, toward candidates who are perceptibly "similar." From Figure 6.1, in contrast to this "jam spoon" curve predicted by inverse resonance and SIT, SAT predicts a more steady decline in preferences as perceived similarity between candidate and host employer, through their respective cultures, declines.

3.5. An empirical test of SIT versus SAT

A test of these two theories, in a context of boundary-less careers and job selection biases against skilled migrants, has been undertaken in East Africa (Carr, Rugimbana, Walkom & Bolitho, 2001). Like many other national economies today, countries co-located in East Africa have formed themselves into trade blocs – in this case, the East African Community (or EAC). Part of the rationale for such blocs, often implicit perhaps, is that they will permit and, indeed, actively facilitate the free movement of goods and labor within the free trade region (Rugimbana, 1997). Assumptions like this are clearly predicated, in a behavioral sense, more on SAT than on SIT. So we tested job preferences across a range of professions relevant to (and needed for) national development, within the region. These preferences were derived after presenting future managers with job selection scenarios (Chapter 3, this volume). In these scenarios, a diversity of candidates, were all equally balanced for the job in terms of KSAOs, relocation costs, etc. The only differences between them concerned their respective countries-of-origin.

Some of the key findings from the study are presented in Figure 6.2. This graphic compares mean rank preferences for equivalently skilled candidates from the "home country" (in this study, Tanzania); versus neighboring countries within the free trade zone (Uganda and Kenya); versus comparatively dissimilar countries-of-origin completely outside of the free trade zone ("the West"). As Figure 6.2 makes clear, the tenets of SAT did not completely hold. There is no gentle downward slope from Tanzania (the home/host country) down to the West – as we might have expected on the basis of SAT alone. Instead, the data display a clear jam spoon shape, an inverse resonance. This inverse resonance effect can be likened to the Motivational Gravity Dip (Chapter 3, this volume). With respect to regional development however, the inversion ironically happens with respect to candidates from the very countries-of-origin that were supposed to be *most* attractive to selectors, namely the countries-of-origin from within the trade bloc itself. Thus, Figure 6.2 supports SIT rather than SAT, brain waste rather than brain gain, and - rather than boundary-less careers - broken promises.

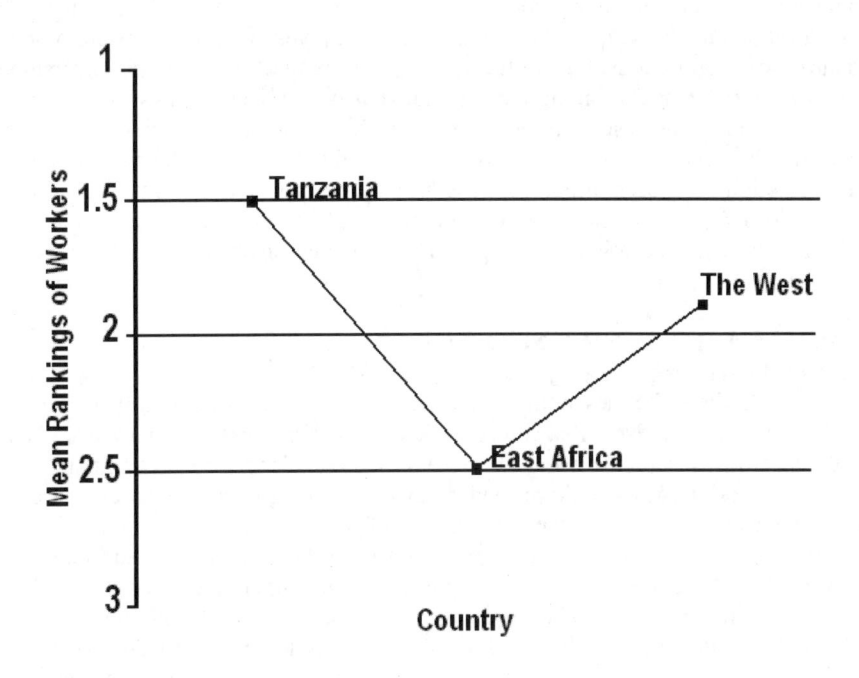

Figure 6.2 Inverse resonance in the EAC

Source: Carr, Rugimbana, Walkom, & Bolitho (2001)

3.6. Social Dominance Theory (or SDT)

The concepts of "developed" and "developing" countries clearly imply an economic hierarchy in migration preferences. To that extent, similarity and dissimilarity are only part of the story with regard to migration choices (Lim & Ward, 2003). Indeed, SIT and SAT are not the only theories with a potential bearing on Figure 6.2 (Carr et al., 2001). According for instance to Social Dominance Theory (or SDT), job selectors will often have an implicit mental model about which countries-of-origin are socio-economically dominant, and in that sense superior versus inferior to each other (Sidanius & Pratto, 1999). In particular, SDT suggests that candidates originating from countries-of-origin that are perceived to be "superior" will have a better chance of being selected, all else being equal, than their equally skilled fellow migrants, originating from countries-of-origin that are perceived to be "lower down" – such as merely "developing" – in their global mental template (Lemieux & Pratto, 2003). Thus, SDT may partly explain why some candidates in Figure 6.2 would experience brain waste, whilst others would enjoy more of a boundary-less transition to their host country.

SDT is often about the psychological and psycho-historical aspects of job selection biases. SDT is a prosaic form of Ben Okri's opening poem, with applications to contemporary job migration. As one study of labour mobility concludes, about the selection advantage being enjoyed by candidates from some countries-of-origin compared to others, "For reasons that are yet to be understood, the 'head start' of British immigrants has not vanished or even diminished over time, despite the fact that past migration from non-British source countries has already substantially diversified New Zealand's society and culture" (Winkelmann, 2000, p. 12). This kind of observation, which is broadly consistent with Kam Chan's story (above), is SDT personified. That personification, and its obvious potential relevance to brain waste, has recently led us to put SDT to an empirical test.

4. An Empirical Test of SAT, SIT & SDT
4.1. Conceptualizing a setting

The three theories outlined above have been tested conjointly in a study conducted recently in New Zealand (Carr & Coates, 2003, research by Coates). This study specifically capitalizes on the fact that New Zealand receives migrants from countries-of-origin whose cultures and standards of living range widely compared to the general cultural environment and quality of living in New Zealand as a whole. For example, in addition to hosting migration from Africa and Asia, and the South Pacific, New Zealand also receives migrants from its larger and wealthier neighbor Australia, with whom it shares numerous cultural and historical traditions, and – to that extent – similarity (Catley, 2001). Theoretically therefore, a study from New Zealand is able to sample, between countries-of-origin and country-of-destination, a representative range of perceived (a) similarities, (b) rivalries (inverse resonances), and (c) power differentials.

4.2. The study

The participants in our study were eighty Human Resource consultants and managers, with an average of 10 years' experience of job selection processes and procedures (Carr & Coates, 2003). These clear subject-matter experts were asked to estimate the probable rankings of job candidates from a wide range of actual countries-of-origin found amongst immigrants to and in the New Zealand context. The jobs we chose are in short supply in the New Zealand economy. This contextual feature minimizes any influence of Realistic Conflict (Chapter 2, this volume), which in this case would be purely economic competition for limited job openings. In our study, it is the people who are in short supply, not the jobs themselves (Taylor & Moghaddam, 1994). Hence the study focused relatively exclusively on (1) the perceived degree of similarity–dissimilarity between (a) New Zealand candidates and (b) the remaining candidates from various other countries-of-origin (Jones, 2000), and (2) the social dominances of those countries-of-origin relative to (a) New Zealand and (b) each other. The latter was defined in terms of perceived standards of living, educational services, health care, etc (after, Pratto, 2002; and Sidanius, 2002). As in the earlier study (Carr et al., 2001), the only ostensible variation between these candidates was their country-of-origin.

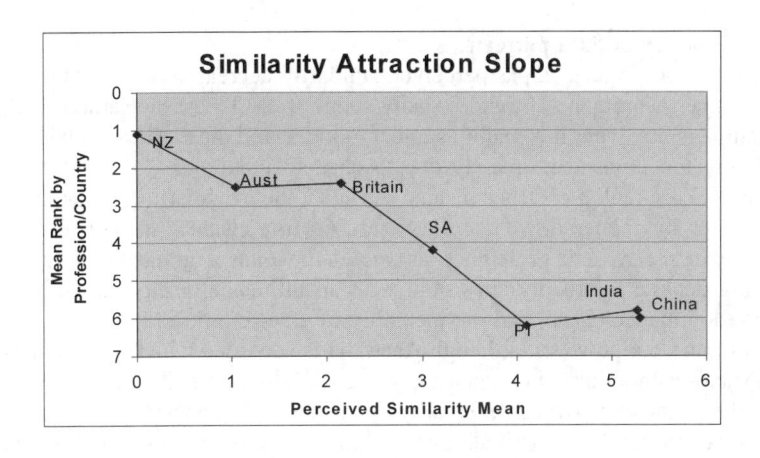

Figure 6.3 Mean rank preference as a function of perceived similarity

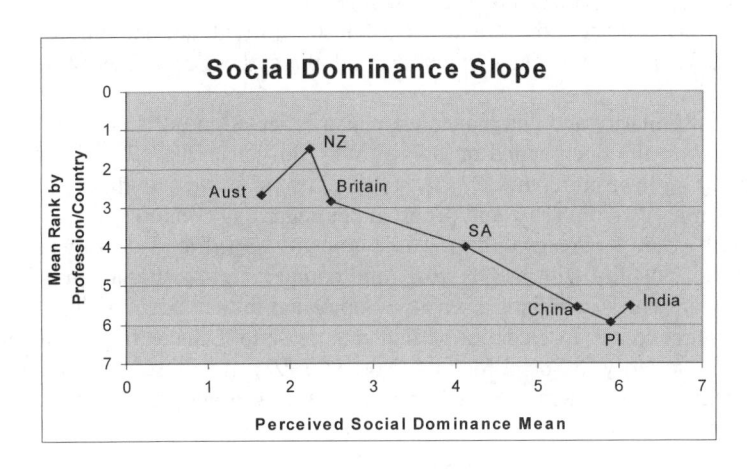

Figure 6.4 Mean rank preference as a function of perceived social dominance

Key

Aust = Australia; SA = Republic of South Africa; PI = Pacific Island nations

Source (for both figures): Carr & Coates (2003)

4.3. Summary of data pattern

From Figure 6.3, as perceived similarity decreases, so, too, does mean rank preference. That general trend broadly supports SAT. At the same time, however, the slope is not even; it is visibly subject to kinks and dips. These kinks and dips are probably too large to be merely due to chance fluctuations, given that the data in Figure 6.3 are rank preference means. As such, the irregularities in the curve suggest influences by moderating factors. Figure 6.4 for instance demonstrates a sloping decline in mean rank preference as *social dominance* gradually decreases. This sloping decline is broadly consistent with an influence being exerted by perceived social dominance (SDT) and the mentality of empire (above p. 133, Okri). As well from Figure 6.4 however, although Australia is accorded a higher standard of living, and socio-economic standing generally, New Zealanders still tend to be preferred for the jobs in question, over their equally skilled and competent counterparts originating from Australia. This particular irregularity signals perhaps the influence of an inverse resonance, and the comparison processes predicted by SIT (Carr & Coates, 2003). That kind of process might possibly explain why, in Figure 6.3, the candidates from Australia are visibly positioned in a slight trough, or motivational gravity dip (Chapter 3, this volume). In other words, Similarity-Attraction is moderated by comparisons in Social Identity.

Overall therefore, Figures 6.3 and 6.4 provide partial support for each of SAT, SIT, and SDT. They imply that all three theories influence selection bias conjointly.

Similarity and dominance were also reflected in our subject-matter experts' responses to the open-ended question, "Why do you think HR and Line Managers would have these preferences?" The top themes in answers to this question included (a) dissimilarity–similarity, and (b) prejudice regarding countries' levels of education and skill (Carr & Coates, 2003). The comments on (a) tended to focus not on any horizontal hostility with neighboring (and comparable) Australia. In New Zealand, the tension with Australia is a sensitive topic, and to that extent perhaps, more latent rather than explicit. Instead, our participants chose to focus on the "meta-contrast" of clear dissimilarity in Social Identity (Turner, 1991). An illustrative example of their comments is, "recruiters in NZ are biased toward races and ethnicities that are *similar* to their own, and discriminate against Pacific Island, Asian and Indian cultures" (SAT, emphasis added). Comments on (b) are typified by, "There is a high level of ignorance regarding education and qualifications in places like India and China" (SDT). Encapsulating (a) and (b), one subject matter expert reflected, "They feel that people who come from a *standard of living* most *similar* to New Zealand will fit into the environment more easily" (emphases added to highlight SAT and SDT, respectively).

4.4. Synopsis

Overall therefore, the data for this study, quantitative and qualitative, are broadly consistent with at least three possible behavioral bases for job selection bias. These bases are: *similarity–attraction; social identity; and social dominance*. Perhaps we can sum this up by saying that inter-group similarity is configured not just along one axis, of similarity and difference (i.e., 'the same as us - uncomfortably like us - comfortably like us - uncomfortably unlike us - exotic'). It is, as well, patterned hierarchically (i.e., 'up or down from us'). Multidimensionality like that would augment the risk of a broken promise, and to that extent raise the stakes on managing it more carefully.

4.5. Limitations

So far, we have only really scratched the surface of what lies behind some countries-of-origin being preferred over others, and the broken promises of "selective brain waste" that these discriminations imply. For example, we have not considered, in our cursory analysis above, the role of Social Facilitation Theory (or SFT) (Chapter 2, this volume). As we learned in that earlier review of SFT, social contact with immigrant groups is a necessary condition for acceptance to be nurtured, but will also facilitate any pre-existing prejudice too (Ying-Yi Hong et al., 2002): A crucial factor in deciding whether acceptance or rejection is facilitated is pre-existing attitude, either 'for' or 'against.' Thus, understanding facilitation processes as a whole is crucial for managing migrant selection fairly. Likewise too of course, facilitation processes include immigrants themselves. They as well bring differing attitudes and expectations with them to the new country. Precisely how those attitudes and expectations are socially facilitated, and thereby influence actual job-hunting behaviors has yet - in this writer's knowledge - to be seriously considered. Hence at a behavioral level, there are many areas still to be plumbed, concerning the motives for and against brain waste generally.

5. Implications for Policy and Practice

Even though the field of brain waste, at a behavioral level, is still formative, there are already some basic implications, for policy, to be drawn from Figures 6.3 and 6.4. As one example, candidates from the Pacific Island (or PI) nations were consistently found at the bottom end of the preference chain. This finding is broadly consistent with wider employment statistics already gathered by the New Zealand government (Ongley & Blick, 2002). Ongley and Blick's report suggests that despite recent rises in the number of qualifications and skills being earned and acquired by young Pacific Islanders, the gain is not being translated into actual jobs: "There are continuing disparities between the occupational and industrial distribution of the Pacific and total populations" (2002: 10). Figures 6.3 and 6.4 converge with this conclusion, and to that extent help to substantiate it. But as well, our data add value to the valuable message in the government paper, by suggesting reasons why this particular brain waste is occurring. The motivational gravity dips in both Figures 6.3 and 6.4 indicate that perceived (a) dissimilarity and (b) lack of social dominance are critical behavioral factors that require concerted recognition and management. Pointers like these will eventually one hopes help to design and implement policies that counteract better the barriers they apparently reflect.

On a more earthly, workplace plan, the data contained in Figures 6.3 and 6.4 have practical implications for training. In New Zealand at the present time, consultancy firms are beginning to respond to the brain waste issue. They are, for instance, providing training about the dynamics of brain waste, both to skilled migrants who are looking for jobs in their domains, and to job selectors in those industries and sectors. Some of this training may help to bridge the two parties, e.g., by raising selectors' awareness about unconscious stereotyping and discrimination. Approaches like that would be going beyond the traditional "helping and caring" approach adopted by some other agencies, in other locations (Cliff, 2000). Whilst the latter clearly have value and utility, they do not directly address one half of the brain waste issue – the attitudes and assumptions of the community of employers. By definition too therefore, they overlook the vital *interaction* between (a) the attitudes and (b) the perceptions of disappointed migrants themselves.

5.1. Content of training

The data in Figures 6.3 and 6.4 indicate that organizations in New Zealand need to find better ways of accommodating the diversity of people who are traveling toward them (Chapter 1, this volume, p. 1). Such needs are probably far from being unique in our global economy today. Consciousness-raising aside, and in addition to stock-in-trade interventions like structuring selection processes (Carr, 2003b), what kinds of training and preparation, exactly, do situations like this require? Clues can be found in the existing literature, for example on EAs. The latest reviews from that literature indicate that cross-cultural training genuinely helps to "make a difference" to travelers' adjustment and performance at work (Morris & Robie, 2001). Moreover, this literature is increasingly recognizing that intercultural encounters are not simply a "one-way street;" that both parties, traveler and host alike, need to learn to respect each other (Selmer, 2001). Selmer's technique is essentially a form of mutual gap analysis (Chapter 2, this volume, p. 36). He suggests that each party not only self-reports its own values, but that it also estimate the positions held by the other group. In this way, any discrepancies between each group's views of self and other can be identified, and made explicit, and to that extent perhaps accommodated and respected. Thus, this new approach focuses on (i) perspective taking (Nickerson, 1999) and (ii) enhancing behavioral flexibility (Marsella, 1997).

5.2. Experiential methods

Techniques such as Selmer's are consistent with an idea explored in the previous chapter of this book, i.e., learning to appreciate what it feels like to experience the broken promise in a workplace team (Chapter 5, this volume). In both cases, the perspective taking entails capitalizing on the power of human imagination. Because it straddles both macro and micro settings, this concept of using the human imagination, to prepare people for the travel they will encounter at work, is robust. A familiar example of this reliance is described in Fox (2003). According to Fox, a key way to make the impact of intercultural training more direct, experiential, real and relevant, is "through the creative use of literature" (2003: 99). This literature includes, for instance, novels that are written from different or similar-though-not-the-same cultural perspectives; and proverbs that are written from a bridging position of "worldly wisdom." The idea of using literature – whether it is fictional, factual, or factional – to improve behavior at work is, of course, embedded in the study of work behavior generally, including the factual writing (and imaginative reading) of this book itself.

5.3. A linking theory

What seems to link all of the ideas in this chapter together is the concept of organizational learning (Murray & Donegan, 2003). A central element in Organizational Learning Theory is the proposition that adopting different, non-routine perspectives on work issues, both raises awareness of alternative solutions to current issues and – in addition – improves work performance (Murray, 2003). A central process by which this change of perspectives occurs is through *double loop learning*. As we saw in Chapter 5 (this volume, p. 129), the essence of double loops in general is the acquisition of a wider and reflexive, more self-critical perspective on pre-existing mental models for working.

5.4. Facilitating double loop learning

Migrants have an inherent potential to help spark double loops. One of the primary catalysts for creating double loops, according to the literature, is the presence of minority points of view, and minority influence. Minority points of view are, by definition, different from, and often critical of, the dominant, "mainstream" view. Skilled immigrants are, ipso facto, representatives of minority groups, and emissaries for different perspectives generally. As such, they potentially have much to offer as catalysts to work group creativity. In the literature on sojourning for instance, the cross-cultural experiences associated with travel tend to bolster both the traveling minorities' creativity (Gurman, 1989) and their emotional resilience (Goldstein & Smith, 1999). Similarly in the literature on OEs (above), it has been argued that the act of traveling to, and living in different countries and working in a diversity of jobs – by definition as a member of the minority – adds significantly to the levels of resilience-under-adversity and creativity available to individuals and work groups alike (Inkson et al., 1997). In the literature on immigration per se, we have already seen that the net impact of influxes in skilled labor, once all infrastructure and other resettlement costs to social services have been computed, tends to be positive (above p. 140, Craig, 2003). According to Menon (2003), this added value, in the occupational sphere, derives in part from the obligatory repeated perspective taking that being an immigrant, and a minority, requires (i.e., compared to the relative safety of being in the "majority").

There is specific theory and research to support the idea that minorities can change and innovate workplace groups and teams. The essence of Minority Influence Theory (Moscovici, 1980), also termed *Dual Process Theory* is that (1) majorities tend to socially facilitate already well-rehearsed and so conventional approaches to group problem solving (Chapter 2, this volume); but that (2) minorities tend to facilitate a norm of originality, and to that extent will generate more novel and creative solutions to work-group issues (Moscovici, 1976). According to Moscovici, minorities that behave as Devil's Advocates will attract attributions of confidence and courage, sneaking admiration, and – eventually – recognition and acceptance. The road to this recognition will not however be easy. First they will need to secure an opportunity to speak and be heard. Second they must be consistent in their behavior, by which Moscovici means assertive and vocal. And third, despite any admiration and intrigue that their minority status and courage wins, they will still encounter hostility. Any positive impressions they create, for example, will for a time be largely covert, including being sometimes implicit. The duplicity happens, according to Moscovici, because the majority at first finds identifying with any deviant out-group - either publicly or in private, consciously to oneself - aversive. Thus minority influence begins with outright rejection; then transits to covert acceptance; and only finally externalizes into an open acceptingness to fresh perspectives (Wood, Lundgren, Ouellette, Busceme & Blackstone, 1994).

5.5. Minorities at work: The evidence

Initially, the literature on minority influence was focused on wider social issues, such as pollution and feminism. Lately however, the research has moved increasingly closer to the influence of minorities at work – for instance in global workplace teams (McLeod et al., 1997), and in multicultural work settings generally (Schippers et al., 2003). Even when they are wrong – provided they are critically consistent – these minorities are capable of stimulating both creativity in the group (Van Dynne & Saavedra, 1996) and more successful problem solving (Nemeth & Rogers, 1996). This positive impact is sometimes attenuated by the majority's cultural positioning – both at the societal level (Ng & Van Dyne, 2001a), and at the level of individual differences (Ng & Van Dyne, 2001b). For example, minority influence is more likely when the majority positions itself as relatively horizontal and individualist (Figure 2.1). That kind of position, it could be argued, is likely to be identified with, by the majority, in a number of local settings toward which people today are migrating.

5.6. How could "migrant minority influences" work?

A hypothetical model for this process is presented for us in Figure 6.5. Each of the various spheres (or single learning loops) in the diagram can be imagined as being potentially connected to any of its three counterparts on the opposite side of the model. Via those imagined linkages, which we are about to describe verbally, the model is intended to link different modes of majority thinking (in this case by local employers) to different phases of minority thinking (in this case by global immigrants) – and vice-versa. The model being proposed in Figure 6.5 is, therefore, both interactive and glocal.

5.7. Key forms of behavior exhibited by the majority

From Figure 6.5, and according to our brief review of Dual Process Theory, the local *majority* (on the left) will tend to run through a broad sequence of reactions to the presence of "outsiders," and the minorities they are perceived to represent, in their *locality*. These reactions may begin with *outright rejection*, or antipathy, and thereafter can progress, in developmental time, from *covert acceptance* through to *open acceptance*. For the progression depicted in Figure 6.5 to happen, according to Moscovici (1980) and Nemeth and Rogers (1996), the majority not only needs minorities, but also needs them to behave in certain ways. Those behaviors, that the minority must display in order to render the majority more tolerant, imaginative and creative at work, are depicted on the right-hand side of Figure 6.5.

MAJORITY   MINORITY

Outright Rejection   Contact Zones   Assimilate & Comply

Covert Acceptance   Backlash Reactance

Open Acceptance   Integrated Balance

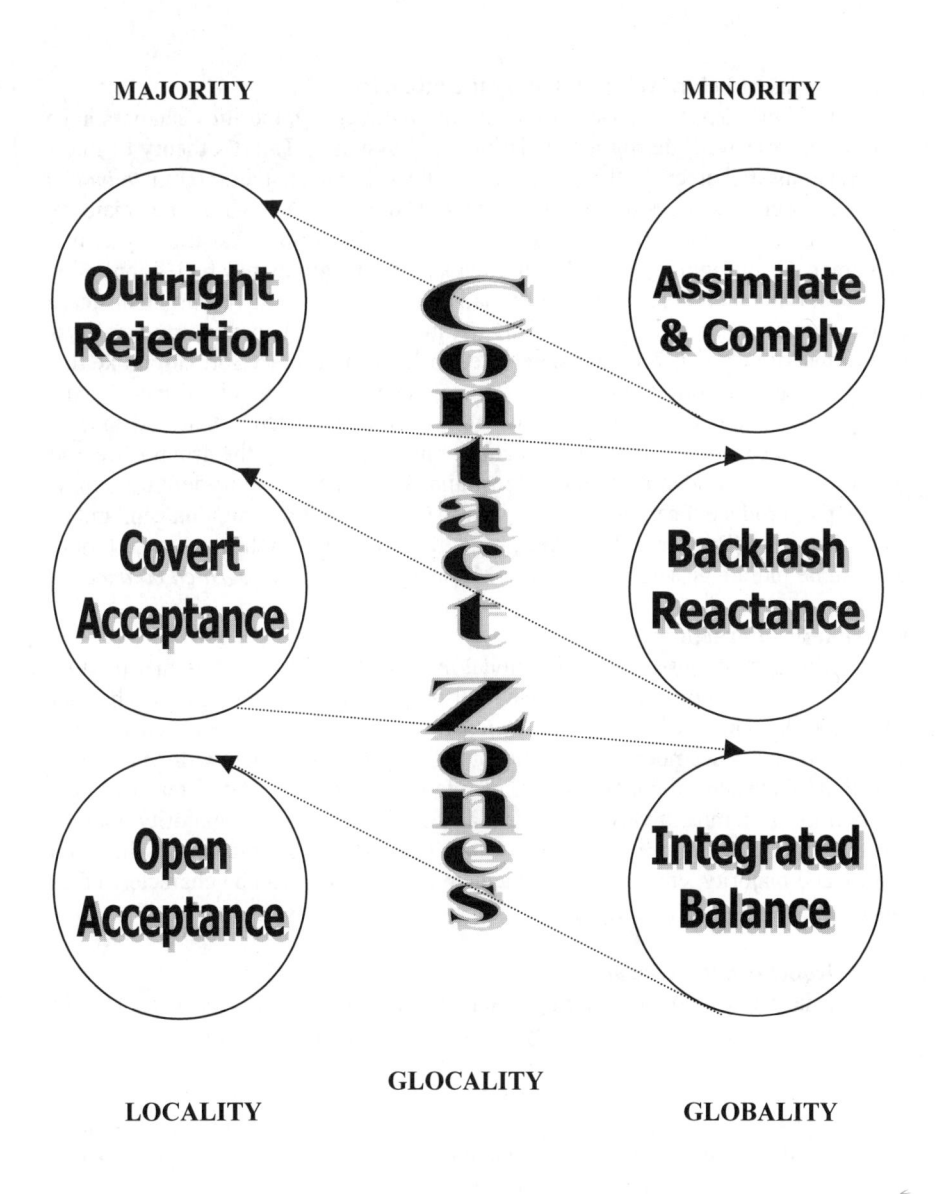

LOCALITY   GLOCALITY   GLOBALITY

Figure 6.5 An integrated perspective on global travel at work

Note

These are relatively broad, recurring forms of positioning only. They are not rigidly programmed dispositions, nor sets of dispositions.

5.8. Key forms of behavior exhibited by the minority

In Figure 6.5, the phases of identity through which minorities can pass have already been reviewed, during a foundational discussion of Tajfel's theory of intergroup relations (Chapter 1, this volume, pp. 8/9). Firstly, an immigrant *minority* might consider the possibility of *assimilate and comply* with the majority mainstream, and to that extent choose *globality*. If that form of positioning is met with perceived 'outright rejection,' as it often is, then the group may be led for a time to *backlash reactance*. Reactance is essentially anti-conformity, involving in this case the transformation of previously negative features of social identity into positive qualities that are cherished in an exaggerated fashion. Reactance formation like this actually belies low self-esteem: The form of identification is still driven by the majority – what we 'are' is defined by what we are 'not.' Once that bad faith is exposed however – for example, by insightful minority leaders – the group is freer to re-determine its own identity without constraint from others. The re-definition may, for example, produce a sense of collectivism balanced against individualism, and of course vice-versa (Brewer, 1993). Thus, what may emerge from the process in Figure 6.5 is a more pluralistic sense of identity (Marsella, 1997), and *integrated balance*.

5.9. Dynamic interactions

The dynamic essence of the model presented in Figure 6.5 is that the two key perspectives, minority and majority, will progressively interact with each other (Ward, 2003). There will from Figure 6.5 be a *"contact zone"* between the two parties (Hermans & Kempen, 1998). In that zone, specifically, there will be repeated interactions between minority points of view that are by definition (through migration itself) comparatively globalized, and on the other hand a majority point of view that is by definition comparatively localized. Thus, the interactions between minority and majority, envisaged with the help of our model, can be characterized as a *glocality*.

5.10. Welcome to your Glocality

One useful way of thinking about the interactions between each half of Figure 6.5 is through the lens of the systems dynamic termed *escalation* (Chapters 2 & 4, this volume). According to this dynamic for example, positioning to 'assimilate and comply,' by a global minority, may actually reinforce rather than rectify the local majority's position of 'outright rejection.' Potential conduits for this hardening of attitude, by the local majority, could include for instance perceived dissimilarity and/or threats to social dominance by the host culture over the candidates' culture-of-origin (Carr, 2003b). Even where there is perceived similarity between groups, and/or parity of social dominance, there may as well be inverse resonance - thereby reinforcing a same escalation dynamic (Senge, 1992).

5.11. Priming for change

According to Moscovici, moving the majority "forwards," from a position of overt rejection, may actually require the minority to become more truculent – to display a consistent 'backlash reactance' (Moscovici, 1980). Faced with that kind of challenge, according to Dual Process Theory, the majority can at least start to move beyond outright rejection, and begin to actually ponder, even if only implicitly at first, that the minority has a point of view, and that their own, by definition, can be questioned.

5.12. Change

The above 'covert acceptance,' that change in the status quo is possible, because the minority has a legitimate point of view, is sufficient to "cool the mark" with respect to previously negatively charged majority–minority relations. From this point onwards, the minority too, itself, is freed up to consider all perspectives and to arrive at a more balanced consideration of them as a whole. Attaining a state of 'integrated balance' enables the local majority to admit to themselves more easily that the minority does actually add value to the group as a whole. This may help to stimulate in and from the majority an 'open acceptance' and recognition of the value of immigrant minorities – an externalization. Through these visible changes on both sides, there can be a positive escalation between majority and minority, of the kind already observed in the literature on work group creativity (Nemeth & Roger, 1996).

5.13. Overall process

To sum up the dynamic presented in Figure 6.5, by moving through the six phases interactively, minority and majority groups can, in principle, "staircase" each other toward a greater recognition of diversity. With that greater recognition of each other's perspective, in principle, the model in Figure 6.5 predicts, on the coattails of Organizational Learning Theory, an enhanced likelihood of organizational learning, morale, and job performance. Of course, the model in Figure 6.5 has significant gaps in it. Whether immigrants themselves actually want to become what Moscovici terms 'consistent' (or vocal and assertive) is a moot point at this stage. So too is government funding to provide skills training in job hunting, and (for employers) on how to make better and fairer job selection and placement decisions. To some extent, these measures are beyond the scope of this book, and are awaiting implementation rather than academic discussion. The essential point though remains - offering a model to begin thinking about the questions in a micro, seriously behavioral way.

6. Beyond Migration

Our opening metaphor of travel suggests that the dynamics of brain waste are not restricted to immigration. The power imbalance depicted in Figure 6.5 can be assumed to be relevant, in principle, to all forms of travel at work – from brain waste to organizational mergers (Chapter 1, this volume). In current merger technology for instance, two groups are brought together, often literally, as part of the merger process. Thereafter, decisions are made about internal placements, and, more generally, the allocation of resources (promotions, etc.) that are not unlike their migrant labor market counterparts. Before, during, and after this process, diagnostic techniques such as Merger Potential Analysis (Chapter 2, this volume, p. 36) make implicit assumptions about these groups. For instance, it is implicitly assumed that similarity will make the merger easier rather than more difficult. Yet Figure 6.5 and our earlier analyses in this chapter suggest that this assumption, of similarity–attraction, is risky. According to SIT for instance, groups that are similar may actually resonate *inversely* with each other, and thus stall prematurely in the model depicted in Figure 6.5. An extant literature on mergers, reviewed in Chapter 1 (this volume), focuses on cross-sectional, survey snapshots. Together, these snapshots present a confusing panoply of contradictory reactions, with minority and majority reactions alike ranging from outright acceptance to outright rejection of the merger itself. Figure 6.5 resolves these apparent contradictions by placing them on a dimension of time, and within a glocality of interacting and transiting identities.

Other applications of this model in Figure 6.5 can be derived and assessed by considering each of the major varieties of glocality introduced throughout the chapters in this book.

7. A Synthesis
7.1. Chapter 1: Glocality

In the opening chapter, it was argued that the people who write about people at work, often stereotype each other and their subject matter. In the print media, the US-based majority presents its own locality as a globality, whilst the other localized minorities present their Indigeneity as a globality. As a result of this standoff, the study of work stands still. It remains unresolvedly, unnecessarily, and unproductively contested. According to Figure 6.5, and as we suggested in Chapter 1 itself, moving beyond this point requires a response from the majority. Rejection may prime reactance, but reactance can also help to prompt the majority, implicitly at least, to begin its own process of reflection. Once this "unfreezing" has begun, the global minority too is free to move on and define itself in a more detached way. This in turn enables the majority to begin externalizing its own (up till now covert) changes, and to face up to its own implicit biases. Thus, rather like a good merger or migration, the study of work behavior eventually requires a reflexive recognition of multiple forms and positionings of identity (Marsella, 1997).

7.2. Chapter 2: Culture

In Chapter 2 of the book we examined more closely the concept of culture at work. Perhaps the central point of the chapter as a whole is that cultural identity shifts from one form of identity to another, even though the core constructed features of the cultural landscape itself – like those features depicted in the Values Grid for instance – do not themselves disappear or cease to serve as navigational aids. Since people at work can and do adopt multiple positions on the culture-scape, they are, in principle, capable of weaving a tapestry of cultural identities within the same organization, e.g., during mergers and through employing skilled immigrants. Figure 6.5 reflects this capacity for variegation by giving a developmental perspective on cultural identity. In that perspective, minorities and majorities are each likely to be rejected at different combinations of positions, but accepted at others. Thus, minorities can attract outright rejection under one set of circumstances, and yet inspire reflexivity at the next.

7.3. Chapter 3: Achievement

The particular glocality discussed in Chapter 3 is that of how relatively individualized (and globalized) forms of achievement interact with their more socialized (and localized) counterparts. A metaphor of "motivational gravity" was introduced, to capture some of the dynamics between dominant and less dominant groups and individuals, in the context of a motivational gravity grid. Figure 6.5

readily assimilates this concept of motivational gravity. Push Down is exerted, for instance by majorities during both outright rejection and - to a lesser extent - covert acceptance, whilst Pull Down is pro-actively exerted by minorities during backlash reactance. Assimilate and comply, meanwhile, can be viewed as a form of Push Up, whilst externalization (open acceptance) reflects a decision to Pull Up. Chapter 3 also discusses a key prospect for attempting to manage an eternal dialectic at work, between individual and social achievement. Specifically, striking a *balance* between social and individual achievement was suggested, for example by respecting traditional metaphors for how work gets organized. Thus, Chapter 3's discussion on managing achievement is consistent with the development of what Figure 6.5 terms (i) integrated balance and (ii) open acceptance.

7.4. Chapter 4: Pay

The essence of Chapter 4, which deals with issues of pay and remuneration, is that pay is relative, and that this relativity positions individuals and groups alike into stratified hierarchies, which they will both defend and resist. Through that process of stratification, pay diversity fosters motivational gravity (Push Down and Pull Down). Stratified positioning like this is readily incorporated into Figure 6.5. In the case studies about pay, for example, we learned that pay diversity fosters antipathy, both rejection (e.g., denigration of hosts' abilities) and reactance (against the perceived injustices of expatriate pay). Our suggestions for managing pay diversity, too, focused on more equitably balancing the available resources for reward amongst the various pay parties. To that extent from Figure 6.5 the recommendations centered on working toward integrated balance and open acceptance. Consideration was also given to an idea called "variegated pay", in which pay diversity becomes so intense that there is no longer any recognizable "majority" to speak of, at a perceptual level. A potential risk with this metaphor concerns the maintenance of upward momentum. Employees who "have a little" success may then "want a little bit more," and in the process become frustrated and disaffected. A more general risk, even if relatively remote, is that total variegation leads to an equally total multitude of divisions. In either of these two events, the dynamics of Figure 6.5 will still continue to be relevant.

7.5. Chapter 5: Power

The idea of variegated pay – and in effect making ultra diversity the microcultural norm in pay relations ("We're all minorities together!") – is inherently applicable also to the idea of (global, virtual) teams. Perhaps the central glocality pinpointed in Chapter 5, on teams, is that what differentiates a "team" from a "group" are their shared assumptions about how teams (a globality) translate into familiar mental models (localities). Specifically for example, we discussed how the concept of "empowerment" has ironically been pedaled as an answer to workers' dreams, when in reality it is often experienced, by the workers themselves, as a faddish broken promise. At the root of this broken promise is possibly reactance. This happens, firstly, through rejection by supervisors who are implicitly (and illogically) asked to disempower themselves; and, secondly, because initially assimilatory workers sense an inequitable attempt to deceive them into producing "more for less." The resulting reactance provokes a clash between more powerful (majority) and less powerful (minority) groups. According to Figure 6.5, the introduction of self-managed work teams should more realistically be pre-viewed as a probably stormy progression from rejection and superficial assimilation of teamwork, through to – potentially – more integrated, balanced and openly accepting ways of working. Thus supervisory power, for example, can be construed as integratively expansive rather than some finite "commodity" that is "handed down" (in a poison chalice) to overworked and underpaid shop floors.

7.6. Chapter 6: Learning

Within this chapter itself, we began by considering the situation of global migrants, whose boundary-less careers are often anything but that. The essential elements in these bounded careers are human factors in the workplace. Those human factors contradict and break the promise of a new and better life, made through points systems and other incentives that are offered as inducements by skills-hungry "Nations Inc.," seeking to benefit from a notional brain gain. Once skilled immigrants arrive in their country- and city-of-destination however, they are not always accepted as bona fide candidates for the jobs that suit their talents, and for the jobs that were promised in the first place. Beliefs in social dominance, for example, may block their way. Such beliefs are clearly signalled in Figure 6.5. Those same kinds of belief may also operate at micro levels, for example during organizational and departmental mergers, and the exact opposite process, organizational extensions /expansions of those departments (e.g., when "HQ" opens new "branch" offices in a new region, either domestically or internationally). Like brain waste, organizational mergers, extensions and other forms of work change each feature majority–minority relations. Whether these relations happen to be societal, inter-organizational or intra-organizational, the minority and majority can always experience a broken promise. Ironically, according to our model, this broken promise may also potentially empower each group to begin moving through the phases depicted in Figure 6.5, eventually assisting both (and the overall community itself) to grow, develop, and learn.

7.7. Caveats

The dynamics in our model entail a twin process of raising awareness about the glocality of travel, and vicariously experiencing that glocality – its diversity of perspectives – so that they themselves become inputs to decision-making and inputs to work action. Through those means, the mentality of glocality may assist both the globalist and the localist to come a little closer together, to experience a genuine double loop (Nemeth & Roger, 1996). Yet we should not overestimate, nor over-promise, on the capacity of such double loops to actually change work behavior. Those changes, as Chapter 5's case study (Spectrum Paints Ltd) all too clearly illustrates, are never easy. Without an awareness of the other's perspective however, attempts to pluralize the workplace will surely stumble and fail. To that extent, appreciating glocality can be considered as a first, vital step toward more integrated and open ways of working generally.

8. Conclusion

Our journey in this book began with a metaphor, so perhaps it is fitting to end it with one as well. Give us a hammer, so the saying goes, and the rest of the world will look like a nail. In that sense, glocality, and indeed even the escalation dynamics implied by Figure 6.5, are merely hammers for "nailing" work behavior. Just like any other theory or concept, they are stereotypes – stereotypes that have both information-managing uses and, as well, prejudice–encouraging limitations. Against these costs, it has been argued consistently throughout the book that one particular hammer – the concept of glocality and the dynamic systems which it implies – is probably less "hard" on its proverbial nails – work behaviors and the people who perform them – than its two main predecessors (globality and locality). Those predecessors, and the combined foibles that they arguably promote, have been delimited in Figure 6.5. If glocality helps to see beyond their boundaries, plus suggests new ways of overcoming them as barriers to human development, then the book will have done its work.

References

Adams, J. S. (1965). Inequity in social exchange. *Advances in Experimental Social Psychology, 2*, 267–99.

Adams, J. S. & Rosenbaum, W. B. (1962). The relationship of worker productivity to cognitive dissonance about wage inequities. *Journal of Applied Psychology, 46*, 161–64.

Adigun, I. (1997). Orientations to work: A cross-cultural approach. *Journal of Cross-Cultural Psychology, 28*, 352–55.

Adkins, C. L. & Naumann, S. E. (2001). Situational constraints on the achievement–performance relationship: A service sector study. *Journal of Organisational Behaviour, 22*, 453–65.

Aiello, J. R. & Douthitt, E. A. (2001). Social facilitation from Triplett to electronic performance monitoring. *Group Dynamics, 5*, 163–80.

Alach, P. & Inkson, K. (2003). *Temping: A study of temporary office workers in Auckland.* Albany and Palmerston North, New Zealand: Labour Market Dynamics Research Programme.

Albert, R. D. (1996). A framework and model for understanding Latin American and Latino/Hispanic cultural patterns. In D. Landis, & R. S. Bhagat (Eds.), *Handbook of intercultural training* (2nd edition) (pp. 327–48). Thousand Oaks, CA: Sage.

Ali, A. J. (1999). The evolution of work ethic and management thought: An Islamic view. In H.S. R.Kao, D. Sinha & B. Wilpert (Eds.). (1999). *Management and cultural values: The Indigenisation of organizations in Asia* (pp. 139–151). New Delhi: Sage.

Alinsky, S. (1972). *Rules for radicals.* New York: Vintage Books.

Ambrose, M. L., Seabright, M. A. & Schminke, M. (2002). Sabotage in the workplace: The role of organisational injustice. *Organisational Behaviour & Human Decision Processes, 89*, 947–65.

Anderson, N. H. (1974). Cognitive algebra: Integration Theory as applied to social attributions. *Advances in Experimental Social Psychology, 7*, 1–101.

Anderson, N. H. (1981). *Foundations of Information Integration Theory.* New York: Academic Press.

Anderson, R. & Alexander, R. (1995). Innovate to grow. *Management: The magazine of the AIM, October*, 8–10.

Argote, L., Turner, M. E. & Fichman, M. (1989). To centralise or not to centralise: The effects of uncertainty and threat on group structure and performance. *Organisational Behaviour and Human Decision Processes, 43*, 58–74.

Argyle, M. (1989). *The social psychology of work.* Harmondsworth, UK: Penguin.

Argyris, C. (1998). A conversation with Chris Argyris: The father of organizational learning. *Organizational Dynamics, 27*, 21–33.

Argyris, C. (1999). Tacit knowledge and management. In R. J. Sternberg & J. A. Horvath (Eds.), *Tacit knowledge in professional practice: Researcher and practitioner perspectives* (pp. 123–40). Mahwah, NJ: Lawrence Erlbaum Associates.

Aronson, E., Willerman, B. *& Floyd, J. (1966).* The effect of a pratfall on increasing interpersonal attractiveness. *Psychonomic Science, 4*, 227–28.

Arthur, M. B. (1994). The boundary-less career: A new perspective for organisational inquiry. *Journal of Organisational Behaviour, 15*, 295–306.

Ashford, S. J. Lee, C. & Bobko, P. (1989). Context, causes, and consequences of job insecurity: A theory-based measure and substantive test. *Academy of Management Journal, 32*, 803–29.

Ashkanasy, N. M. (1994). Automatic categorisation and causal attribution: The effect of gender bias in supervisor response to subordinate performance. *Australian Journal of Psychology, 46*, 177–82.

Ashkanasy, N. M., Broadfoot, L. E. & Falkus, S. (2000). Questionnaire measures of organizational culture. In N. M. Ashkanasy, C. Wilderom, & M. F. Peterson (Eds.), *Handbook of organizational culture* (pp. 131–46). Thousand Oaks, CA: Sage.

Ashkanasy, N. M. & Falkus, S. (2003). The Australian enigma. In J. Chokar, F. Brodbeck, & R. J. House (Eds.), *The GLOBE research project: Country anthology* (in press). Thousand Oaks, CA: Sage.

Ashkanasy, N. M. & Holmes, S. (1995). Perceptions of organizational ideology following merger: A longitudinal study of merging accounting firms. *Accounting, Organizations, and Society, 20*, 19–34.

Ashkanasy, N. M., Trevor–Roberts, E. & Earnshaw, L. (2001). The Anglo cluster: legacy of the British Empire. *Journal of World Business, 37*, 28–39.

Ashkanasy, N. M., Wilderom, C. P. M. & Peterson, M. F. (Eds.). (2000). *Handbook of organizational culture and climate*. Thousand Oaks, CA: Sage.

Atkins, S. G. & Fletcher, R. B. (2003, July). *I/O psychology and skill recognition*. Fifth Australian Industrial and Organisational Psychology Conference, Melbourne.

Atkinson, J. W. & Rayner, J. O. (1974). *Motivation and achievement*. Washington, DC: Winston.

Austin J., Kessler, M. L., Riccobono, J. E. & Bailey, J. (1996). Using feedback and reinforcement to improve performance and safety of a roofing crew. *Journal of Organisational Behaviour Management, 16*, 49–75.

Austin, W., McGinn, N. C. & Susmilch, C. (1980). Internal standards revisited: Effects of social comparisons and expectancies on judgements of fairness and satisfaction. *Journal of Experimental Social Psychology, 16*, 426–41.

Australian Broadcasting Corporation. (1998). *Papua New Guinea academics to take industrial action*. ABC News home page, Monday August 10th, 1998 (accessed at 4.19 am Australian Eastern Standard Time, AEST).

Aycan, Z., Kanungo, R. N. & Mendonca, M. (2000). Impact of culture on human resource management practice: A 10-country comparison. *Applied Psychology: An International Review, 49*, 192–221.

Aycan, Z. & Kanungo, R. N. (2001). Cross-cultural industrial and organisational psychology: A critical appraisal of the field and future directions. In N. Anderson (Ed.), *Handbook of industrial, work, and organisational psychology* (pp. 386–408). London: Sage Publications.

Aycan, Z., Kanungo, R. N. & Sinha, J. B. P. (1999). Organisational culture and human resource management practices. *Journal of Cross–cultural Psychology, 30*, 501–26.

Aycan, Z. & Koc, U. (1999). Effects of workforce integration on immigrants' psychological wellbeing and adaptation. *Turk Psikolji Dergisi, 14*, 17—33. [English abstract only].

Bachiochi, P. D. & Weiner, S. P. (2002). Qualitative data collection and analysis. In S. G. Rogelberg (Ed.), *Handbook of research methods in industrial and organisational psychology* (pp. 161–183). Malden, MA: Blackwell.

Baker, K. W. (1995). Allen and Meyer's 1990 longitudinal study: A re-analysis and reinterpretation using structural equation modelling. *Human Relations, 48*, 169–86.

Bales, R. F. (1956). How people interact in conferences. *Scientific American, 192*, 31–5.

Baldwin, T. T., Magjuka, R. J. & Loher, B. T. (1991). The perils of participation: Effects of choice of training on trainee motivation and learning. *Personnel Psychology, 44*, 51–65.

Barker, J. R. (1993). Tightening the iron cage: Concertive control in self-managing teams. *Administrative Science Quarterly, 38*, 408–437.

Baron, R. (1986). Self-presentation in job interviews: When there can be 'too much of a good thing.' *Journal of Applied Social Psychology, 16*, 16–28.

Barrick, M. R., Stewart, G. L., Neubert, M. J. & Mount, M. K. (1998). Relating member ability and personality to work-team processes and team effectiveness. *Journal of Applied Psychology, 83*, 377–391.

Barsade, S. G., Ward, A. J., Turner, J. D. F. & Sonnenfeld, J. A. (2000). To your heart's content: A model of affective diversity in top management teams. *Administrative Science Quarterly, 45*, 802–36.

Bassman, E. & London, M. (1993). Abusive managerial behaviour. *Leadership & Organisation Development Journal, 14*, 18–24.

Bau, L. P. & Dyck, M. J. (2002). Predicting the peacetime performance of military officers in the Papua New Guinea Defence Force. In F. H. Bolitho, S. C. Carr, & B. O'Reilly (Eds.), *South Pacific Psychology: Global, local, and glocal applications* (pp. 93–101). http://spjp.massey.ac.nz/.

Beaverstock, J. V. & Smith, J. (1996). Lending jobs to global cities: Skilled international labour migration, investment banking and the City of London. *Urban Studies, 33*, 1377–1394.

Becker, G. S. (1975). *Human capital: A theoretical and empirical analysis, with special reference to education* (2nd edition). New York: Columbia University Press.

Bedeian, A. G. (1995). Workplace envy. *Organizational Dynamics, 23*, 49–56.

Belbin, R. M. (1997). *Teams at work*. Melbourne: Butterworth-Heinemann.

Bell, B. S. & Kozlowski, S. W. J. (2002). A typology of virtual teams. *Group & Organization Management, 27*, 14–49.

Berke, J. H. (1988). *The tyranny of malice: Exploring the dark side of character and culture*. New York: Summit Books.

Berkowitz, L., Fraser, C., Treasure, P. & Cochran, S. (1987). Pay, equity, job gratifications, and comparisons in pay satisfaction. *Journal of Applied Psychology, 72*, 544–551.

Berry, J. W. (1997). Immigration, acculturation, and adaptation. *Applied Psychology: An International Review, 46*, 5–34.

Beyerlein, M. M., Johnson, D. A. & Beryerlein, S. T. (2001). *Virtual teams*. Amsterdam: JAI Press.

Bhawuk, D. P. S. (2001). Evolution of culture assimilators: Toward theory-based assimilators. *International Journal of Intercultural Relations, 25*, 141-163.

Bird, A. (1994). Careers as repositories of knowledge: A new perspective on boundary-less careers. *Journal of Organisational Behaviour, 15*, 325–44.

Bloor, G. & Dawson, P. (1994). Understanding professional culture in organizational context. *Organization Studies, 15*, 279–299.

Bluedorn, A. C., Kalliath, T. J., Strube, M. J. & Martin, G. D. (1998). Polychronicity and the Inventory of Polychronic Values (IPV): The development of an instrument to measure a fundamental dimension of organisational culture. *Journal of Managerial Psychology, 14*, 205–30.

Bochner, S. & Perks, R. W. (1971). National role evocation as a function of cross-national interaction. *Journal of Cross-Cultural Psychology, 2*, 157–64.

Boggs, L., Carr, S. C., Fletcher, R. B. & Clarke, D. (2003). *Broken promises in communication networks: Rejuvenation of a classic paradigm*. Auckland: Massey University.

Bolitho, F. H. & Carr, S. C. (2003). A dysfunctional workplace. In S. C. Carr, *Social Psychology: Context, communication, and culture* (p. 387). Brisbane: John Wiley.

Bond, R & Smith, P. B. (1996) Culture and Conformity: A meta-analysis of studies using Asch's (1952/3,1956) Line Judgement Task. *Psychological Bulletin, 119*, 111–137.

Borg, W. R. (1957). The behaviour of emergent and designated leaders in situational tests. *Sociometry, 20*, 95–104.

Bourhis, R. Y., Moïse, L. C., Perrault, S. & Senécal, S. (1997). Towards an interactive acculturation model: A social psychological approach. *International Journal of Psychology, 32*, 369–86.

Bowa, M. & MacLachlan, M. (1994). *No 'congratulations' in Chichewa: Deterring achievement motivation in Malawi*. Zomba, Malawi: University of Malawi.

Bowers, C. A., Pharmer, J. A. & Salas, E. (2000). When member homogeneity is needed in work teams: A meta-analysis. *Small Group Research, 31*, 305–27.

Brewer, A. M. (1995). *Change management: Strategies for Australian organisations*. Sydney: Allen & Unwin.

Brewer, M. B. (1993). The role of distinctiveness in social identity and group behaviour. In M. A. Hogg & D. Abrams (Eds.), *Group motivation: Social psychological perspectives* (pp. 1–16). London: Harvester-Wheatsheaf.

Brockner, J., Mannix, E. A., Leung, K. & Skarlicki, D. R. (2000). Culture and procedural fairness: When the effects of what you do depend on how you do it. *Administrative Science Quarterly, 45*, 138–59.

Brown, K. A. & Huber, V. L. (1992). Lowering floors and raising ceilings: A longitudinal assessment of the effects of an earnings-at-risk plan on pay satisfaction. *Personnel Psychology, 45*, 279–311.

Brown, R. & Williams, J. (1984). Group identification: The same thing to all people? *Human Relations, 37*, 547–64.

Buckley, M. R., Fedor, D. B. & Carraher, S. M. (1997). The ethical imperative to provide recruits with realistic job previews. *Journal of Management Issues, 9*, 468–84.

Buckley, M.R., Fedor, D. B., Veres, J. G., Wiese, D. S. & Carraher, S. M. (1998). Investigating newcomer expectations and job-related outcomes. *Journal of Applied Psychology, 83*, 452–61.

Burroughs, S. M. & Eby, L. T. (1998). Psychological sense of community at work: A measurement system and exploratory framework. *Journal of Community Psychology, 26*, 509–32.

Byrne, D. (1971). *The attraction paradigm*. New York: Academic Press.

Capelli, P. & Chauvin, K. (1991). An interplant test of the efficiency wage hypothesis. *The Quarterly Journal of Economics, CVI*, 769–87.

Carr, S. C. (1994). Generating the velocity to overcome motivational gravity in LDC business organizations. *Journal of Trans-national Management Development, 1*, 33–56.

Carr, S. C. (1996). Social psychology and culture: Reminders from Africa and Asia. In H. Grad, A. Blanco, & J. Georgas (Eds.), *Key issues in cross-cultural psychology* (pp. 68–85). Lisse, Netherlands: Swets & Zeitlinger.

Carr, S. C. (1999). Review of management and cultural values: The indigenisation of organisations in Asia. *South Pacific Journal of Psychology, 11*, 78–9.

Carr, S. C. (2003a). Poverty and justice. In S. C. Carr & T. S. Sloan (Eds.), *Poverty and psychology: From global perspective to local practice* (pp. 45–68). New York: Kluwer Academic Publishers.

Carr, S. C. (2003b). *Social psychology: Context, communication, and culture*. Brisbane: John Wiley.

Carr, S. C. & Bolitho, F. H. (2003). A dysfunctional workplace. In S. C. Carr, *Social psychology: Context, communication, and culture*. Brisbane: John Wiley.

Carr, S. C., Bolitho, F. H. & Purcell, I. P. (1999). *Organisational behaviour*. Darwin: School of Humanities, Social Sciences, and Management.

Carr, S. C., Chipande, R. & MacLachlan, M. (1998). Expatriate aid salaries in Malawi: A doubly de-motivating influence? *International Journal of Educational Development, 18*, 133–43.

Carr, S. C. & Coates, K. (2003, July). *I/O psychology and migrant selection*. Fifth Australian Industrial and Organisational Psychology Conference, Melbourne (peer-reviewed).

Carr, S. C., Ehiobuche, I., Rugimbana, R. O. & Munro, D. (1996). Expatriates' ethnicity and their effectiveness: "Similarity–attraction" or "inverse resonance"? *Psychology and Developing Societies, 8*, 265–82.

Carr, S. C., Fletcher, R. B., Atkins, S. G. & Clarke, S. J. (2002, July). *From groups to teams: A cross-contextual prototypes model*. XXV International Congress of Applied Psychologists, Singapore.

Carr, S. C., Fletcher, R. B., Atkins, S. G. & Clarke, S. J. (2003, July). *Are teams any different from groups?* Fifth Australian Industrial/Organisational Psychology Conference, Melbourne (peer-reviewed).

Carr, S. C., Hodgson, M. R., Vent, D. H. & Purcell, I. P. (2001). *Income inequity between groups: A doubly de-motivating influence?* Darwin: Northern Territory University.

Carr, S. C. & Jones, S. (2002). Reconstructing regional meanings of work: Myths, illusions, and economic crisis. *The Asian Psychologist, 2*, 17–8.

Carr, S. C. & MacLachlan, M. (1993/4). The social psychology of development work: The double de-motivation hypothesis. *Malawi Journal of Social Science, 16*, 1–8.

Carr, S. C. & MacLachlan, M. (1997). Motivational gravity. In D. Munro, J. F. Schumaker, & S. C. Carr (Eds.), *Motivation and culture* (pp. 133–58). New York: Routledge.

Carr, S. C. & MacLachlan, M. (1999). Work motivation in Malawi: Neither flat earth nor Babel. *Journal of International Development, 11*, 141–46.

Carr, S. C., MacLachlan, M., Zimba, C. G. & Bowa, M. (1995a). Motivational gravity in Malawi. *Journal of Social Psychology, 135*, 659–67.

Carr, S. C., MacLachlan, M., Zimba, C. G. & Bowa, M. (1995b). Community aid abroad: A Malawian perspective. *Journal of Social Psychology, 135*, 781–83.

Carr, S. C., McAuliffe, E. & MacLachlan, M. (1998). *Psychology of aid*. London: Routledge.

Carr, S. C., McLoughlin, D., Hodgson, M. & MacLachlan, M. (1996). Effects of unreasonable pay discrepancies for under and overpayment on double de-motivation. *Genetic, Social and General Psychology Monographs, 122*, 477–94.

Carr, S. C., Powell, V., Knezovic, M., Munro, D. & MacLachlan, M. (1996). Measuring motivational gravity: Likert or scenario scaling? *Journal of Managerial Psychology, 11*, 43–7.

Carr, S. C., Purcell, I. P., Bolitho, F. H., Moss, N. D. & Brew, S. E. (1999). Managing attitudes toward high achievers: The influence of group discussion. *Asian Journal of Social Psychology, 2*, 237–44.

Carr, S. C., Rugimbana, R. O., Walkom, E. & Bolitho, F. H. (2001). Selecting expatriates in developing areas: "Country-of-origin" effects in Tanzania? *International Journal of Intercultural Relations, 25*, 441–57.

Carrell, M. R. & Dittrich, J. E. (1978). Equity theory: The recent literature, methodological considerations, and new directions. *Academy of Management Review, April*, 202–10.

Carrington, W. J. & Detragiache, E. (1999). How extensive is the brain drain? *Finance & Development, 36*, 46–50.

Carter, A. (2002, July). *Making life better for team-workers: A challenge for interventionists?* XXV International Congress of Applied Psychologists, Singapore.

Cassidy, T. & Lynn, B. (1989). A multifactorial approach to achievement motivation: The development of a comprehensive measure. *Journal of Occupational Psychology, 62*, 301–12.

Catley, B. (2001). *Waltzing with Matilda: Should Australia join New Zealand?* Wellington, NZ: Dark Horse.

Ceremalus, N. (1994). Why we need talent. *Management, 41*, 74–5.

Chan, K. (2001). Utilising the immigrants we already have. Adapted for *Managing Human Resources Today, 65*, 14–5.

Chavez, D. N. J. (1997). *Exploring team and group dynamics within an organizational context.* San Francisco, CA: Golden Gate University. (Doctoral Thesis).

Chen, C. C., Choi, J. & Chi, S. C. (2002). Making justice sense of local–expatriate compensation disparity: Mitigation by local referents, ideological explanations, and interpersonal sensitivity in China–foreign joint ventures. *Academy of Management Journal, 45*, 807–17.

Chidgey, J. E. (1995). *Managing motivational gravity using a sporting metaphor in Australia.* Newcastle, Australia: University of Newcastle.

Chi-Yue Chiu, & Yong-Yi Hong. (1997). Justice in Chinese societies: A Chinese perspective. In H. S. R. Kao & D Sinha (Eds.), *Asian perspectives on Psychology* (pp. 164–75). New Delhi: Sage.

Choi, J. N. & Kim, M. U. *(1999).* The organisational application of groupthink and its limitations in organizations. *Journal of Applied Psychology, 84*, 297–306.

Clarke, E. (2001). Role conflicts and coping strategies in care–giving: A symbolic interactionist view. *Journal of Psychosocial Nursing, 39*, 28–37.

Clarke, S. J. (2002, June). Personal correspondence.

Cliff, D. (2000). Helping refugees, asylum seekers and migrants to use their wealth of talents and experience. *Local Economy, 15*, 339–42.

Clifford, J. (1997). *Routes: Travel and translation in the late 20th century.* Cambridge, MA: Harvard University Press.

Clore, G. L. & Ortony, A. (1991). What more is there to emotion concepts than prototypes? *Journal of Personality and Social Psychology, 60*, 48–50.

Cohen, R. L. (1985). Procedural justice and participation. *Human Relations, 3*, 643–63.

Cohen, S. G. & Ledford, G. E. (1994). The effectiveness of self–managing teams: A quasi–experiment. *Human Relations, 47*, 13–43.

Cohen, S. G., Ledford, E. E. & Spreitzer, G. M. (1996). A predictive model of self–managing work team effectiveness. *Human Relations, 49*, 643–76.

Colquitt, J. A., Conlon, D. E. & Wesson, M. J. (2001). Justice at the millennium: A meta-analytic review of organizational justice research. *Journal of Applied Psychology, 86*, 425–45.

Colquitt, J. A., Hollenbeck, J. R., Ilgen, D. R., LePine, J. A. & Sheppard, L. (2002). Computer-assisted communication and team decision making performance: The moderating effect of openness to experience. *Journal of Applied Psychology, 87*, 402–10.

Conway, N. & Briner, R. B. (2002). A daily diary of affective responses to psychological contract breach and exceeded promises. *Journal of Organisational Behaviour, 23*, 287–302.

Cooper, C. (2000). Introduction. *Journal of Managerial Psychology, 15*, 197–201.

Cowherd, D. M. & Levine, D. I. (1992). Product quality and pay equity between lower–level employees and top management: An investigation of Distributive Justice Theory. *Administrative Science Quarterly, 37*, 302–20.

Cox, S. E. (2003, July). *Effective online discussion groups: Roles and skills for facilitators*. 29th Interamerican Congress of Psychology, Lima, Peru.

Coyle–Shapiro, J. A. M. (2002). A psychological contract perspective on organisational citizenship behaviour. *Journal of Organisational Behaviour, 23*, 927–46.

Craig, G. (2003, October). *Social justice, poverty and the response of New Labour: A critique*. Albany, Auckland: College of Humanities and Social Science Massey University Seminar Series.

Cromie, S. (2000). Assessing entrepreneurial inclinations: Some approaches and empirical evidence. *European Journal of Work & Organisation Psychology, 9*, 7–30.

Cunha, M. P. E. & Da Cunha, J. V. (2001). Managing improvisation in cross-cultural virtual teams. *International Journal of Cross–Cultural Management, 1*, 187–208.

Cushner, K. & Brislin, R. W. (1996). *Intercultural interactions: A practical guide* (2nd edition). London: Sage.

Daroesman, I. P. & Daroesman, R. (1992). *Degrees of success*. Canberra: AIDAB/IDP.

Das, G. (1993). Local memoirs of a global manager. *Harvard Business Review, March/April*, 38–47.

Daun, A. (1991). Individualism and collectivity among Swedes. *Ethnos, 56*, 165–72.

Davidson, M., Manning, M., Timo, N. & Ryder, P. (2001). The dimensions of organisational climate in four- and five-star Australian hotels. *Journal of Hospitality & Tourism Research, 25*, 444–61.

Deci, E.L. (1975). *Intrinsic Motivation*. New York: Plenum Publishing.

Deci, E. L., Koestner, R. & Ryan, R. M. (1999). The undermining effect is a reality after all – extrinsic rewards, task interest, and self-determination: Reply to Eisenberger, Pierce, and Cameron (1999), and Lepper, Heiderlong, and Gingras (1999). *Psychological Bulletin, 125*, 692–700.

Deci, E. L. & Ryan, R. M. (1990). A motivational approach to self: Integration in personality. *Nebraska Symposium on Motivation, 1990*, 237–88.

Department of Labour. (2003). *Skilled migrants: Labour market experiences*. Wellington: New Zealand Immigration Service.

Deutsch, M. (1975). Equity, equality, and need: What determines which value will be used as the basis for distributive justice? *Journal of Social Issues, 31*, 137–49.

Devine, D. J. (2002). A review and integration of classification systems relevant to teams in organizations. *Group Dynamics, 6*, 291–310.

De Fillippi, R. J. & Arthur, M. B. (1994). The boundary-less career: A competency-based perspective. *Journal of Organisational Behaviour, 15*, 307–324.

De Vries, M. F. R. K. (1999). High performance teams: Lessons from the Pygmies. *Organizational Dynamics, 27*, 66–77.

Dexter, C. (1999). *The remorseful day*. London: Pan Books.

Diaz–Guerrero, R. (1977). A Mexican psychology. *American Psychologist, 32*, 934–44.

Donohue, R. (2003, July). *An evaluation of the Career Attitudes and Strategies Inventory and Holland's propositions in terms of predicting career change and career persistence*. Fifth Australian Industrial & Organisational Psychology Conference, Melbourne (peer-reviewed).

Donovan, J. J. (2001). Work motivation. In N. Anderson, D. S. Ones, H. K. Sinangil, & C. Viswesvaran (Eds.), *Handbook of industrial, work and organisational psychology, vol. 2* (pp. 53–76). London: Sage.

Dore, R. (1994). Why visiting sociologists fail. *World Development, 22*, 1425–36.

Dovidio, J. F. & Esses, V. M. (2001). Immigrants and immigration: Advancing the psychological perspective. *Journal of Social Issues, 57*, 378–87.

Dowling, P. J., Schuler, R. S. & Welch, D. E. (1994). *International dimensions of human resource management.* Belmont, CA: Wadsworth.

Drucker, P. F. (1954). *The practice of management.* New York: Harper & Row.

Drucker, P. F. (1988). *Management.* London: Heinemann.

Druskak, V.U. & Pesconsolido, A. T. (2002). The content of effective teamwork mental models in self-managing teams: Ownership, learning and heedful interrelating. *Human Relations, 55*, 283–315.

Duffy, M. F., Ganster, D. & Pgon, M. (2002). Social undermining in the workplace. *Academy of Management Journal, 45*, 331–51.

Dunphy, D. C. & Dick, R. (1987). *Organisational change by choice.* Sydney: McGraw-Hill.

Dunphy, D. C. & Stace, D. (1993). The strategic management of corporate change. *Human Relations, 46*, 905–20.

Eagly, A. H. (1999, July). *Few women at the top: Is prejudice a cause?* XXVII Interamerican Congress of Psychology, Caracas, Venezuela.

Eagly, A. H. (2003). Transformational, transactional, and laissez–faire leadership styles: A meta-analysis comparing women and men. *Psychological Bulletin, 129*, 569–91.

Earley, P. C. (1993). East meets West meets Mid East: Further explorations of collectivistic and individualistic work groups. *Academy of Management Review, 36*, 319–48.

Earley, P. C. (2002). Refining interactions across cultures and organizations: Moving forward with cultural intelligence. In B. M. Staw and R. M. Roderick (Eds.), *Research in organisational behaviour* (pp. 271-99). New York: Elsevier Science/JAI Press.

Earley, P. C. & Mosakowski, E. (2000). Creating hybrid team cultures: An empirical investigation of transnational team functions. *Academy of Management Journal, 43*, 26–49.

Eby, L. T., Butts, M. & Lockwood, A. (2003). Predictors of success in the era of the boundary-less career. *Journal of Organisational Behaviour, 24*, 689–708.

Edmondson, A. (2000). Review of Theory and research on small groups. *Administrative Science Quarterly, 45*, 636–637.

Einarsen, S. E., Hoel, H., Zapf, D. & Cooper, C. L. (2003). The concept of bullying at work: The European tradition. In S. E. Einarsen, J. Hoel, D. Zapf, & C. L. Cooper (Eds.), *Bullying and emotional abuse in the workplace: International perspectives in research and practice* (pp. 3–30). London: Taylor & Francis.

Empson, L. (2001). Fear of exploitation and fear of contamination: Impediments to knowledge transfer in mergers between professional service firms. *Human Relations, 54*, 839–62. [special issue on knowledge management in professional service firms].

Ensley, M. D. & Pearce, C. L. (2001). Shared cognition in top management teams: Implications for new venture performance. *Journal of Organisational Behaviour, 22*, 145–60.

Exline, J. J. & Lobel, M. (1999). The perils of out-performance: Sensitivity about being the target of a threatening upward comparison. *Psychological Bulletin, 125*, 307–37.

Fadil, P. A. & Moss, S. E. (1998). An integrative framework of cognitive stereotypes in the bicultural leader/member dyad. In T. A., Scandura & M. G. Serapio (Eds.), *Research in international business and international relations: Leadership and innovation in emerging markets* (pp. 87–115). Stamford, CT: Jai Press.

Fazio, R. H., Jackson, J. R., Dunton, B. C. & Williams, C. J. (1995). Variability in automatic activation as an unobtrusive measure of racial attitudes: A bona fide pipeline? *Journal of Personality and Social Psychology, 69*, 1013–27.

Feather, N. T. (1993). Success and failure in the labour market: Some comments. *Journal of Organisational Behaviour, 14*, 573–76.

Feather, N. T. (1994). Attitudes toward high achievers and reactions to their fall: Theory and research concerning tall poppies. *Advances in Experimental Social Psychology, 26*, 1–73.

Fehr, B. & Russell, J. A. (1991). The concept of love viewed from a prototype perspective. *Journal of Personality and Social Psychology, 60*, 425–38.

Feltz, D. L. & Lirrg, C. D. (1998). Perceived team and player efficacy in hockey. *Journal of Applied Psychology, 83*, 557–64.

Ferrin, D. L. (2003). The use of rewards to increase and decrease trust: Mediating processes and differential effects. *Organization Science, 14*, 18–31.

Ferris, G. R., Perrewe, P. I. Anthony, W. P. & Gilmore, D. G. (2000). Political skill at work. *Organizational Dynamics, 28*, 25–37.

Finholt, T. & Spoull, L. S. (1990). Electronic groups at work. *Organization Science, 1*, 41–64.

Fiore, S. M., Salas, E. & Cannon-Bowers, J. A. (2001). *Group dynamics and shared mental model development*. In M. London (Ed.), *How people evaluate others in organizations* (pp. 309–336). Mahwah, NJ: Lawrence-Erlbaum Associates.

Fisher, K. (1993). *Leading self-directed work teams: A guide to developing new team leadership skills*. New York: McGraw-Hill.

Fisher, C. D. & Boyle, G. J. (1997). Personality and employee selection: Credibility regained. *Asia-Pacific Journal of Human Resources, 35*, 26–40.

Fisher, S. G., Hunter, T. A. & Macrosson, W. D. K. (1998). The structure of Belbin's team roles. *Journal of Occupational and Organisational Psychology, 71*, 283–88.

Fisher, S. G., Macrosson, W. D. K., & Wong, J. (1998). Cognitive styles and team role preferences. *Journal of Managerial Psychology, 13*, 544–57.

Fiske, A. P. (1991). *Structures of social life: The four elementary forms of human relations: Communal sharing, authority ranking, equality matching, market pricing*. New York: The Free Press.

Fletcher, R. B. & Atkins, S. G. (2002, June). Personal correspondences.

Folger, R., Rosenfeld, D., Grove, J. & Corkran, L. (1979). Effects of voice and peer opinions on responses to inequity. *Journal of Personality and Social Psychology, 37*, 2253–61.

Fontaine, G. (2002, July). *Teams in Teleland: Working effectively in geographically dispersed teams 'in' the Asia Pacific*. XXV Congress of Applied Psychology, Singapore (to appear in Team Performance Management, 2002, 8[5/6]).

Fox, F. F. (2003). Reducing intercultural friction through fiction: Virtual cultural learning. *International Journal of Intercultural Relations, 27*, 99–123.

Frandsen, A. (1969). Group facilitation of individual learning. *Psychology In The Schools, 6*, 292–97.

Franken, R. E. & Brown, D. J. (1995). Why do people like competition? The motivation for winning, putting forth effort, improving one's performance, performing well, being instrumental, and expressing forceful/aggressive behaviour. *Personality & Individual Differences, 19*, 175–84.

Fried, Y. & Ferris, G. R. (1987). The validity of the Job Characteristics Model: A review and meta-analysis. *Personnel Psychology, 40*, 287–322.

Friese, M. (2003, June). *Keynote address on Entrepreneurial studies in the new Millennium*. Fifth Australian Industrial/Organisational Psychology Conference, Melbourne (peer-reviewed).

Fryer–Keene, S. & Simpson, B. (1997). Using metaphor to clarify emerging roles in patient care management teams. *Canadian Journal of Nursing Administration, 10*, 67–76.

Fukuda, J. (1999). 'Bushido:' The guiding principle of new Japan. In H. S. R. Kao, D. Sinha, & B. Wilpert (Eds.), *Management and cultural values: The Indigenisation of organisations* in Asia (pp. 73–85). New Delhi: Sage.

Gaertner, S. L., Dovidio, J.F. & Bachman, B. A. (1996). Revisiting the contact hypothesis: The induction of a common in-group identity. *International Journal of Intercultural Relations, 20*, 271–90.

Gallois, C., Callan, V. J. & Palmer, J. A. M. (1992). The influence of applicant communication style and interviewer characteristics on hiring decisions. *Journal of Applied Social Psychology, 22*, 1041–60.

Garcia-Prieto, P. Bellard, E. & Schneider, S. C. (2003). Experiencing diversity, conflict, and emotions in teams. *Applied Psychology: An International Review, 52*, 413–40.

Garman, A. N., Davis-Lenane, D. & Corrigan, P. W. (2003). Factor structure of the transformational leadership model in human service teams. *Journal of Organisational Behaviour, 24*, 803–12.

Gergen, K. J. (1994a). Metaphor, meta-theory, and the social world. In D. E. Leary (Ed.), *Metaphors in the history of psychology* (pp. 267–99). Cambridge, MA: Cambridge University Press.

Gergen, K. J. (1994b). *Toward transformation in social knowledge* (2nd edition). London: Sage.

Gergen, K. J., Morse, S. J. & Bode, K. A. (1974). Overpaid or overworked? Cognitive and behavioural reactions to inequitable rewards. *Journal of Applied Social Psychology, 4*, 259–74.

Geurts, S., Schaufeli, W. & De Jonge, J. (1998). Burnout and intention to leave among mental health–care professionals: A social psychological approach. *Journal of Social & Clinical Psychology, 17*, 341–62.

Giacalone, R. A. & Beard, J. W. (1994). Impression management, diversity, and international management. *American Behavioural Scientist, 37*, 621–36.

Giacobbe-Miller, J. K., Miller, D. J. & Victorov, V. I. (1998). A comparison of Russian and U.S. pay allocation decisions, distributive justice judgements, and productivity under different payment conditions. *Personnel Psychology, 51*, 137–63.

Gibson, C. B. & Cohen, S. G. (2003). *Virtual teams that work: Creating conditions for virtual team effectiveness*. San Francisco, CA: Jossey-Bass.

Gibson, C. B. & Zelmer-Bruhn, M. E. (2001). Metaphors and meaning: An intercultural analysis of the concept of teamwork. *Administrative Science Quarterly, 46*, 274–303.

Gilchrist, J. A. & White, K. D. (1991). Policy development and satisfaction with merit pay: A field study in a university setting. *College Student Journal, 24*, 249–54.

Gitel'makher, Z. (1988). A through team: Psychological barriers and ways of removing them. *Psikologicheski Zhurnal, 9*, 53–62 [Abstract only in English].

Glynn, T. & Carr, S. C. (1999). Motivation and performance in teams: Transforming loafing into resonance. *South Pacific Journal of Psychology, 11*, 71–77. [http://www.spjp.massey.ac.nz/].

Goldstein, D. L. & Smith, D. H. (1999). The analysis of the effects of experiential training on sojourners' cross-cultural adaptability. *International Journal of Intercultural Relations, 23*, 157–73.

Gould, S. J. (1994). Science without taxonomy is blind. *The Sciences, March/April*, 38–39.

Greenberg, J. (1993). Stealing in the name of justice: Informational and interpersonal moderators of theft reactions to underpayment inequity. *Organisational Behaviour & Human Decision Processes, 54*, 81–103.

Greenberg, J. & Ornstein, S. (1983). High status job title compensation for underpayment: A test of equity theory. *Journal of Applied Psychology, 68*, 285–97.

Grey, G. & Pratt, R. (1995). *Issues in Australian Nursing* (No. 4). Sydney: Churchill-Livingstone.

Grove, J. R. & Paccagnella, N. H. (1995). Tall poppies in sport: Attitudes and ascribed personality traits. *Australian Psychologist, 30*, 89–91.

Gupta, R. K. (1999). The truly familial work organization: Extending the organisational boundary to include employees' families in the Indian context. In H. S. R. Kao, D. Sinha, & B. Wilpert (Eds.), *Management and cultural values: The indigenisation of organisations in Asia* (pp. 86–101). New Delhi: Sage.

Gurman, E. B. (1989). Travel abroad: A way to increase creativity. *Educational Research Quarterly, 13*, 12–16.

Hackman, J. R. & Oldham, G. (1976). Motivation through the design of work: Test of a theory. *Organisational Behaviour and Human Performance, 16*, 250–79.

Hall, V. (2001). Management teams in education: An unequal music. *School Leadership & Management, 21*, 327–42.

Hallier, J. & Butts, S. (1998). Employers' discovery of training: Self-development, employability and the rhetoric of partnership. *Employee Relations, 21*, 80–94.

Halpern, D. & Osofsky, S. (1990). A dissenting view of MBO. *Public Personnel Management, 19*, 321–30.

Hambrick, D. C. & Cho, T. (1996). The influence of management team heterogeneity on firms' competitive moves. *Administrative Science Quarterly, 41*, 659–75.

Harpaz, I. (1989). Non-financial employment commitment: A cross-national comparison. *Journal of Occupational Psychology, 62*, 147–50.

Harrington, L. & Liu, J. H. (2002). Self-enhancement and attitudes toward high achievers: A bicultural view of the independent and interdependent self. *Journal of Cross-Cultural Psychology, 33*, 37–55.

Harrison, D. A., Price, K. H. & Bell, M. P. (1998). Beyond relational demography: Time and the effects of surface-level and deep-level diversity on work group cohesion. *Academy of Management Journal, 41*, 96–107.

Harrod, W. J. (1980). Expectations from unequal rewards. *Social Psychology Quarterly, 43*, 126–30.

Harthill, P. (1998). A hypocritical host. *Migration Economics, September*, 24–5.

Haslam, S. A. (2001). *Psychology in organizations: The Social Identity approach*. New Delhi: Sage.

Harvey, M. & Novicevic, M. (2002). The role of political competence in global assignments of expatriate managers. *Journal of International Management, 8*, 389–406.

Headay, B. (1991). Distributive justice and occupational income: Perceptions of justice determine perceptions of fact. *British Journal of Sociology, 42*, 581–96.

Hegtvedt, K. A. (1989). Fairness conceptualisations and comparable worth. *Journal of Social Issues, 45*, 81–97.

Helmreich, R., Aronson, E. & LeFan, J. (1970). To err is humanizing sometimes: Effects of self-esteem, competence, and a pratfall on interpersonal attractions. *Journal of Personality and Social Psychology, 16*, 259–64.

Heneman, R. L., Fay, C. H. & Zhong-Ming Wang. (2001). Compensation systems in the global context. In Anderson, D. S. Ones, H. K. Sinangil, & C. Viswesvaran (Eds.), *Handbook of industrial, work and organisational psychology, vol. 2* (pp. 77–91). London: Sage.

Heneman, R. L., Ledford, E. E. & Gresham, M. (2000). The changing nature of work and its effects on compensation design and delivery. In S. Rynes & B. Gerhart (Eds.), *Compensation in organizations: Current research and practice* (pp. 195–240). San Francisco, CA: Jossey-Bass.

Hermans, H. J. M. & Kempen, H. J. G. (1998). Moving cultures: The perilous problems of cultural dichotomies in a globalizing society. *American Psychologist, 53*, 1111–20.

Herriot, P. (1991). The selection interview. In P. Warr (Ed.), *Psychology at work* (pp. 139–59). Harmondsworth, UK: Penguin.

Hertel, G. & Kerr, N. L. (2001). Priming in-group favouritism: The impact of normative scripts in the minimal group paradigm. *Journal of Experimental Social Psychology, 37*, 316–24.

Hickson, J. & Pugh, D. S. (2001). *Management worldwide: Distinctive styles amid globalisation*. St. Ives, UK: Penguin.

Hill, M. E. & Augoustinos, M. (1997). Re-examining gender bias in achievement attributions. Australian Journal of Psychology, 49, 85–90.

Hines, G. H. (1973a). Achievement motivation, occupations, and labour turnover in New Zealand. *Journal of Applied Psychology, 58*, 313–17.

Hines, G. H. (1973b). Motivational correlates of Pacific Islanders in urban environments. *Journal of Psychology, 83*, 247–49.

Hines, G. H. (1973c). The persistence of Greek achievement motivation across time and culture. *International Journal of Psychology, 8*, 285–88.

Hines, G. H. (1976). Cultural influences on work motivation. *Massey University Occasional Papers, 3*, 10.

Hofstede, G. (1980). *Culture's consequences*. London: Sage.

Hofstede, G. (1997). Motivation, leadership, and organization; Do American theories apply abroad? In D. S. Pugh (Ed.), *Organization theory: Selected readings* (4th edition) (pp. 233–50). Harmondsworth, UK: Penguin.

Hofstede, G. (2001). *Culture's consequences* (2nd edition). Thousand Oaks, CA: Sage.

Hofstede, G. & Bond, M. H. (1988). The Confucius connection: From cultural roots to economic growth. *Organizational Dynamics, 16*, 4–21.

Hofstede, G., Triandis, H. C., Smith, P. B., Bond, M. H., Fu, P. P. & Pasa, S. K. (2001). Special commentary: The study of cross-cultural management and organization: past, present, and future. *International Journal of Cross-Cultural Management, 1*, 11–30.

Hogg. M. A. (2001). A social identity theory of leadership. *Personality and Social Psychology Review, 5*, 184–200.

Hogg, M. A., & Terry, D. J. (Eds.). (2000). *Social identity processes in organizational contexts*. Philadelphia: Psychology Press.

Hogg, M. A. & Williams, K. D. (2000). From I to we: Social identity and the collective self. *Group Dynamics: Theory, Research, and Practice, 4*, 81–97.

Holt, N. L. & Sparkes, A. C. (2001). An ethnographic study of cohesiveness in a college soccer team over a season. *The Sport Psychologist, 15*, 237–59.

House, R. J. & Aditya, R. N. (1997). The social scientific study of leadership: Quo Vadis? *Journal of Management, 23*, 409–73.

Howard, S. (2003). Personal correspondence. August, Wellington.

Huang, W. W., Wei, K. K., Watson, R. T. & Tan, B. C. Y. (2002). Supporting virtual team-building with a GSS: An empirical investigation. *Decision Support Systems, 34*, 359–67.

Hui, C. H. (1988). Measurement of individualism–collectivism. *Journal of Research in Personality, 22*, 17–36.

Hui, C. H. & Triandis, H. C. (1986). Individualism–collectivism: A study of cross-cultural researchers. *Journal of Cross-Cultural Psychology, 17*, 225–28.

Huseman, R. C., Hatfield, J. D. & Miles, E. W. (1985). Test for individual perceptions of job equity: Some preliminary findings. *Perceptual and Motor Skills, 61*, 1055–64.

Huseman, R. C., Hatfield, J. D. & Miles, E. W. 91987). A new perspective on Equity Theory: The Equity Sensitivity construct. *Academy of Management Review, 17*, 222–34.

Imel, S. (2001). Career development of free agent workers. *ERIC Digest, 228*. http://www.ericacve.org/fulltext.asp (accessed May 27, 2002).

Ingram, S. & Parker, A. (2002). The influence of gender on collaborative projects in an engineering classroom. *IEEE Transactions on Professional Communication, 45*, 7–20.

Inkson, K. (2001). The interim manager: Prototype of the 21st–century worker? *Human Relations, 54*, 259–84.

Inkson, K. & Arthur, M. B. (2001). How to be a successful career capitalist. *Organizational Dynamics, 30*, 48–62.

Inkson, K., Arthur, M. B., Pringle, J. & Barry, S. (1997). Expatriate assignment versus overseas experience: Contrasting modes of international human resource development. *Journal of World Business, 32,* 351–68.

Inkson, K., Arthur, M. B., Pringle, J. K., & Barry, S. (1997). Expatriate assignment versus overseas experience: Contrasting models of human resource development. *Journal of World Business, 32,* 351–68.

Inkson, K. & Myers, B.A. (in press). The Big OE: International travel and career development. *Career Development International.*

Insko, C. A., Schopler, J., Graetz, K. A. & Drigotas, S. M. (1994). Inter-individual and inter-group discontinuity in the prisoner's dilemma game. *Journal of Conflict Resolution, 38*, 87–116.

Invernizzi, G. (2001). New concepts in the psychology of workplace relationships: The so-called "mobbing." *New Trends in Experimental and Clinical Psychiatry, 16*, 5–6.

Ivory, B. (2003). Poverty and enterprise. In S. C. Carr & T. S. Sloan (Eds.), *Poverty and psychology: Emergent critical perspectives* (pp. 251-66). New York: Kluwer–Plenum.

Jackall, R. (1988). *Moral mazes.* New York: Oxford University Press.

Janis, I. (1982). Groupthink. In D. Krebs (Ed.), *Readings in social psychology: Contemporary perspectives* (pp. 172–75). New York: Harper & Row.

Jarvenpaa, S. L. & Leidner, D. E. (1998). Communication and trust in global virtual teams. *Journal of Computer-Mediated Communication, 3*, e–journal.

Javidan, M. & House, R. J. (2001). Cultural acumen for the global manager: Lessons from Project G.L.O.B.E [Global Leadership and Organisational Behaviour Effectiveness]. *Organizational Dynamics, 29*, 289–305.

Jetten, J., Postmes, T. & Mc Auliffe, B. J. (2002). We're all individuals: Group norms of individualism and collectivism, levels of identification, and identity threat. *European Journal of Social Psychology, 32*, 189–207.

Joerin, S. *(2003, July). Personality and job: Systematic mismatch of Holland's dimensions?* Fifth Australian Industrial and Organisational Psychology Conference, Melbourne (peer-reviewed).

Joiner, T. A. (2001). The influence of national culture and organizational culture alignment on job stress and performance: Evidence from Greece. *Journal of Managerial Psychology, 16*, 229–42.

Jones, A. R. (2000, August). Personal correspondence.

Jones, G. (2002). Performance excellence: A personal perspective on the link between sport and business. *Journal of Applied Sport Psychology, 14*, 268–81.

Jordan, P. C. (1986). Effects of an extrinsic reward on intrinsic motivation: A field experiment. *Academy of Management Journal, 29*, 405–412.

Kalimo, R., Taris, T. W. & Schaufeli, W. B. (2003). The effects of past and anticipated future downsizing on survivor wellbeing: An equity perspective. *Journal of Occupational Health Psychology, 8*, 91–109.

Kanungo, R. N. & Mendonca, M. (Eds.). (1994). *Work motivation: Models for developing countries*. New Delhi: Sage.

Kao, H. S. R., Sinha, D. & Wilpert, B. (Eds). (1999). *Management and cultural values: The indigenisation of organisations in Asia.* New Delhi: Sage.

Karau, S. J. & Williams, K. D. (1993). Social loafing: A meta-analytic review and theoretical integration. *Journal of Personality and Social Psychology, 65*, 681–706.

Karotkin, D. & Paroush, J. (2003). Optimum committee size: Quality versus quantity dilemma. *Social Choice & Welfare, 20*, 429–42.

Kashima, Y. & Callan, V. J. (1994). The Japanese work group. In H. C. Triandis & D. Dunnette (Eds.), *Handbook of Industrial and Organizational Psychology* Vol. 4 (2nd edition), (pp. 609–46). Palo Alto, CA: Consulting Psychologists' Press.

Kaur, R. & Ward, C. (1992). Cross-cultural construct validity of "fear of success:" A Singaporean case study. In S. Iwawaki, Y. Kashima, & K. Leung (Eds.), *Innovations in cross-cultural psychology* (pp. 214–225). Lisse, Netherlands: Swets & Zeitlinger.

Kayworth, T. & Leidner, D. (2000). The global manager: A prescription for success. *European Management Journal, 18*, 183–194.

Kealey, D. J. (1989). A study of cross-cultural effectiveness: Theoretical issues, practical applications. *International Journal of Intercultural Relations, 13*, 387–428.

Kennedy, P. W. (1995). Performance, pay, productivity, and morale. *The Economic Record, 1995*, 240–47.

Kichuk, S. L. & Wiesner, W. H. (1998). Work teams: Selecting members for optimal performance. *Canadian Psychology, 39*, 23–32.

Kickul, J. & Lester, S. W. (2001). Broken promises: Equity sensitivity as a moderator between psychological contract breach and employee attitudes and behaviour. *Journal of Business Psychology, 16*, 191–217.

King, W. C. & Miles, E. W. (1994). The measurement of Equity Sensitivity. *Journal of Occupational and Organisational Psychology, 67*, 133–42.

King, W. C., Miles, E. W. & Day, D. D. (1993). A test and refinement of the Equity Sensitivity construct. *Journal of Organisational Behaviour, 14*, 301–17.

Kirkman, B. L., Gibson, C. B. & Shapiro, D. L. (2001). "Exporting" teams: Enhancing the implementation and effectiveness of work teams in global affiliates. *Organizational Dynamics, 30*, 12–29.

Kirkman, B. L., Jones, R. G. & Shapiro, D. L. (2000). Why do employees resist teams? Examining the "resistance barrier" to work team effectiveness. *The International Journal of Conflict Management, 11*, 74–92.

Kirkman, B. L. & Shapiro, D. L. (1997). The impact of cultural values on employee resistance to teams: Toward a model of globalised self-managing work team effectiveness. *Academy of Management Review, 22*, 730–57.

Klein, O. & Azzi, A. (2001). Do high-status groups discriminate more? Differentiating between social identity and equity concerns. *Social Behaviour and Personality, 29*, 209–22.

Kleven, A. & Jenssen, M. A. (2001). Personality as a predictor of team performance: A meta-analysis. *Norwegian Journal of Psychology, 38*, 16–23. (English Abstract only).

Klimoski, R. & Mohammed, S. (1994). Team mental model: Construct or metaphor? *Journal of Management, 20,* 403–37.

Kluckhohn, C. (1951). The study of culture. In D. Lerner & H. D. Lasswell (Eds.), *The policy sciences* (pp. 86-101). Stanford, CA: Stanford University Press.

Kohn, A. (1998). Challenging behaviourist dogma: Myths about money and motivation. *Compensation & Benefits Review, March/April*, 1–8.

Kohnert, D. (1996). Magic and witchcraft: Implications for democratisation and poverty-alleviating aid in Africa. *World Development, 24*, 1347–55.

Komin, S. (1999). The Thai concept of effective leadership. In H. S. R. Kao, D. Sinah, & B. Wilpert (Eds.). (1999). *Management and cultural values: The indigenisation of organisations in Asia* (pp. 265–286). New Delhi: Sage.

Kosmitzki, C. (1996). The re-affirmation of cultural identity in cross-cultural encounters. *Personality & Social Psychology Bulletin, 22*, 238–48.

Kratz, M. S. & Moore, J. H. (2002). Executive migration and institutional change. *Academy of Management Journal, 45*, 120–43

Kunda, G. (1992). *Engineering culture: Control and commitment in a high-tech corporation.* Temple University Press.

Lalonde, R. N. (2002). Testing the social identity-inter-group differentiation hypothesis: "We're not American eh!" *British Journal of Social Psychology, 41*, 611–30.

Langens, T. A. (2001). Predicting behaviour change in Indian businessmen from a combination of need for Achievement and Self-Discrepancy. *Journal of Research in Personality, 35*, 339–52.

Langfred, C. W. (2000). The paradox of self-management: Individual and group autonomy in work groups. *Journal of Organisational Behaviour, 21*, 563–85.

Larson, J. R., & Schaumann, L. J. (1993). Group goals, group coordination, and group member motivation. *Human Performance, 6*, 49–69.

Latham, G. P. & Blades, J. (1975). The "practical significance" of Locke's theory of goal setting. *Journal of Applied Psychology, 60*, 122–124.

Lawler, E. E., Koplin, C. A., & Young, T. F. (1968). Inequity reduction over time in an induced overpayment situation. *Organizational Behaviour & Human Decision Processes, 3,* 253–268.

Lawler, E. E. & Finegold, D. (2000). Individualizing the organization: past, present, and future. *Organizational Dynamics, 29*, 1–15.

Lawrence, T. E. (1997). *Seven pillars of wisdom.* Ware, UK: Wordsworth Editions Limited.

Lawuyi, O. B. (1992). Vehicle slogans as personal and social thought: A perspective on self-development in Nigeria. *New Directions for Education Reforms, 1*, 91–8.

Leavitt, H. J. (1951). Some effects of certain communication patterns on group performance. *Journal of Abnormal and Social Psychology, 46*, 38–50.

Lee, D. (2000). An analysis of workplace bullying in the UK. *Personnel Review, 29*, 593–612.

Lee, R. T. & Martin, J. E. (1996). When a gain comes at a price: Pay attitudes after changing tier status. *Industrial Relations, 35*, 218–26.

Lemieux, A. & Pratto, F. (2003). Poverty and prejudice. In S. C. Carr & T. S. Sloan (Eds.), *Poverty and psychology: From global perspective to local practice* (147-61). New York: Kluwer-Plenum Academic Press.

Lemons, M. A. (1997). Work groups or work teams? Cultural and psychological dimensions for their formation. In M. M. Beyerlein, & D. A. Johnson (Eds.), *Advances in Interdisciplinary Studies of Work Teams, vol 4* (pp. 97–113). Stamford, CT: JAI Press, Inc.

LePine, J. A. & Van Dyne, L. (1998). Predicting voice behaviour in work groups. *Journal of Applied Psychology, 83*, 853–68.

Lerner, M. J. (1980). *The belief in a just world: A fundamental illusion.* New York: Plenum.

Leung, K., & Bond, M. H. (1984). *The impact of cultural collectivism on reward allocation.* Journal of Personality and Social Psychology, 47, 793–804.

Leung, K. Wang, Z. & Smith, P. B. (2001). Job attitudes, and organisational justice in joint venture hotels in China: The role of expatriate managers. *International Journal of Human Resource Management, 12*, 926–45.

Leventhal, G. S. & Michaels, J. W. (1969). Extending the Equity model: Perception of inputs and allocation of regard as a function of duration and quantity of performance. *Journal of Personality and Social Psychology, 12,* 303–09.

Levi, D. (2001). *Group dynamics for teams.* Thousand Oaks, CA: Sage Publications.

Levine, D. I. (1993). What do wages buy? *Administrative Science Quarterly, 38*, 462–83.

Levine, J. M. & Moreland, R. L. (1990). Progress in small group research. *Annual Review of Psychology, 41*, 585–634.

Lewin, K. (1947). Group decision making and social change. In E. E. Maccoby, T. M. Newcomb, & E. G. Hartley (Eds.) (1966). *Readings in social psychology* (pp. 197–211). London: Methuen.

Lewin, K., Lippitt, R. & White, R. K. (1939). Patterns of aggressive behaviour in experimentally created "social climates." *Journal of Social Psychology, 10*, 271–99.

Lewis, J. (1991). Re-evaluating the effects of N-Ach on economic growth. *World Development, 9,* 1269–127.

Lewis, R. D. (1999). *When cultures collide: Managing successfully across cultures.* London: Nicholas Brealey.

Leymann, H. (1990). Mobbing and psychological terror at workplaces. *Violence & Victims, 5*, 119–26.

Lim, A., & Ward, C. (2003). The effects of nationality, length of residence, and occupational demand on the perceptions of "foreign talent" in Singapore. In Yang, Kuo-Shu, & Hwang, Kwang-Kuo (Eds.), *Progress in Asian social psychology: Conceptual and empirical contributions* (pp. 247-259). Westport, CT: Praeger/Greenwood.

Littig, L. W. (1963). Effects of motives on probability preferences. *Journal of Personality, 31*, 417–27.

Liu, C. (1999). The concept of Bao and its significance in organisational research. In H. S. R. Kao, D. Sinha, & B. Wilpert (Eds.). *Management and cultural values: The indigenisation of organisations in Asia (*pp. 152–168). New Delhi: Sage.

Locke, E. P. (1991). The motor sequence, the motivation hub, and the motivation core. *Organisational Behaviour & Human Decision Processes, 50,* 288–299.

Locke, E. P. & Latham, G. P. (2002). Building a practically useful theory of goal setting and task motivation. *American Psychologist, 57,* 705–717.

Maani, K. E. & Benton, C. (1999). Rapid team learning: Lessons from Team New Zealand America's Cup campaign. *Organizational Dynamics, 27*, 48–62.

MacLachlan, M. (1993a). Splitting the difference: How do refugee workers survive? *Changes: International Journal of Psychology and Psychotherapy, 11,* 155–57.

MacLachlan, M. (1993b). Sustaining human resource development in Africa: The influence of expatriates. *Management Education and Development, 24*, 153–57.

MacLachlan, M. (2003). Personal correspondence, June.

MacLachlan, M. & Carr, S. C. (1993). De-motivating the doctors: The double de–motivation hypothesis in Third World health services. *Journal of Management in Medicine, 7*, 6–10.

MacLachlan, M. & Carr, S. C. (1999). The selection of international assignees for development work. *The Irish Journal of Psychology, 20*, 39–57.

MacLachlan, M., Mapundi, J., Zimba, C. G. & Carr, S. C. (1995). Trialing the MAPP in Malaŵi A cross–cultural investigation of face validity. *Journal of Social Psychology, 135*, 645–48.

MacLachlan, M., Nyirenda, T. & Nyando, C. (1995). Attributions for admission to Zomba Mental Hospital: Implications for the development of mental health services in Malawi. *International Journal of Social Psychiatry, 41*, 79–87.

Mahroum, S. (2000). Highly skilled globetrotters: Mapping the international migration of human capital. *R & D Management, 30*, 23–32.

Mann, L. (1988). Cross-cultural studies of rules for determining majority and minority decision rights. *Australian Journal of Psychology, 38*, 319–28.

Manning, M. R., & Avolio, B. J. (1985). The impact of blatant pay disclosure in a university environment. *Research in Higher Education, 23*, 135–49.

Manz, C. C., Keating, D. E. & Donnellon, A. (1990). Preparing for an organizational change to employee self-management: The managerial transition. *Organzsational Dynamics, 19*, 15–26.

Marai, L. (2002/3). Double de-motivation and negative social affect among teachers in Indonesia. *South Pacific Journal of Psychology, 14*(1), 1-7.

Marin, G. (1985). The preference for equity when judging the attractiveness and fairness of an allocator: The role of familiarity and culture. *Journal of Social Psychology, 125*, 543–49.

Markus, H. R. & Kitayana, S. (1991). Culture and the self: Implications for cognition, emotion, and motivation. *Psychological Review, 98*, 224–53.

Marrow, A. (1948). Group dynamics in industry: Implications for guidance and personnel workers. *Occupations, 26*, 472–76.

Marrow, A. J. (1964). Risks and uncertainties in action research. *Journal of Social Issues, 20*, 5-20.

Marsella, A. J. (1997). Migration, ethno-cultural diversity and future work-life: Challenges and opportunities. *Scandinavian Journal of Work and Environmental Health, 23*, 8–46.

Mathieu, J. E., Marks, M. A. & Zaccaro, S. J. (2001). Multi-team systems. In N. Anderson, D. S. Ones, K. Sinangil, & C. Viswesvaran (Eds.), *Handbook of industrial, work and organisational psychology, vol 2* (pp. 289–313). London: Sage.

Mayo, E. (1933). *The human problems of an industrial civilisation*. New York: MacMillan.

McClelland, D. C. (1961). *The achieving society*. Princeton, NJ: Van Nostrand.

McClelland, D. C. (1965). Achievement and entrepreneurship: A longitudinal study. *Journal of Personality and Social Psychology, 1*, 389–92.

McClelland, D. C. (1987a). Characteristics of successful entrepreneurs. *Journal of Creative Behaviour, 21*, 219–33.

McClelland, D. C. (1987b). *Human motivation*. New York: Cambridge University Press.

McClelland, D. C. & Boyatzis, R. E. (1982). Leadership motive pattern and long-term success in management. *Journal of Applied Psychology, 67*, 737–43.

McClelland, D. C. & Winter, D. (1969). *Motivating economic achievement*. New York: Free Press.

McCleod, P. L., Baron, R. S., Marti, M. W. & Yoon, K. (1997). The eyes have it: Minority influence in face-to-face and computer-mediated group discussion. *Journal of Applied Psychology, 82*, 706–18.

McCrae, R. R. & Allik, J. (Eds.). (2002). *The five-factor model of personality across cultures*. New York: Kluwer-Plenum.

McEntire, M. H. & Bentley, J. C. (1996). When rivals become partners: Acculturation in a newly merged organization. *International Journal of Organisational Analysis, 4*, 154–74.

McGrew, J. F. Bilotta, J. G., & Deeney, J. M. (1999). Software team formation and decay: Extending the standard model for small groups. *Small Group Research, 30*, 209–34.

McLoughlin, D. & Carr, S. C. (1994). *The Buick Bar & Grill*. Melbourne: University of Melbourne Graduate Case Study Library.

McLoughlin, D. & Carr, S. C. (1997). Equity sensitivity and Double De-motivation. *Journal of Social Psychology, 137*, 668–70.

Meaning of Work (MoW). (1987). The meaning of working. London: Academic Press.

Mehta, P. (1977). Employee motivation and work satisfaction in a public enterprise. *Vikalpa (Indian Institute of Management), 2*, 223–36.

Melamed, T. (1995). Barriers to women's career success: Human capital, career choices, structural determinants, or simply sex discrimination? *Applied Psychology: An International Review, 44*, 295–314.

Menon, K. (2003). Personal correspondence. December.

Mento, A., Locke, E. P. & Klein, H. (1992). Relationship of goal level to valence and instrumentality. *Journal of Applied Psychology, 77*, 395–405.

Middlemist, D. R. & Peterson, R. R. (1976). Test of equity theory by controlling for comparison co-workers' efforts. *Organisational Behaviour & Human Decision Processes, 15*, 335–354.

Misumi, J. & Peterson, M. F. (1985). The performance–maintenance (PM) theory of leadership: Review of Japanese research program. *Administrative Science Quarterly, 30*, 198–223.

Mitchell, T. (1993). The effects of acceptance vs. rejection of subordinate input on task performance and perceptions of management. *Journal of Social Behaviour & Personality, 8*, 155–67.

Montoya-Weiss, M. M., Massey, A. P. & Song, M. (2001). Getting it together: Temporal coordination and conflict management in global virtual teams. *Academy of Management Journal, 44*, 1251–62.

Montreuil, A. & Bourhis, R. Y. (2001). Majority acculturation orientations toward "valued" and "de-valued" immigrants. *Journal of Cross-Cultural Psychology, 32*, 698–719.

Moran, E. T. & Volkwein, J. F. (1992). The cultural approach to the formation of organisational climate. *Human Relations, 45*, 19–47.

Morgan, B. B. & Salas, E. (1993). An analysis of team evolution and maturation. *Journal of General Psychology, 120*, 277–87.

Morris, M. A. & Robie, C. (2001). A meta-analysis of the effects of cross-cultural training on expatriate performance and adjustment. *International Journal of Training and Development, 5*, 112–25.

Morris, M. W. & Leung, K. (2000). Justice for all? Progress and research on cultural variation in the psychology of distributive and procedural justice. *Applied Psychology: An International Review, 49*, 100–32.

Morse, N. C. & Weiss, R. S. (1955). The function and meaning of work and the job. *American Sociological Review, 20*, 151–98.

Moscovici, S. (1976). *Social influence and social change.* London: Academic Press.

Moscovici, S. (1980). Toward a theory of conversion behaviour. *Advances in Experimental Social Psychology, 13*, 209–39.

Muchinksy, P. (2003). *Psychology applied to work* (7th edition). Belmont, CA: Thomson–Wadsworth.

Mueller, S. L. & Clarke, L. D. (1998). Political-economic context and sensitivity to equity: Differences between the United States and the transition economies of Central and Eastern Europe. *Academy of Management Journal, 41*, 319–29.

Munro, D. (1983). Developing "La conscience professionelle" in cultures with a history of vocational disadvantage. In F. Blackler (Ed.), *Social psychology and developing countries* (pp. 51–69). Chichester, UK: Wiley.

Munro, D., Carr, S. C., MacLachlan, M., Kwang, N. A., & Bishop, G. D. (1997). A brief history of T.I.M.E.: The Inventory for Monitoring Efficiency. In K. Leung, U. Kim, S. Yamaguchi, & Y. Kashima (Eds.), *Progress in Asian social psychology vol. 1* (pp. 261-70). Singapore: John Wiley & Sons.

Murray, H. A. (1938). *Explorations in personality.* New York: Oxford University Press.

Murray, H. A. (1943). *Thematic Apperception Test.* Cambridge, MA: Harvard University Press.

Murray, P. (2003). Organizational learning, competencies, and firm performance: Empirical observations. *Learning Organization, 10*, 305–17.

Murray, P. & Donegan, K. (2003). Empirical linkages between firm competencies and organisational learning. *Learning Organization, 10*, 51–63.

Naim, M. (2000). The digital drain. *Foreign Policy, 120*, 120–124.

Navara, G. S. & James, S. (2002). Sojourner adjustment: Does missionary status affect acculturation? *International Journal of Intercultural Relations, 26*, 695–709.

Neck, C. P. & Manz, C. C. (1994). From groupthink to teamthink: Toward the creation of constructive thought patterns in self-managing work teams. *Human Relations, 47*, 929–52.

Neck, C. P., Connerley, M. L. & Manz, C. C. (1997). Toward a continuum of self-managing team development. In M. M Beyerlein, & D. A. Johnson (Es.), *Advances in interdisciplinary studies of work teams, vol. 4* (pp. 193–216). Stamford, CT: JAI Press, Inc.

Nemeth, C. & Rogers, M.S. (1996). Dissent and the search for information. *British Journal of Social Psychology, 35*, 67–76.

Ng, K. Y. & Van Dyne, L. (2001a). Culture and minority influence: Effects on persuasion and originality. In C. K. W. De Dreu & N. K. De Vries (Eds.), *Group consensus and minority influence: Implications for innovation* (pp. 284–306). Malden, MA: Blackwell Publishers.

Ng, K. Y. & Van Dyne, L (2001b). Individualism–collectivism as a boundary condition for effectiveness of minority influence decision making. *Organisational Behaviour & Human Decision Processes, 84*, 198–225.

Nickerson, R. S. (1999). How we know – and sometime misjudge – what others know: Imputing one's own knowledge to others. *Psychological Bulletin, 125*, 737–59.

Nohria, N. & Eccles, R. G. (1992). Face-to-face: Making network organizations work. In N. Nohria & R. G. Eccles (Eds.), *Networks and organizations* (pp. 288–308). Boston, MA: Harvard Business School Press.

Ogbonna, E. (1996). Managing organisational culture: Fantasy or reality? In J. Billsberry (Ed.), *The effective manager: Perspectives and illustrations* (pp. 113-18). Milton Keynes, UK: Open University Press/Sage.

Ogbonna, E. & Harris, L. C. (2002). Organizational culture: A ten-year, two-phase study of change in the IK food-retailing sector. *Journal of Management Studies, 39*, 673-706.

Oliver, P. (2000). *Employment for professional migrants to New Zealand: Barriers and opportunities.* Wellington: Work and Income NZ/Centre for Operational Research and Evaluation.

O'Neil, G L. (1995). Linking pay to performance: Conflicting views and conflicting evidence. *Asia-Pacific Journal of Human Resources, 33*, 20-35.

O'Neill, B. S. & Morne, M. A. (1995). Investigating equity sensitivity as a moderator of relationships between self-efficacy and workplace attitudes. *Journal of Applied Psychology, 83*, 805-16.

Ones, D. S. & Viswesvaran, C. (1999). Relative importance of personality dimensions for expatriate selection: A policy capturing study. *Human Performance, 12*, 275-94.

Ongley, P. & Blick, G. (2002). Employment and income of Pacific peoples in New Zealand. *Key Statistics, December*, 9-14.

Ook Lee. (2002). Cultural differences in e-mail use of virtual teams: A Critical Social Theory perspective. *Cyber Psychology & Behaviour, 5*, 227-32.

Orpen, C. (1986). Improving organizations through team development. *Management & Labour Studies, 11*, 1-12.

Orpen, C. (1995). The Multifactorial Achievement Scale as a predictor of salary growth motivation among middle managers. *Social Behaviour and Personality, 23*, 159-62.

Oshodi, J. E. (1999). The construction of an Africentric sentence completion test to assess the need for achievement. *Journal of Black Studies, 30*, 216-31.

Ottati, V. Rhoads, S., & Graesser, A. C. (1999). The effect of metaphor on processing style in a persuasion task: A motivational resonance model. *Journal of Personality and Social Psychology, 77*, 688-97.

Oyserman, D., Coon, H. M., & Kemmelmeier, M. (2002). Rethinking individualism and collectivism: Evaluation of theoretical assumptions and meta-analyses. *Psychological Bulletin, 128*, 3-72.

Partington, D. & Harris, H. (1999). Team role balance and team performance: An empirical study. *Journal of Management Development, 18*, 694-705.

Paton, D. & Stephens, C. (1996). Training and support for emergency responses. In D. Paton & J. M. Violanti (Eds.), *Traumatic stress in critical occupations* (pp. 173-205). Springfield, IL: Charles C. Thomas.

Paul, R. J., Niehoff, B. P. & Turnley, W. H. (2000). Empowerment, expectations, and the psychological contact – managing the dilemmas and gaining the advantages. *Journal of Social-Economics, 29*, 471-85.

Payne, B. M., Nielsen, J. F. & Kristi, L. T. (2002). An investigation of cultural cohesion in a community bank. *International Journal of Human Resource Management, 13*, 677-96.

Peck, D. (1975). *Approaches to personality theory.* London: Methuen.

Perry, L. S. (1993). Effects of inequity on job satisfaction and self-evaluation in a national sample of African-American workers. *Journal of Social Psychology, 133*, 565-73.

Phillips, J. M. (1998). Effects of realistic job previews on multiple organisational outcomes: A meta-analysis. *Academy of Management Journal, 41*, 673-90.

Posthuma, A. C. (1995). Japanese techniques in Africa? Human resources and industrial restructuring in Zimbabwe. *World Development, 23*, 103-16.

Power, V. (1994, October). *Gender bias and the "glass ceiling."* 29th Annual Conference of the Australian Psychological Association, Wollongong, Australia.

Prapavessis, H. & Carron, A. V. (1997). Sacrifice, cohesion, and conformity to norms in sport teams. *Group Dynamics: Theory, Research, & Practice, 1*, 231–40.

Pratto, F. (2002, April 2). Personal correspondence.

Printz, R. A. & Waldman, D. A. (1985). The merit of merit pay. *Personnel Administrator, 30*, 84–90.

Pritchard, R. D. (Ed.). (1995). *Productivity measurement and improvement: Organisational case studies.* College Station, TX: Texas A & M University Press.

Probst, T., Carnevale, P. J. & Triandis, H. C. (1999). Cultural values in inter-group and single-group social dilemmas. *Organizational Behavior & Human Decision Processes, 77*, 171–91.

Pun, A. S. (1990). Managing the cultural differences in learning. *Journal of Management Development, 9*, 35–40.

Punnett, B. J. (1986). Goal setting: An extension of the research. *Journal of Applied Psychology, 71*, 171–72.

Purser, R. E. & Cabana, S. (1998). *The self-managing organization: How leading companies are transforming the work of teams for real impact.* New York: Free Press.

Quine, L. (2001). Workplace bullying in nurses. *Journal of Health Psychology, 6*, 73–84.

Randolph, A. W. (2000). Re–thinking empowerment: Why is it so hard to achieve? *Organizational Dynamics, 29*, 94–113.

Ratner, C. & Hui, L. (2003). Theoretical and methodological problems in cross-cultural psychology. *Journal for the Theory of Social Behaviour, 33*, 67–94.

Rayner, C. (1997). The incidence of workplace bullying. *Journal of Community and Applied Social Psychology, 7*, 199–208.

Reddy, P., Langan–Fox, J. & Code, S. (2003). *The 5th Australian Industrial & Organisational Psychology Conference: Advancing Creative Solutions in Science and Practice* (pp. 1–83). Melbourne: Australian Psychological Society (Refereed Conference Proceedings).

Reeve, J. M. (1992). *Understanding motivation and emotion.* Orlando, FL: Holt, Rinehart, & Winston.

Robbins, S. P., Waters-Marsh, T., Cacioppe, R. & Millett, B. (1994). *Organisational behaviour: Concepts, controversies, and applications.* Sydney: Prentice–Hall.

Robbins, T. L. & Fredenhall, L. D. (1995). The empowering role of self-directed work teams in the quality-focused organization. *Organisational Development Journal, 13*, 33–42.

Roberts, J. A. & Chonko, L. B. (1996). Pay satisfaction and sales force turnover: The impact of different facets of pay on pay satisfaction and its implications for sales force management. *Journal of Managerial Issues, 8*, 154–69.

Robertson, R. (1995). *Globalization: Social theory and global culture.* London: Sage.

Robinson, M. D. & Clore, R. (2001). Simulation, scenarios, and emotional appraisal: Testing the convergence of real and imagined reactions to emotional stimuli. *Personality & Social Psychology Bulletin, 27*, 1520–32.

Rogelberg, S.G. & O'Connor, M. S. (1995). Extending the stepladder technique: An example of self-paced stepladder groups. *Group Dynamics, 2,* 82–91.

Rogers, J. & Ward, C. (1993). Expectation–experience discrepancies and psychological adjustment during cross-cultural re-entry. *International Journal of Intercultural Relations, 17*, 185–96.

Rokeach, M. C. (1973). *The nature of human values.* New York: Free Press.

Rosenfeld, J. M. & Smith, M. J. (1967). Participative management: An overview. *Personnel Journal, 46,* 101–04.

Rousseau, D. M. & Arthur, M. B. (1999). The boundary-less human resource function: Building agency and community in the new economic era. *Organizational Dynamics, Spring,* 7–18.

Ruber, P. (2000). The great foreign IT worker debate. *Information Week, 814,* 153–57.

Rudmin, F. W. (2003). Critical history of the acculturation psychology of assimilation, separation, integration, and marginalisation. Review of General Psychology, 7, 3-37.

Rugimbana, R. O. (1996). Marketing psychology in developing countries. In S. C. Carr & J. F. Schumaker (Eds.), *Psychology and the developing world* (pp. 140–59). Westport, CT: Praeger.

Rugimbana, R. O. (1997, July). *Marketing within developing areas: A "consumer cringe" in Tanzania?* XXVI Interamerican Congress of Psychology, São Paulo, Brazil.

Rugimbana, R. O. (1998). *The Case.* In S. C. Carr, E. McAuliffe, & M. MacLachlan, 1998, Psychology of aid (pp. 1–2). London: Routledge.

Rutland, A. & Brown, R. (2001). Stereotypes as justifications for prior inter-group discrimination: Studies of Scottish national stereotyping. *European Journal of Social Psychology, 31,* 127–41.

Sackett, P. R. & DeVore, C. J. (2001). Counterproductive behaviours at work, vol. 1. In N. Anderson, D. S. Ones, H. K. Sinangil, & C. Viswesvaran (Eds.), *Handbook of industrial, work and organisational psychology,* vol. 2 (pp. 145–64). London: Sage.

Sadler-Smith, E., El-Kot, G. & Leat, M. (2003). Differentiating work autonomy facets in a non-Western context. *Journal of Organisational Behaviour, 24,* 709–31.

Salas, E., Rozell, D., Mullen, B. & Driskell, J. E. (1999). The effect of team building on performance: An integration. *Small Group Research, 30,* 309–29.

Salovey, P. (Ed.). (1991). *The psychology of jealousy and envy.* New York: Guilford Press.

Sauley, K. S., & Bedeian, A. G. (2000). Equity sensitivity: Construction of a measure and examination of its psychometric properties. *Journal of Management, 26,* 885–910.

Schalk, R., & Rousseau, D. M. (2001). Psychological contracts in employment. In N. Anderson, D. S. Ones, H. K. Sinangil, & C. Viswesvaran (Eds.), *Handbook of industrial, work and organisational psychology,* vol. 2 (pp. 133–42). London: Sage.

Schein, E. H. (1990). Organizational culture. *American Psychologist, 45,* 109–19.

Schein, E. H. (1996). Culture: The missing concept in organization studies. *Administrative Science Quarterly, 41,* 229–40.

Schein, E. H. (2000). Sense and nonsense about culture and climate. In N. M. Ashkanasy, C. P. M. Wilderom, & M. F. Peterson (Eds.), *Handbook of organisational culture and climate* (pp. xiii–xxx). Thousand Oaks, CA: Sage.

Schippers, M. C. Den Hartog, D. N. D., Koopman, P. L., & Wienk, J. A. (2003). Diversity and team outcomes: The moderating effects of outcome interdependence and group longevity and the mediating effect of reflexivity. *Journal of Organisational Behaviour, 24,* 779–802.

Schlaeger, S. (2002, March). *Merger Potential Analysis.* IONet (Industrial/Organisational Psychology Network) Professional Seminar Series, Auckland, New Zealand.

Schneider, S. C. (1991). National vs. corporate culture: Implications for Human resource management. In M. Mendenhall & G. Oddou (Eds.), *Readings and cases in International Human Resource Management* (pp. 13–27). Boston, MA: PWS–Kent.

Schneider, S. (2001). Introduction to the International Human Resource Management Special Issue. *Journal of World Business, 36*, 341–45. [special issue on the process of expatriate assignments].

Schwartz, S. H. (1994). E–correspondence sent to, and distributed by, the listserv termed 'XCUL' (XCUL@UACSC2.ALBANY.EDU), accessed December 6th, 15:31:31.

Schwartz, S. H. (1997). Values and culture. In D. Munro, J. F. Schumaker, & S. C. Carr (Eds.), *Motivation and culture* (pp. 69–84). New York: Routledge.

Scott, S. E., & Einstein, W. O. (2001). Strategic performance appraisal in team-based organizations: One size does not fit all. *Academy of Management Executive, 15*, 107-116.

Searle, W. & Ward, C. (1990). The prediction of psychology and socio-cultural adjustment during cross-cultural transitions. *International Journal of Intercultural Relations, 3*, 15–47.

Selmer, J. (2001). Antecedents of expatriate/local relationships: pre-knowledge vs. socialisation tactics. *International Journal of Human Resource Management, 12*, 916–25.

Semler R. (2002). *The seven-day weekend.* London: Century.

Senge, P. (1992). *The fifth discipline.* Sydney, Australia: Random House.

Sessa, V. I. (1996). Using perspective taking to manage conflict and affect in teams. *Journal of Applied Behavioural Science, 32*, 101–15.

Shaw, M. E. (1964). Communication networks. *Advances in Experimental Social Psychology, 1*, 111–147.

Shaw, G. (2001). Who let the plug out? *NZ Marketing Magazine, 20*, 38–9.

Shaw, J. B. & Barrett-Power, E. (1998). The effects of diversity on small work group processes and performance. *Human Relations, 51*, 1307–1325.

Sheridan, J. E. (1992). Organizational culture and employee retention. *Academy of Management Journal, 35*, 1036–56.

Shubik, M. (1986). Cooperative game solutions: Australian, Indian, and US opinions. *Journal of Conflict Resolution, 30*, 63–76.

Sidanius, J. (2002, April). Personal correspondence.

Sidanius, J. & Pratto, F. (1999). *Social dominance: An inter-group theory of social hierarchy and oppression.* Cambridge, MA: Cambridge University Press.

Sinangil, H. K. & Ones, D. S. (2001). Expatriate management. In N. Anderson, D. S. Ones, A K. Sinangil, & C. Viswesvarn (Eds.), *Handbook of industrial, work and organisational psychology*, vol. 1 (pp. 424–43). London: Sage.

Sinclair, A. (1992). The tyranny of team ideology. *Organization Studies, 13*, 611–26.

Singelis, T. M., Triandis, H. C., Bhawuk, D., & Gelfand, M. J. (1995). Horizontal and vertical dimensions of individualism and collectivism: A theoretical and measurement refinement. *Cross-Cultural Research, 29*, 240–75.

Singer, M. S. & Coffin, T. K. (1996). Cognitive and volitional determinants of job attitudes in a voluntary organnisation. *Journal of Social Behaviour & Personality, 11*, 313–28.

Sinha, D. (1989). Cross-cultural psychology and the process of indigenisation: A second view from the Third World. In D. M. Keats, D. Munro, & L. Mann (Eds.), *Heterogeneity in cross–cultural psychology* (pp. 24–40). Lisse, Netherlands: Swets & Zeitlinger.

Sinha, J. B. P. (1990). A model of effective leadership in India. In A. M. Jaeger & R. N. Kanungo (Eds.), *Management development in developing countries* (pp. 252–63). Chippenham, UK: Routledge.

Sligo, F. (1991). *Spectrum Paints.* Palmerston North, NZ: Massey University.

Smith, P.B. & Bond, M.H. (1993) *Social psychology across cultures*. Hemel Hempstead, U.K: Wheatsheaf.

Smith, B. J. & Carr, S. C. (2002). Selection in equalitarian Australia: Weighted average or motivational gravity? In F. H. Bolitho, S. C. Carr, & B. O'Reilly (Eds.), South Pacific Psychology: Global, Local, and Glocal applications (pp. 93–100). Special publication of the South Pacific Journal of Psychology (http://spjp.massey.ac.nz/).

Smith, P. B., Peterson, M. F., Akande, D., Callan, V. J. Cho, N. G., Jesuino, J., D'Amorim, M. A., Koopman, P. & Laing, K. (1994). Organisational event management in fourteen countries: A comparison with Hofstede's dimensions. In A. M.Bouvy & F. Van de Vijver (Eds.), *Journeys into cross-cultural psychology* (pp. 364–73). Lisse, Netherlands: Swets & Zeitlinger.

Smith, P. B., Peterson, M. F. & Schwartz, S. H. (2002). Cultural value, sources of guidance, and their relevance to managerial behaviour. *Journal of Cross-Cultural Behaviour, 33*, 188–208.

Snodgrass, J. G., Levy–Berger, G. & Haydon, M. (1985). *Human experimental psychology*. New York: Oxford University Press.

Sokolova, E. E. & Akkuratov, E. P. (1995). Envy used as power: Reflections on some psychological mechanisms in the practice of crudely egalitarian communism. *Journal of Russian and East European Psychology, 33*, 5–20.

Solomon, C. M. (2001). Managing virtual teams. *Workforce, 80*, 60–67.

Sparks, K., Faragher, B. & Cooper, C. L. (2001). Wellbeing and occupational health in the 21st century workplace. *Journal of Occupational and Organisational Psychology, 74*, 489–509.

Spector, P. E. & Cooper, C. L. (2002). The pitfalls of poor psychometric properties: A rejoinder to Hofstede's reply to us. *Applied Psychology: An International Review, 49*, 174–78.

Spreitzer, G. M. (1995). Psychological empowerment in the workplace: Dimensions, measurement, and validation. *Academy of Management Review, 38*, 1442–65.

Stahl, M. J. (1983). Achievement, power and managerial motivation: Selecting managerial talent with the job choice exercise. *Personnel Psychology, 36*, 775–89.

Stanne, M. B., Johnson, D. W. & Johnson, R. T. (1999). Does competition enhance or inhibit motor performance: A meta-analysis. *Psychological Bulletin, 125*, 133–54.

Stepina, L. P. & Perrewe, P. L. (1987). The impact of inequity on task satisfaction, internal motivation, and perceptions of job characteristics. *Journal of Social Behaviour & Personality, 2*, 117–25.

Stevens, M. J. & Campion, M. A. (1999). Staff and work teams: Development and validation of a selection test for teamwork settings. *Journal of Management, 25*, 207–28.

Stewart, P. A., & Moore, J. C. (1992). Wage disparities and performance expectations. *Social Psychology Quarterly, 55*, 78–85.

Stouffer, S. A., Suchman, E. A., De Vinnay, L. C., Star, S. A. & Williams, R. M. (1949). *The American soldier: Adjustment during army life*, vol. 1. Princeton, NJ: Princeton University Press.

Stricker, L. J. & Rock, D. A. (1998). Assessing leadership potential with a biographical measure of personality traits. *International Journal of Selection & Assessment, 6*, 164–84.

Stroh, L. K. & Reilly, A. H. (1997). Rekindling organisational loyalty: The role of career mobility. *Journal of Career Development, 24*, 39–54.

Strohschneider, S. (1999). On the cultural relativity of problem-solving styles: Explorations in India and Germany. In W. J. Lonner, D. L. Dinnel, D. K. Forgays, & S. A. Hayes (Eds.), *Merging past, present and future in cross-cultural psychology* (pp. 188–204). Lisse, Netherlands: Swets & Zeitlinger.

Tai, S. H. C. & Wong, Y. H. (1998). Advertising decision making in Asia: "Glocal" versus "Regcal" approaches. *Journal of Managerial Issues, 10*, 318–39.

Taggar, S., Hackett, R., & Saha, S. (1999). Leadership emergence in autonomous work teams: Antecedents and outcomes. *Personnel Psychology, 52*, 899–926.

Tajfel, H. (1978). *Differentiation between social groups*. London: Academic Press.

Tan, S. L. & Moghaddam, F. M. (1996). Reflexive positioning and culture. *Journal for the Theory of Social Behaviour, 25*, 388–400.

Taylor, D. M. & Moghaddam, F. M. (1994). *Theories of inter-group relations: International social psychological perspectives*. Westport, CT: Praeger.

Taylor, F. W. (1912). *Testimony to the House of Representatives Committee*. Washington, DC: Harper & Row (1947, In *Scientific management*, pp. 39–73).

Taylor, R. & Yavalanavanua, S. (1997). Linguistic relativity in Fiji: A preliminary study. *South Pacific Journal of Psychology, 9*, 69–74.

Templer, A., Beaty, D. & Hofmeyr, K. (1992). The challenge of management development in South Africa: So little time and so much to do. *Journal of Management Development, 11*, 32–41.

Terav, T., & Keltikangas-Jaervinen, L. (1998). Social decision-making strategies among Finnish and Estonian adolescents. *Journal of Social Psychology, 138*, 381-94.

Terry, D. J. & Callan, V. J. (1998). In-group bias in response to an organizational merger. *Group Dynamics, 2*, 67–81.

Terry, D. J., Carey, C. J. & Callan, V. J. (2001). Employee adjustment to an organisational merger: An inter-group perspective. *Personality & Social Psychology Bulletin, 27*, 267–80.

Terry, D. J. & O'Brien, A. T. (2001). Status, legitimacy, and in-group bias in the context of an organisational merger. *Group Processes and Inter–group Relations, 4*, 271–89.

The Afro-centric Alliance. (2001). Indigenizing organizational change: Localization in Tanzania and Malawi. *Journal of Managerial Psychology, 16*, 59–78.

The Afro-centric Alliance. (2003). Psychosocial barriers to female leadership: Motivational Gravity in Ghana and Tanzania. *Psychology and Developing Societies, 15*, 201-220 (special issue on Gender & Development).

The Chinese Culture Connection. (1987). Chinese values and the search for culture–free dimensions of culture. *Journal of Cross-Cultural Psychology, 18*, 143–64.

The Economist. (2002). South African immigration: Want them, throw them out. *The Economist, 363*, 43–4.

Thompson, L. L., Nadler, J. & Kim, P. H. (1999). Some like it hot: The case for the emotional negotiator. In L. L. Thompson, J. M. Levine (Eds.). *Shared cognition in organizations: The management of knowledge* (pp. 139–61). Evanston, IL: Northwestern University.

Tindale, R. S. et al (Eds.). (1998). *Theory and research on small groups*. New York: Plenum.

Tjosvold, D., Coleman, P. T. & Sun, H. F. (2003). Effects of organizational values on leaders' use of informational power to affect performance in China. *Group Dynamics, 7*, 152–67.

Toh, S. M. & Denisi, A. S. (2003). Host country national reactions to expatriate pay policies: A model and implications. *Academy of Management Review, 28*, 606–21.

Trevor, C. O., Gerhart, B. & Boudreau, J. W. (1997). Voluntary turnover and job performance: Curvilinearity and the moderating influences of salary growth and promotions. *Journal of Applied Psychology, 82*, 44–61.

Triandis, H. C. (1995). The importance of contexts in studies of diversity. In S. E. Jackson & M. N. Ruderman (Eds.), *Diversity in work teams* (pp. 225–33). Washington, DC: American Psychological Association.

Triandis, H. C. (2002, May). *Culture, conflict, and negotiation*. Visiting Researcher Seminar, Auckland University of Technology, New Zealand.

Triandis, H. C., Bontempo, R., Villareal, M. J. Asai, M., & Lucca, N. (1988). Individualism and collectivism: Cross–cultural perspectives on self-/in-group relationships. *Journal of Personality and Social Psychology, 54*, 323–38.

Triandis, H. C. & Gelfand, M. J. (1998). Converging measurement of horizontal and vertical individualism and collectivism. *Journal of Personality and Social Psychology, 74*, 118–28.

Triandis, H. C., McCusker, C. & Hui, C. H. (1990). Multi-method probes of individualism and collectivism. *Journal of Personality and Social Psychology, 59*, 1006–20.

Trist, E. L. & Bamforth, K. W. (1951). Some social psychological consequences of the Long Wall method of coal getting. *Human Relations, 4*, 3–38.

Trist, E. L., Susman, G. I. & Brown, E. R. (1977). An experimental in autonomous working in an American underground coal mine. *Human Relations, 30*, 201–36.

Trompenaars, F. (1994). *Riding the waves of culture*. Burr Ridge, ILL: Irwin Professional Publishers.

Trompenaars, F. & Hampden-Turner, C. (1998). *Riding the waves of culture* (2nd edition). New York: McGraw-Hill.

Trudgett, S. (2000). Resignation of women managers: Dispelling the myths. *Asia–Pacific Journal of Human Resource Management, 38*, 67–83.

Tubbs, S. (2002). The historical roots of self-managing work teams in the twentieth century: An annotated bibliography. In M. M. Beyerlein & D. A. Johnson (Eds.), *Advances in Interdisciplinary studies of teams: Theories of self-managing work teams*, vol 1 (pp. 39–66). Stamford, CT: JAI Press, Inc.

Tuckman, B. W. (1965). Developmental sequence in small groups. *Psychological Bulletin, 63*, 384–99.

Tuckman, B. W. & Jensen, M. A. (1977). Stages of small-group development revisited. *Group & Organisation Studies, 2*, 419–27.

Turner, J. C. (1975). Social comparison and social identity: Some prospects for inter-group behaviour. *European Journal of Social Psychology, 5*, 5–34.

Turner, J. C. (1991). *Social influence*. Milton Keynes, UK: Open University Press.

Van den Bos, K. & Spruijt, N. (2002). Appropriateness of decisions as a moderator of the psychology of voice. *Journal of Social Psychology, 32*, 57–72.

Van den Bos, K., Lind, E. A., Vermunt, R. & Wilke, H. A. M. (1997). How do I judge my outcome when I do not know the outcome of others? The psychology of the Fair Process Effect. *Journal of Personality and Social Psychology, 72*, 1034–46.

Van den Bos, K., Vermunt, R. & Wilke, H. A. M. (1996). The consistency rule and the voice effect: The influence of expectations on procedural fairness judgements and performance. *European Journal of Social Psychology, 26*, 411–28.

Van der Zee, K. I. & Van Oudenhoven, J. P. (2001). The Multicultural Personality Questionnaire: Reliability and validity of self- and other ratings of multicultural effectiveness. *Journal of Research in Personality, 35*, 278–88.

Van Dierendonck, D., Schaufeli, W. B. & Buunk, B. P. (2001). Burnout and inequity among human service professionals. *Journal of Occupational Health Psychology, 6*, 43–52.

Van Dyne, L. & Saavedra, R. (1996). A naturalistic minority influence experiment: Effects of divergent thinking, conflict, and originality in work groups. *British Journal of Social Psychology, 35*, 151–67.

Van Knippenberg, D., van Knippenberg, Monden, L. & de Lima, F. (2002). Organizational identification after a merger: A social identity perspective. *British Journal of Social Psychology, 41*, 233–52.

Vargo, L. G. (1976). Generalisations of the back-to-the-wall effect in series competitions. *International Journal of Sport Psychology, 7*, 107–12.

Vartia, M. A. L. (2001). Consequences of workplace bullying with respect to the wellbeing of its targets and the observers of bullying. *Scandinavian Journal of Work, Environment, and Health, 27*, 66–9.

Vecchio, R. P. (1981). An individual–differences interpretation of the conflicting predictions generated by equity and expectancy theory. *Journal of Applied Psychology, 66*, 470–81.

Vroom, V. H. (1964). *Work and motivation.* New York: Wiley.

Wageman, R. (1997). Critical success factors for creating superb self-managing teams. *Organizational Dynamics, Summer*, 49–61.

Wallace, R. W. (2001). The dynamics of team formation. *BioMedNet (bmn.com), 113* (55pp, accessed 30/10/2001).

Wanous, J. P. (1973). Effects of a realistic job preview on job acceptance, job attitudes, and job survival. *Journal of Applied Psychology, 58*, 327–32.

Wanous, J. P. (1992). *Organisational entry: Recruitment, selection, orientation, and socialisation of newcomers* (2nd edition). Reading, MA: Addison-Wesley Publishing Company.

Ward, C. (2003, May). Personal correspondence. Observation offered during Carr, S. C. (2003, May), *Culture and work psychology: A pro-social perspective.* Wellington: Victoria University of Wellington, Research Seminar Series.

Ward, C. & Kennedy, A. (1994, July). *Before and after cross-cultural transitions: A study of New Zealand volunteers on field assignments.* XII Congress of Cross-Cultural Psychology, Pamplona, Spain.

Ward, C. & Rana-Deuba, A. (1999). Acculturation and adaptation revisited. *Journal of Cross–Cultural Psychology, 30*, 422–42.

Warr, P. (1982). A national study of non-financial work employment commitment. *Journal of Occupational Psychology, 55*, 297–312.

Webber, S. S. & Donahue, L. M. (2001). Impact of highly and less job-related diversity on work group cohesion and performance: A meta-analysis. *Journal of Management, 27*, 141–62.

Weber, Y. (2000). Measuring cultural fit in mergers and acquisitions. In N. M. Ashkanasy, C. P. M. Wilderom, & M. F. Peterson (Eds.), *Handbook of organizational culture and climate* (pp. 309–20). London: Sage.

Weinberg, R. & McDermott, M. (2002). A comparative analysis of sport and business organizations: Factors perceived critical for organisational success. *Journal of Applied Sports Psychology, 14*, 282–98.

Werner, S. & Ones, D. S. (2001). Determinants of perceived pay inequities: The effects of comparison other characteristics and pay-system communication. *Journal Applied Social Psychology, 30*, 1281–1309.

West, M. A. (2001). The Human team: Basic motivations and innovations. In N. Anderson, D. S. Ones, H. K. Sinangil, & C. Viswesvaran (Eds.), *Handbook of industrial, work, and organisational psychology*, vol. 2 (pp. 270–88). London: Sage.

White, J. B. & Langer, E. J. (1999). Horizontal hostility: Relations between similar minority groups. *Journal of Social Issues, 55*, 537–59.

Wikan, U. (1989). Managing the heart to brighten face and soul: Emotions in Balinese morality and health care. *American Ethnologist, 16*, 294–312.

Wilke, H. & van Knippenberg, A. (1990). Group performance. In M. Hewstone, W. Stroebe, J. P. Codol, & G. M. Stephenson (Eds.), *Introduction to social psychology* (pp. 315–49). Oxford, UK: Basil Blackwell Ltd.

Winkelmann, R. (2000). The labour market performance of European immigrants in New Zealand in the 1980s and 1990s. *The International Migration Review, 34*, 33–58.

Winter, D. G. (2002). The motivational dimensions of leadership: Power, achievement, and affiliation. In R. E. Riggio, S. E.Murphy, & F. J. Pirozzolo (Eds.), *Multiple intelligences and leadership* (pp. 119–38). Mahwah, NJ: Lawrence Erlbaum Associates.

Wong, M. M. L. (2001). Internationalising Japanese expatriate managers: Organisational Learning through International Assignment. *Management Learning, 32*, 237–52.

Wood, W., Lundgren, S., Ouellette, J. A., Busceme, S. & Blackstone, T. (1994). Minority influence: A meta-analytical review of social influence processes. *Psychological Bulletin, 115*, 323–45.

Workman, J. (1993). Marketing's limited role in new product development in one computer systems firm. *Journal of Marketing Research, 30*, 405–21.

Xin, K. (2001). Review of *Management and Cultural Values: The Indigenisation of Organisations in Asia. Administrative Science Quarterly, September*, 571–75.

Ying-yi Hong, Wong, R. Y. M., Chen, G., Chi-Yue Chiu, Ip, G., Ho-Ying Fu & Hansen, I. .G. (2002, July). *When two national groups meet: Prior out–group attitudes predicted subsequent social identification.* XXV International Congress of Applied Psychology, Singapore.

Yoo, B. & Donthu, N. (2002). Review of 'culture's consequences,' 2nd edition. *Journal of Marketing Research, 39*, 388–89.

Zigurs, I. (2003). Leadership in virtual teams: Oxymoron or opportunity? *Organizational Dynamics, 31*, 339–51.

INDEX

Abuse of power, 56
Acculturation, 134, 136
Achievement, 11, 24, 49, 154
Acquisitiveness, 22, 51
Adversity-affiliation, 45
Afro-centric Alliance, 67, 52
Aggression, 21
All-channel networks, 122
Anti-conformity, 8, 110
Ascription, 24
Assertiveness, 24, 60
Assimilation, 8
Association principle, 76
Attribution theory, 26
Australia, 53, 54, 61, 144
Authority-ranking, 29
Averaging, 62

Backlash, 3, 7, 40, 43, 87, 110, 134, 152
Backward inference, 85
Bad faith, 8
Belief in a Just World, 101
Belief in equality, 83
Belief in equity, 83
Belief in need, 83
Big five in personality, 108
Boundary-less careers, 4, 14, 20, 51, 133
Brain gain, 156
Brain waste, 14, 140, 153
Broken promise, 14, 19, 21, 121, 133, 135, 142, 155
Buick Bar & Grill, 15, 53, 70

Canada, 139, 141
Career capital, 133, 135
Case methodology, 34
Centripetal values, 53
CEOs, 36
Channel theory, 106
China, 44
Chinese Confucianism, 3, 23
Chinese Culture Connection, 23
Climate, 21
Cognitive evaluation theory, 78
Cohesion, 113
Collectivism, 5, 22, 23, 28, 29, 34, 38, 47, 48, 54, 109, 152
Communal sharing, 29
Communication networks, 125
Companionship, 22
Conformity 8, 24, 35
Confucian Work Dynamism, 23

Consumerism, 55
Contiguity, 78
Continuous improvement, 51
Controlling feedback, 82
Counter-productive work behavior, 82
Cross-cultural communication, 43
Cross-cultural management, 5
Cultural cringe, 8
Cultural identity, 7
Cultural integrity, 7
Cultural mediation, 110
Cultural myths, 50
Cultural positioning, 11, 40, 43, 45, 47, 150
Cultural repertoires, 6
Cultural repositioning, 10, 38, 45, 86
Cultural transitions, 22, 27
Culture, 10
Culture fit analysis, 36
Culture's consequences, 23
Cultures of work, 6
Cyber teams, 111

Developing economies, 3
Diaspore, 37
Diffuseness, 38
Discourse, 7, 8, 75
Disempowerment, 54, 118, 127
Distributed leadership, 103, 106, 111
Distributive justice, 12, 80
Distributive justice theory, 12
Diversity, 104
Double de-motivation, 12, 13, 19, 21, 85, 94
Double loop learning, 145
Double Pygmalion effects, 42
Downsizing, 129
Dual process theory, 145, 148

EAC (East African Community), 142
Ecological approach, 26, 27, 32, 33
Economic recession, 3
Educational services, 2, 25, 144
Egality vs. hierarchy, 29
Emic vs. etic, 5, 6
Emotional labor, 13, 112
Empowerment, 13, 37, 78, 79, 105, 106, 110, 115, 155
Engineering culture, 37, 44
Engineers, 36, 37
Enterprise bargains, 77, 89
Envy, 53, 70
Equality matching, 29
Equity restoration process, 84
Equity, 12
Equity sensitivity, 55, 97

Equity theory, 12, 84, 86, 91,100
Escalation, 40, 152
Escalation dynamics, 40, 136, 157
Espoused theory, 14, 123
Espoused values, 22, 34
Ethnography, 34, 109
Executives, 36, 37
Expatriate assignment (EA), 14, 33, 93, 97, 134
Expatriation, 135
Expectancy theory, 79

Face validity, 61
Fair process effect, 83
Fear of success, 69
Flow in performance, 43
Foreign workers, 4
Free-riding, 44, 46
Frustration effect, 125
Fuzzy concepts, 116

Gain sharing, 77
Gender, 2
    and achievement, 67
    in leadership, 69
    and motivational gravity dip, 66
    differences, 2
    discrimination, 2, 56
    in teams, 44
Gendered social identities, 44
Ghana, 54, 68
Glass ceiling, 67
Global economy, 55
Global migration, 14
Global work culture, 6
GLOBE project, 24, 25, 27
Globalization, 1, 3, 4, 5, 7, 10, 51, 55, 110
    of individualism, 2
Glocal, 41
Glocal consciousness, 4
Glocal interactions, 59
Glocality, 5, 13, 20, 40, 45, 55, 62, 70, 74, 75, 120, 133, 151, 154
Glocalization, 4, 22, 49
Glocal lens, 6, 12, 20, 69
Glocal perspective, 4, 11, 13, 97
Glocal repositioning, 11, 18, 47
Glocal standoff, 40
Goal setting theory, 78
Groupthink
    in organizations, 109
    in teams, 113, 115, 116
Hawthorne studies, 106
Hedonism, 25
Hegemony, 7, 93

Homogeneity vs. diversity, 34/35
Hong Kong, 44
horizontal collectivism vs. individualism, 29, 47, 150
Horizontal hostility, 141
Humaneness, 26
Human capital theory, 80, 134
Humanitarian organizations, 11

Imperialism, 7
Impression formation, 62
Impression management, 51, 62, 73
INDCOL, 28
India, 3
Indigenisation, 8
Indigenous values, 3
Individual differences, 26, 32, 54
Individualization, 1/2, 7, 56, 77, 110
Individualism, 2, 18, 22, 23, 25, 26, 28, 29, 34, 37, 38, 44, 47, 54, 86, 109, 152
Industrial/organizational (I/O) psychology, 33
Informational feedback, 82
Interactional justice, 82
Interactive acculturation model (AIM), 136
Internal-external, 24, 25, 79
International HRM, 33
Inverse resonance effect, 15, 19, 20, 21, 141, 142, 152
Islamic values, 3
Israel, 44

Jam spoon curve, 141
Japan, 3, 53, 73
Jealousy, 55, 73, 77
Job characteristics theory, 106
Job insecurity, 55, 71, 73
Job satisfaction, 89, 98, 100, 125
Job security, 55
Job selection
    and double de-motivation, 97

Knowing whom, 134, 135
Knowledge wave, 13

Labor economics, 77
Labor mobility, 51, 144
Leadership, 3, 6, 11, 109
Leadership styles, 6
Libertarianism, 2
Likert scales, 61
Line of sight, 78
Local culture, 10
Localization, 3, 4, 8, 85, 110
Localized perspective, 7
Locus of control, 25, 79
Looseness-tightness, 28

Lottery question, 80, 89

Malaŵi, 60
Malaysia, 54
Māori worldviews, 9
Management by Objectives (MbO), 79, 124
Market pricing, 29
Masculinity-femininity, 22, 23
Mateship, 18, 19, 49
Meaning of work, 78
Mental models for teams, 118
Mentoring, 79
Merger potential analysis, 36
Mergers, 8, 153
Merit pay, 77
Meta contrast, 146
Metaphor, 1, 13, 19, 47, 56, 58, 73, 100, 114, 120, 130, 153, 157
Middle managers and n ach, 51
Migrants, 6
Migration, 51, 133
Minimal group effect, 43
Minority and majority groups, 7
Minority influence, 149
Mobbing, 56
Motivation, 21
Motivational gravity, 11, 19, 21, 58, 60, 84, 85, 90, 128
Motivational gravity dip, 62, 64, 69, 142, 146
Motivational gravity grid, 56, 57, 155
Motivational gravity scenario scale, 60, 71
Motivational gravity theory, 62
Motivational pluralism, 27

National consciousness, 27
Need for achievement (n Ach), 49, 50, 53, 55
       and discrepancy, 51
Neo colonialism, 93
Netherlands, 45
Neutral-affective, 24, 25, 34, 39
New Zealand, 53, 54, 144

Oasis metaphor, 100
Occupational culture, 21, 36, 41, 42, 69
Occupational values, 22
Occupational health/wellbeing, 91
Occupational work culture, 41
OE, 135
Online measures, 60
Operators, 36
Orchestral metaphor, 114
Organizational anthropologists, 33
Organizational citizenship behavior, 81
Organizational climate, 7, 21, 59, 61
Organizational culture, 21, 32, 33, 35, 36, 106

Organizational learning, 59, 148
Organizational learning theory, 123, 148, 153
Outdoor training, 44
Outward bound, 45
Over-assertiveness, 61
Over-promise/under-delivering empowerment,14, 19, 121, 124

Pay discrepancy, 77
Pay diversity, 4, 11, 77
Pay equality, 4
Pay for performance, 11, 77
Pay performance matrix, 13, 102
Performance orientation, 5, 26, 37, 39, 41
Performance pyramid, 2
Perspective taking, 129, 148, 149
Pluralism, 9, 26
Positioning, 5, 8, 42
Power distance, 22, 23, 24, 26, 34, 54, 84, 111, 112
Priming, 118, 152
Procedural justice, 82
Profit sharing, 75\7
Prototype theory, 13, 116
Pseudo participation, 124, 128
Psychological contract, 82
Pull Him Down (PHD), 54
Pull down, 56
Pull up, 56
Push down, 56
Push up, 56
Pygmalion effect, 42

Quality circles, 105, 106, 121, 122, 124
Quality of work life, 36, 58, 105, 110

Radical egalitarianism, 19
Radical individualism, 11
Reaffirmation, 43
Red eye disease, 54
Reflexivity norm, 10, 113, 129
Regional trade blocs, 15
Realistic conflict theory (RCT), 42, 45, 144
Reinforcement theory, 78
Relative deprivation, 101
Remuneration, 11
Repatriation, 135
Resilience, 149
Resistance to teams, 129
Reverse process, 85
Rhetoric of empowerment, 14, 120, 121, 123, 128
Rhetoric of teams, 105, 120
Royal Swedish envy, 59, 70

Scenario scaling, 59, 73, 94

Scientific management, 6
Self-direction, 35
Self-perception, 81, 97
Shoe sock man, 54
Short- vs. long-term orientation, 23
Similarity attraction theory (SAT), 140,142, 143, 144
Skilfully incompetent, 130
Skilfully unaware, 129
SME's, 50
Social achievement (s Ach), 3, 11, 65
Social capital, 5, 14, 42, 74
Social constructivism, 26
Social desirability effects, 60, 80
Social dominance theory (SDT), 143, 144, 146
Social equity theory (SET), 86
Social facilitation, 13, 44, 45
Social facilitation theory (SFT), 11, 42, 147
Social identification, 44, 45
Social identification with individualism, 3
Social identity, 2, 146, 152
Social identity theory (SIT), 7, 12, 15, 42, 99, 113, 140, 142, 144, 146
Social loafing, 44, 46, 109
Social support, 13
Societal identity, 22
Socio-technical systems theory, 106
Software engineering teams, 42
Specificity-diffuseness, 24, 25
Sporting metaphor, 74
Stereotyping, 5, 11, 40, 41, 43, 45, 49, 108, 147
Stimulation, 25
Stimulus response theory, 77, 78
Stratified positioning, 155
Sublimation of motivational gravity, 74
Supervisors, 14
Systems theory, 39, 70, 93, 128

Tall poppy syndrome, 19, 53
Tanzania, 68
Team New Zealand, 109
Teams, 49
Technical assistance, 135
Temporal orientation, 23
Test utility, 98
Thailand, 3
Theory-in-use, 14, 123
Theory X, 121, 123, 128
Theory Y, 123, 129
Thematic Apperception Test (TAT), 49
Threatening upward comparison, 70
Tightness-looseness, 34
Too much of a good thing, 61, 64
Trade blocs, 142
Tradition orientation, 25

Transactional pay, 81
Transformational leadership, 123
Transition economies, 98
Transitivity in identity, 36
Travel metaphor, 1, 6, 19, 40, 47, 153
Trust, 21
Turnover, 90, 124
Type A personality, 55

Uncertainty avoidance, 22, 23
United Kingdom, 141
Upward mobility, 72, 98
USA, 1, 3, 8, 29, 44, 49, 84, 98, 99, 140, 141

Values grid, 31, 38
Variegation metaphor
    in pay, 100
    in virtual teams, 111
    in migration and mergers, 154
Vertical collectivism vs. individualism, 29, 37
Vertical individualism, 47
Vicious circles, 42, 130
Virtuous circle, 131
Vocational fit, 135
Voice, 13, 83, 113

Weighted averaging, 62
Whānau, 9
Whānau interviewing, 9
Wheel networks, 125
Women are wonderful, 69
Work dynamics, 26
Work events, 23
Work group culture, 33
Work justice, 12
Workplace bullying, 56, 70, 82
Work justice theory, 77
Work stress, 56, 70
Work values, 22

Zero sum game, 4